AF505654

ATLANTIC STUDIES ON SOCIETY IN CHANGE

NO. 96

Editor in Chief, Béla K. Király
Associate Editor in Chief, Peter Pastor

THE APPEAL OF SOVEREIGNTY

Hungary, Austria and Russia

Edited by

Csaba Gombár
Elemér Hankiss
László Lengyel
Györgyi Várnai

Social Science Monographs, Boulder, Colorado
Atlantic Research and Publications, Inc.
Highland Lakes, New Jersey

Distributed by Columbia University Press, New York
1998

EAST EUROPEAN MONOGRAPHS, NO. DIII

The publication of this volume was made possible by a grant from
Pénzügykutató Alapítvány [Financial Research Foundation],
Budapest

Originally published as *A szuverenitás káprázata*
© 1996 Korridor, Politikai Kutatások Központja,
Budapest

© 1998
by Atlantic Research and Publications, Inc.
All rights reserved.

Library of Congress Catalog Card Number 97–76982
ISBN 0–88033–401–0

Printed in the United States of America

CONTENTS

CONTENTS

PREFACE TO THE SERIES

The present volume is a component of a series which when completed will constitute a comprehensive survey of the many aspects of East Central European society.

The books in the series deal with the peoples whose homelands lie between the Germans to the west, the Russians to the east and the Mediterranean and Adriatic Seas to the south. They constitute a particular civilization, one that is at once an integral part of Europe, yet substantially different from the West. The area is characterized by a rich variety in language, religion, and government. The study of this complex area demands a multidisciplinary approach and, accordingly, our contributors to the series represent several academic disciplines. They have been drawn from universities and other scholarly institutions in the United States and Western Europe, as well as East Central Europe.

The editor in chief, of course, takes full responsibility for ensuring the comprehensiveness, cohesion, internal balance, and scholarly quality of the series. He cheerfully accepts this responsibility and intends this work to be neither a justification nor condemnation of the policies, attitudes, and activities of any persons involved. At the same time, because the contributors to the series represent so many disciplines, interpretations, and schools of thought, his policy in this, as in the past and future volumes, is to present their contributions without major modifications.

Béla K. Király

TO THE READER

According to linguists, the word *szuverenitás* (sovereignty) first occurred in the Hungarian language in 1796, and the less abstract adjective *szuverén* (sovereign) was applied to a person only in 1806. Linguistic data are not crucial facts in the history of politics and political ideas, but neither can they be disregarded. The fact that a concept, in use for centuries in the Western half of Europe, appears so late in a language, reveals much about the context. Throughout its modern history, Hungary was not a sovereign state, though it always possessed the important attributes of statehood within the given imperial framework.

This situation was to change in the twentieth century. After World War I, Hungary, diminished in size and population, became an independent state. But not for long: in the wake of the German occupation in 1944 and the subsequent Soviet occupation, the country lost its independence for decades to come, even though it had the formal attributes of sovereignty. Since 1989, however, Hungary can again be called sovereign by all criteria of international legal norms and political reality.

Hungary became a *de facto* sovereign state in a period when important political integrative processes were taking place all over the world, and in Europe in particular, characterized simultaneously by globalization and fragmentation. These circumstances prompt the question: What does, what could sovereignty mean in today's Hungary, striving for integration?

The phrase striving for integration is, deceptive and dubious, and refers only to a feeling, without seriously taking into account the facts, that many entertain a desire to attain security and would like to see an end to the country's historical vicissitudes and exposure. The bulwark of the European Union (EU) seems to provide such security for its members. Our questions about the meaning of sovereignty and integration are formulated in line with this approach.

The question we have come to ask is: What historical, economic, cultural, and attitudinal requisites does Hungary possess for meeting the conditions of an international or supranational union? During the debates on these issues the statement of some politicians that integration helps assert sovereignty was raised not only as a question, but also proved to be questionable. Another major issue is the following: While the concept of sovereignty is very much a part of everyday political discourse, to what extent and in what way can we speak of the sovereignty of a nation, or of the sovereignty of a nation-state, which is not exactly the same thing, or of the sovereignty of only a state? As a result of extensive reading and a series of debates the concept of sovereignty has become questionable even when applied to Hungary in 1996.

We were aware from the start that this dispute is, indeed, an old one, but it was a challenge to find out whether or not we could add anything new to the issue here and now. While parliamentary and government organizations are busy working out strategies of integration, while politicians in Hungary and abroad issue contradictory statements about the possibility and timetable of integration, while NATO troops are stationed in the country, while we see graffiti saying "McDonald's eats us" on the walls of dilapidated buildings in Budapest, what we were curious to learn was this: What do the concepts of sovereignty and integration actually mean to Hungarians today?

What Have We Accomplished so Far?

The contributors to the present volume have, in the course of their work, formulated firm if divergent opinions; they are united by the conviction that a country's sovereignty lies in its political status and not in its wealth or cultural state. In brief, sovereignty is a political category. Consequently, international integrations that can have an impact on the conditions of sovereignty, and this is especially true of the European Union, raise primarily political questions, among them an intention to avoid conflicts that would lead to war between nation-states. In economic debates, these integration achievements prove the viability of an integration which was conceived and organized by politicians, and developed in line with political values but, from the start, the reason for its existence, and also its influence and success transcends the principle of economic self-interest.

In addition to taking into account the history of concepts and ideas, we also have had to take sides in debates conducted in the literature and practice of international law. If we had any illusions—and we did have some—that legal thinking, so matter-of-fact and aiming at precision—can be of greater help to us than cumbersome philosophical and theological approaches, these soon disappeared. Neither legal institutions, nor any philosophy of law can change the political nature of the exalted concept of sovereignty, in itself always contradictory. Albeit sovereignty cannot be understood without a knowledge of law, yet international law refrains, with good reason, from the interpretation of sovereignty as a merely legal category. Sovereignty conceived as supremacy is more than a legal institution, because those who exercise sovereignty in the main current of politics are not only legislators acting in accordance with their own political nature but, in a number of cases, political actors who consciously transcend the law.

By reason of the foregoing, we had to study the political actors intellectual character, embedded in history, as well as the palpable conclusions of Hungarian public opinion concerning sovereignty and the integrations modifying the country's sovereignty. Like politicians busy with the technical tasks of integration, we were curious to know what the citizens think of, and to what degree they care about Hungary's sovereignty and her chances of integration into Europe. Amid deteriorating opportunities and declining job security people do not brood over the concept of sovereignty, but the barometer of public fears and public aspirations clearly shows the desire for manifold security. War is the primary cause of fear. Thus, whether Hungary does or does not belong to an international integration which promises peace and protection, but not necessarily immediate material well-being, is an important problem affecting everyone.

The obvious conclusion derived from the national surveys is that the political stand of citizens concerning sovereignty and integration is determined mostly by an emotionally charged concept of nationhood. This is a complex, difficult, and admittedly sensitive question. Sovereignty, which for two hundred years has existed in Europe mostly within the framework of nation-states has released great creative energies. But it was also a source of a number of conflicts, including two world wars. The idea of European integration and its political institutional system, in the process of evolution over decades, are directed at the elimination of these very conflicts. This integrative effort, through establishing and invigorating supranational decision-making forums, affects the very core of the idea and practice of nation-states. For this reason, the realm of problems dealing with the question of nation and nation-state deserves special attention in clarifying the conceptual relations between sovereignty and integration.

Globalization, manifest in a number of spheres, rendering nation-state borders and decisions increasingly less substantial, sheds new light on the question of small statehood, an important issue in the case of Hungary. In the course of these planetary developments there seems to be something new under the sun: the scope of mobility of small states has increased in an unprecedented way. We gave this question special attention because it means that perception and judgment of the size of a country has changed and because this has occurred simultaneously with the integrational processes.

Two studies in this volume deal with Russia and Austria, contributing to a better understanding of the problem of sovereignty. Russia was chosen because it has been nearly ten years since the country turned firmly toward the West, yet we cannot predict whether the process is irreversible or not. The former Soviet Union was a challenge for Western Europe. European integration today is a challenge for Russia to which it will respond one way or another. It is not indifferent whether Hungary is inside or outside the integration when Russia does react. As for Austria, it is a particularly important point of reference for Hungary because it is a neighboring country of similar size, a militarily neutral nation and a brand-new member of the European Union.

The integrative process in Western Europe erodes the idea and practice of the welfare state and of the nation-state alike. Both processes are painful. There is a price to be paid for integration accompanied by diminishing sovereignty. The price paid for relative security is political. This could be expressed in monetary terms, but that would be only the metaphoric expression of a political event. A unified Europe, free of internal wars, is costly but, after all, it is not a matter of finances. It would be worth a great deal to Hungary to join this union. And exclusion would cost even more.

We attempted to weigh these problems, and to analyze the future of integration as a mixture of perspectives and imponderables that Hungary is bound to face. However, we must admit that we have not discussed a number of questions. The maze of seemingly technical affairs, from military policy through diplomacy to agrarian regulations, conceals a number of theoretical issues also relating to the matter discussed. We do not believe it is our task to delve into these issues here. We tried only to define the fundamental questions of the principles of sovereignty and integration, and to answer them as thoroughly as we could from a Hungarian viewpoint (in 1996).

Methods of Interpretation

Our research group has already published two volumes over the past few years, so our methods are more or less established. Albeit previously we had focussed on evaluating the performance of the government, and this led us to investigate a mostly unexplored field, whereas now we had to find our bearings in an intricate maze of types of knowledge and opinion, a set of ideas that has grown for centuries, we did not change our methods. This means in essence that we invited well-known experts to write the various chapters. However, we are skeptical not only of political, but also of professional authority. No one was allowed to remain satisfied with past achievements. The challenge of a new problem demanded that the authors prove their expertise once again. Professional debates served this purpose, wherein two well-prepared commentators presenting real counterarguments introduced each of the critical essays. This was seldom pleasant for the author whose essay was dissected, but extremely useful for the work as a whole. These contributors rarely find readers who would give their works such serious and deep analysis.

Sometimes our authors, commentators, and critics represented fields far removed from one another. By organizing these sessions of collective reflection, our aim was not only to satisfy routine interdisciplinary requirements in analyzing the questions of sovereignty and integration, but also to promote understanding between the disciplines. As a result, participants in the debates could never fall back on the terminology of their special field and rely on tacit understanding, a practice often leading to abstruseness. In the case of politically significant questions, it is not enough for the experts to understand one another, even if they disagree; it is important that people without any special training should be able to comprehend the problems. Therefore, we also paid attention to a clear and comprehensible style.

The English language translation was revised by Professors Mario D. Fenyo and Peter Pastor. The index was prepared by Edit Völgyesi. Their assistance is greatly appreciated.

We hereby express our gratitude to all those who agreed to act as commentators: Gáspár Bíró, László Csaba, Péter Kende, Tamás Kende, György Matolcsy, Gusztáv Molnár, Boldizsár Nagy, Peter Pastor, George Schöpflin, Zoltán Sz. Bíró, and Péter Szigeti. We have invited to the debates on the individual essays not only recognized specialists, but also young researchers whose expertise and critical verve have helped our work considerably. We have recorded the views of the participants and made use of the transcripts in the final phrasing of the studies. We must note, however, that the final version of each study is the author's own work and responsibility. Our collective enterprise and memorable debates do not infringe upon the sovereignty of authorship in any way. Although many of us came to doubt the significance of the concept of the sovereignty of the nation-state we have inherited, we firmly believe in the importance of recognizing the sovereignty of the individual.

The volume presents to the reader different views on what sovereignty means in 1996 in Hungary, a nation with an opportunity to join the process of European integration. Thus anyone can form, so to speak, a sovereign opinion on the issue.

Budapest, June 1996   *Csaba Gombár*

Csaba Gombár

BY THE TIME SOVEREIGNTY FELL INTO OUR LAPS IT HAD BECOME OBSOLETE
On the Sovereignty of Hungary

Sovereignty is a historical category with connotations which command respect; many interpretations and emotions have been attached to it over the centuries. Recently, however, the importance of this concept in the interpretation of international power relations has decreased considerably, though it has preserved a dignified resonance in everyday usage.

Traditionally, a distinction is made between the internal and the external sovereignty of a country. Historically, internal sovereignty, that is, the centralized and recognized supremacy of the state, was established first, and it became the foundation of external sovereignty, that is, the country's power demonstrated and recognized internationally as well. For a long time, however, the concept of sovereignty has mainly been used when speaking of the international system of power relations. While the internal sovereignty of states is rendered anachronistic by the democratic legitimation of power, the integration processes are leading to the same result in foreign policy.[1]

1. Introductory Remarks

As far as the state is concerned, the problem of sovereignty revolves around the following questions: who has the last say, who makes the

---

[1] We know full well that although the applicability and the significance of the concept of sovereignty have been discussed many times, people still show great concern for it. See David Kennedy, "Some Reflections on The Role of Sovereignty in the New International Order," Conference paper, Canadian Society of International Law, October 17, 1992.

ultimate decisions. Sovereignty is a qualified state of the supreme authority in a political system circumscribed by state boundaries, where the central authority is recognized not only internally but externally as well. A sovereign agent enacts laws and grants exceptions to the law; the one that is above everything and everyone and is not under any power. Sovereignty is the result of aversion to anarchy and the yearning for order and civil peace. A sovereign state promises peace and security within its province of authority. Sovereignty is a special state of supremacy because it consists of both a real position of force and its acceptance, not only within the political boundaries, but internationally as well.[2]

Sovereignty is a basic feature of territorially defined monarchies, eventually nation-states of Europe, which evolved from the sixteenth and seventeenth centuries and particularly among the great powers, an essential component of the system of international relations characteristic of the modern era. The elements of the system of international relations were sovereign states with the right of war and peace at least in Europe. By the end of the twentieth century, the concept of sovereignty has changed considerably. On the political scene, one can see the international organizations of integration emerge as "new sovereigns." In communication, economy, security policy, environment protection, the field of non-governmental organizations and non-governmental movements, it is not the global networks but some of the international regional unions that have actual power, that is, they have more than just influence as far as their membership and environment are concerned. It is not the international community as a whole that constitutes a kind of world center of power to harness the conflicts between the multiplying states; the regional organization of integration has the opportunity and capability of occupying the position of the "new sovereign."[3]

---

[2] We are also aware that theoretically it is risky to give a definition. We would only like to indicate that our approach is closer to the points that refer to sovereignty as a fact, than to the one that is based upon a "pure" legal theory. Cf. Martti Koskenniemi, *From Apology to Utopia: The Structure of International Legal Argument* (Helsinki, 1989), pp. 192–263.

[3] The new sovereign we mention in the text always between quotation marks, that is, the regional organizations of international integration, can be referred to as sovereigns only partially, metaphorically, or as projects (for the time being).

Hungary is a nation-state but, historically speaking, it was never sovereign. During the sixteenth and seventeenth centuries, while the territorial system of states stabilized and the problem of sovereignty became a topic for theoretical debates, Hungary was an occupied country, subjugated by empires. Nobody considered the Hungarian kingdom, which existed as one of the titles of the Habsburg emperors and one of the parts of the empire, to be sovereign, not even the subjects of the kingdom themselves.[4]

Only as late as the interwar period in the twentieth century was the country free of foreign troops. (Previously the deployed troops of the emperor—from the aspect of international law—were not for-

---

[4] Theoretically, it seems possible to use the category of sovereignty "retrospectively" concerning the Middle Ages. That is what Jenő Szűcs does in his essay where presenting the splendid thirteenth century, he analyzes the separation process of "state" and "society." "There remained only one institution that was not torn asunder by development—the Church" (p. 139). "The theoretical sovereignty of monarchical power, derived from divine grace, hovered empty above the whole social fabric, like the Augustinian legitimation of power as the 'safeguarding of peace and justice' on this earth. The power of the king was a real power only insofar as the monarch exercised it not as a sovereign but as a suzerain....no longer resembled any kind of sovereignty, and the exclusively vertical formula of feudal society had scarcely anything in common with any kind of coherent 'political society'....In the West the feudal components of the medieval 'corpus politicum' gave up the struggle gradually and unwillingly,...so that the state was only able to come out on the top in the 17th century." Jenő Szűcs, "The Three Historical Regions of Europe: An Outline," *Acta Historica Academiae Scientiarum Hungaricae* 29, nos. 2–4 (1983), p. 142. Afterwards, when it was already possible to find real sovereignty and real state in Europe, the part of Hungary which had been attached to the Habsburg empire was not sovereign, let alone the other two parts, the one occupied by the Ottoman Empire, and Transylvania, which was said to be the "invention of Emperor Suleyman." In this respect, we agree with Domokos Kosáry who wrote: "We can refer to the smaller or bigger political units with some extent of autonomy, proper political institutions, traditions and 'the idea of state' as states even if they belonged to a wider political organization and were in a more or less subordinated position. In this respect, we are entitled to consider, for example, Hungary a state even in the period when it belonged to the Habsburg monarchy and thus did not have internationally recognized sovereignty and diplomatic missions of its own." Domokos Kosáry, *Az európai kis államok fejlődési típusai* (Budapest, 1990), pp. 75.

eign, nevertheless they were seen ever as oppressors by Hungarians yearning for a sovereign Hungarian state.) Hungarian consciousness, however, was dominated not by the joy of regained independence but by the loss of much of its historical territories and its consequence, a huge deficit in sovereignty. Being defeated again in World War II and occupied first by the Germans in 1944, then by the Soviets for decades to come, neither Hungary's citizens nor its politicians ever considered Hungary a sovereign state.[5]

Such a sequence of events is nothing extraordinary on the eastern side of Europe. Sovereignty, whether that of a state, a nation, or a nation-state, was only a distant goal, a vague ideal for the semi- or non-independent states within the sphere of the Habsburg, the Ottoman, the Russian and, from 1945, the Soviet empires. Real sovereignty was a privilege granted to the Western part of Europe, and even there primarily to the great powers.

After 1989, Hungary also became a sovereign state. In this historical period, however, sovereignty has lost much of its value. Because of varying developments and conditions, the local evaluation of sovereignty varies markedly. In a world which is becoming globalized and institutionally internationalized, a new order is

---

[5] From the formal point of view of international law, both in the interwar period and after 1962, that is, after the recuperation of United Nations membership, Hungary was a sovereign country. Independent Hungary, established after World War I, existed under conditions of isolation. Hungary had managed to escape from isolation but she did not use this new situation for strengthening her sovereignty but appealed for help to a "higher" power for the restoration of the lost territories. In this respect, the ultimate decisions were made in Berlin, not in Budapest. It is a rhetorical question again whether the Hungary that belonged to the Soviet sphere of interest was sovereign or not. Neither the veil of the international law nor the much emphasized notion of national independence could conceal the substantial lack of sovereignty. Before the end of the 1930s Hungary had more room for maneuvering than in the Soviet bloc after the war—but in both cases lacked genuine sovereignty. For further elaboration see Ákos Szilágyi's paper on the question of national independence and sovereignty as an inherent component of the official Soviet doctrine of foreign policy. The same is demonstrated by István Vida's analysis of the Marshall Plan. See István Vida, "A Szovjetunió és a Marshall-terv," *BIGIS Nemzetközi Tanulmányok*, no. 1 (1995).

unfolding, in which the value of the concept of sovereignty attached to the nation-state, just like its historically sophisticated significance, is decreasing dramatically.

Sovereignty, although in a state of functional division, has shifted upwards to the level of integrations above the nation-states. Thus, for considerations of security, the now sovereign Hungary may renounce several components of her sovereignty in due time to join the organizations of integration that promise "sustainable growth." But it is as difficult to renounce sovereignty as it is to achieve it.

Sovereignty, given special glow by the attributes of independence, integrity and self-determination,[6] has traditionally been associated with the nation-state. The political concept of the nation is the fundamental question of the integrative process. In a world that is globalizing and fragmenting at the same time, the organizations of political integration present a united front against the idea of the nation-state, and they do it in cooperation with the nation-states that are already their members. Hungary is not an exception to that paradoxical tendency. Those processes prevailing globally take effect through the individual, internal conditions. An idea which loses its value in the imaginary stock exchange of notions may still be quite valuable in the eyes of its "owners."

2. *Discourses on Sovereignty and Integration*

In September 1995, according to a rumor, a study was circulating among the ambassadors of the NATO countries in Budapest, with the conclusion that the governing coalition should be maintained. The parliamentary parties, whether in the government or in opposition, claim to support Hungary's integration into the European Union. When this rumor came to the open, the president of an opposition

---

[6] Independence, integrity, self-determination, as notions, are not synonyms of sovereignty, they are its inherent conditions. The essence of sovereignty is what is called legibus solutus, that is, the capability of making the ultimate, unappealable decisions.

party immediately issued a statement within and outside Parliament, declaring the case an interference in Hungary's internal affairs and a violation of sovereignty. The existence of the study was denied officially, though it would be strange if the NATO countries were not interested in signs of crisis within the government of a NATO partner, and if they did not have strong opinions regarding any of the decisions. Such cases raise the question: What should be considered an internal matter and what is an external matter? It is sovereignty that is actually behind the problem. What is sovereignty and where does it reside?

On October 3, 1995, the newspapers printed the statement of the Hungarian prime minister: his party is sovereign and it is inadmissible that another party, in this case the other party in the coalition, should decide whether a candidate of his own party is suitable or not for a position in the government. The prime minister also affirmed that Hungary was a sovereign country, and the opinion of Russia could not influence the chances of Hungarian NATO membership. According to a radio commentary concerning the same topic, Russia was free to express her opinion opposed to that of NATO since she was a sovereign country. Reading such claims we can draw the conclusion that there are sovereign parties and sovereign countries, and there are parties and countries without sovereignty.

Late November, the minister of finance offered his resignation because of the decisions adopted by the Constitutional Court and suggested that in the present situation "the government and Parliament should regain their sovereignty over economic policy."[7] Concerning the same subject, the prime minister claimed that the government should regain its sovereignty over economic policy (the claims quoted above would suggest that sovereignty had shifted to the Constitutional Court). The logic of such agitated political declarations suggests that, in the Hungarian state, sovereignty is sometimes here, sometimes there, it is fought for, but the politicians quoted seem to agree that it should be somewhere (presumably, it should be where they are speaking). It does not seem to bother them that the separa-

---

[7] *Népszabadság*, November 24, 1995.

tion of powers and the presence of checks and balances in the institutional system of democratic state authority render the concept of sovereignty irrelevant. In that kind of usage, we can see a shift in meaning: the notion of position or authority is dignified by being raised to the level of sovereignty. But if any kind of forum can have sovereignty, what significance can the concept have any more?

At the beginning of 1992, the justification for the Gulf War from the point of view of international law was that the sovereignty of Kuwait had to be restored. Nowadays, during the recent protracted war in the Balkans, the international bodies decided that a sovereign state called Bosnia and Herzegovina, consisting of two autonomous parts, a Bosnian and a Serbian one, should be created; that would be "the world's first bi-confederated condominium state."[8] In this case, certain bodies grant sovereignty to somebody else who is lacking it.[9]

Since the fall of the Soviet empire and the fragmentation of its sphere of interest, the concept of sovereignty has been used often in Eastern European public discourse. That discourse is not meaningless, however vague the boundaries and contents of the notions may be. Since 1989, in this region, the word sovereignty has been used mostly in connection with the fact that the countries that had depended on the Soviet Union to various degrees, and certain other political units became independent. Independent of the late Soviet Union, at least. Under such historical circumstances, the word sovereignty expresses feelings of joy and of liberation. Sovereignty is a sublime, lofty and triumphant notion. We may not know where sublimity's home is, and in what way it triumphed, but the word has an aura that suggests solemn dignity. It is quite natural then that those longing for it, whether persons, organizations or states, like to use the word to characterize themselves, and they are also willing to use it as a not too substantial compliment to persuade or to court somebody else.

---

[8] *Newsweek*, November 27, 1995.

[9] According to a lopsided legal argument, it is no more than just an international recognition of declared independence. Bosnia has never had real sovereignty that could be recognized. The legal fiction of recognition seeks to force (by the military help of NATO) the parties to establish real sovereignty. If there is to be Bosnian sovereignty, it will be bestowed by NATO.

Sovereignty is, of course, a political category. Nevertheless, since political conditions and institutions do have their impact on the development of personality, and since they can be used as simile, because of their definite meaning, political terms are frequently used to characterize persons. One hears about autocratic or democratic personality, technocratic mentality, and so on.

Usage of the term sovereignty was a custom even when in common Hungarian political discourse no one, not even the official propaganda, used the adjective to denote the state of the nation. The attribute sovereign is, of course, a positive epithet whereas it does not seem to be an elaborate psychological category. One may use it to characterize a person who is independent in her/his ideas and deeds. Somebody may be described as a sovereign personality if he/she is of integral character, that is, complete, intact, inviolable and unimpeachable. The person who can be characterized this way may be so independent that it may harm her/his, but one owes respect to her/his autonomy and supposed spotless character by declaring him/her a sovereign. The conceptual content of this qualification used in private speech rarely comes closer to the classical features of the concept than the version used in public discourse nowadays; the ease and lack of inhibitions with which different political entities or agents apply this attribute to themselves or others, might well be called frivolous.[10]

The international literature that used to interpret sovereignty using the Latin word *maiestas*, meaning glory and grandeur, sounds

---

[10] It is no use condemning the everyday usage of the word. Discussion is justified, however, if somebody claims that sovereignty as a political category should be understood and used as it has been for centuries. The conceptual structure of sovereignty was determined thoroughly by absolutism. The European absolute monarchs were actual and recognized sovereigns, that is, their supremacy and its internal and external recognition bore all the marks of the concept of sovereignty. That concept has recently lost its meaning because the internal sovereignty of state is inconsistent with pluralistic democracy, and it is questionable to speak about the significance of external sovereignty when we are witnessing the deconstruction of the nation-state. It is understandable, however, that one may apply that attribute to political entities which are considered important; the concept does have an aura of respectable dignity.

rather awkward nowadays. It increasingly questions the applicability of the concept of sovereignty, referring to its deterioration and corrosion.[11] Even the titles of the volumes suggest a transition from sovereignty to integration, and the volumes collect papers in which the authors speak about the decrease of the significance of sovereignty, the decline of the sovereign nation-state, and about the state that tries to defend itself against those tendencies.[12]

"Sovereignty is a worn-out problem." This was the assumption in the West already in sixties.[13] Even the writings that apply a global perspective and argue against the withering away of the state, speaking rather about diversification and development, take it for granted that after hundreds of years both the fact and the concept of the nation-state and consequently that of sovereignty have recently lost their importance.[14]

What one reads in the specialized literature is one thing, and what one feels in everyday politics is another. In Hungary, we have seen the national rhetoric and the political, governmental emphases on ethnic matters strengthen over the past five years, and we can also observe that the political debates refer to the concept of sovereignty

---

[11] J. A. Camilleri and J. Falk, *The End of Sovereignty? The Politics of a Shrinking and Fragmenting World* (Aldershot, 1992).

[12] See *Between Sovereignty and Integration*, ed. Ghita Ionescu (London, 1974); Allan Rosas, "The Decline of Sovereignty: Legal Perspectives," in *The Future of Nation States in Europe*, ed. Jyrki Livonen (Aldershot, 1993); see also Vincent Cable, "The Diminished Nation State," and Susan Strange, "The Defective State," in *Daedalus* (Spring 1995). These also dwell upon the disappearance of sovereignty. Gusztáv Molnár expresses the demand of the dissolution of the mystic unity between state and nation. He writes: "From the moment when the state ceases to be a kind of superindividual 'emanation' of the nation as a collective subjectivity, it consists of citizens and not of the nation, it becomes free, not 'soil-bound' any more; to put it bluntly: it goes wherever it wants to," (Gusztáv Molnár, A belső és a külső integrációról," in *Autonómia és integráció*, eds. Gáspár Bíró et al. (Budapest, 1993), p. 6; Gusztáv Molnár, "Az új leviatán jogara alatt," *Magyar Hírlap*, October 13, 1995.

[13] See Carl J. Friedrich, *Trends of Federalism in Theory and Practice* (New York, 1968), p. 159.

[14] Michael Mann, "Nation-States in Europe and Other Continents: Diversifying, Developing, Not Dying," *Daedalus* (Summer 1993).

more and more often. Hungary joined the International Monetary Fund (IMF) and the World Bank in 1982, and political denunciations of those two international institutions of integration have been heard regularly ever since. According to the unanimous grumbling of the parliamentary parties, Hungary seems to want to join the European Union and NATO, yet on both sides of the Parliament the emphasis on sovereignty and on the actual or alleged harms to sovereignty sound stronger than the arguments in favor of the steps needed for integration, in spite of the alleged support by every party. Lately a party with no members in Parliament initiated a referendum regarding Hungary's NATO membership.[15] That move caused a remarkable silence of embarrassment among the parties that are supporting integration. It is safe to say, however, that there is a continuous and intense discourse on the question of sovereignty in Hungary.[16]

To this discourse belongs the Constitution, which declares independence, territorial integrity, the sovereignty of the people through elected representatives and direct participation, and assures harmony between international legal obligations taken by the country and internal legislation. Luring and courting various multinational corporations to Hungary, as well as expressing fear of them and condemning them, are all part of this discourse. Another part of this discourse is the desire to be a member of a union that is supposed to provide Hungary with tranquillity, stability and wealth, even if that step may curtail the sovereignty of the state; and without doubt many measures have been taken in this direction from thorough

---

[15] Miklós Haraszti, "Thürmer Gyula kesztyűje," *Népszabadság*, November 6, 1995; László Valki, "Felvesszük-e a kesztyűt?," *Népszabadság*, November 17, 1995; László Vit, "Belépni vagy kívülmaradni," *Magyar Hírlap*, November 21, 1995; M. Haraszti, "NATO, hozzánk közeledőben," *Népszabadság*, December 18, 1995; T. Csapody, "Érvek Magyarország NATO-csatlakozása ellen" and Imre Mécs, "Ellenérvek dzsungele," *Mozgó Világ*, no. 11 (1995).

[16] The discourse on sovereignty, some examples of which we have mentioned above, deserves attention anyway. While we are concentrating in this paper, on the original and substantial political content of sovereignty, it is advisable not to ignore everyday speech in which, even if with a different meaning, the concept shines bright. And if it shines, it will always enlighten the situation of the country enough to raise the question: What about the sovereignty of the state?

analysis to the step towards harmonizing legislation. To that discourse belong the plans, aspirations and nightmares about the state boundaries, whether they should be fixed or, on the contrary, changed, easier to cross, perhaps abolished. And the discourse covers the ideas involved by the answers to the question whether the Hungarian nation is able to fit within these boundaries or whether they should be widened so that the country could embrace the whole of the imaginary nation.[17]

Thus, in this proliferating discourse one can find a mixture of different usages of the notion of sovereignty; some speak about the sovereignty of the Hungarian nation-state, others about that of the nation, or the country constituted by Hungarian citizens.[18] The mixture of different traditions, ideas, ambitions, deeds, wills, and wishes is rather chaotic and full of conflicts, but it does not mean that its discrete components are confused in themselves. Anyway, it is difficult for us to participate in an articulated public discourse on sovereignty; we did not have enough time to learn it.

---

[17] Parliamentary speech by MP Zsolt Lányi (FKGP); see the Hungarian newspapers of November 22, 1995.

[18] Why do the different interpretations of sovereignty (the sovereignty of the state, or of the nation, or that of the nation-state) mix in public political discourse? According to some, the state is a means for the existence and development of the nation, and according to others, the state that is strengthened by the idea of nation is but a stage in the development of the state. The notions of "political nation" and "state-nation" are the key categories of the nation-state period and the corresponding type in the development of state; they express the institutional whole of the state from the point of view of the nation, that is, from that of the "sovereignty of the nation." This author thinks, on the contrary, that nation-state is only one of the stages of the development of state. There was state before nation state and there will be state after nation-state. We should not forget, however, that one can find opinions according to which the subject of sovereignty is different. See László Lengyel's paper in this volume, in which the author examines the different points of view that emphasize the state or the nation.

3. Evoking the History of the Concept of Sovereignty

The sixteenth and the seventeenth centuries saw the beginning of a new stage in the development of the state. In the age of absolutism, the state got the upper hand over the syncretic forms of feudal society. Time and again one comes across references to the Treaty of Westphalia in the studies on sovereignty. The writings on the new international units of integration and on international power relations refer to the famous peace treaties of 1648 which settled the wars of religion as a milestone in European history.[19] That treaty can be regarded as the birth of states as we know them today. Sovereign states having the right of war and peace were not only *de facto* tolerated but were recognized *de jure*. And that was also the era when international law was born.

Consequently, new assumptions ceased to consider the group of countries as a system of "dependencies" but saw them as a set of sovereign states. It was the rather haphazard foreign policy and the still fledgling international law that provided the sovereign states with connections. Foreign policy was the continuation of internal policy of sovereign states at a time when internal sovereignty of the territorially fixed states was itself a new development which needed enforcement, recognition, and institutionalization.[20] Afterwards, the West-

---

[19] By the Treaty of Westphalia, the emperor of the Holy Roman Empire recognized the sovereignty of the German principalities. As Paul Kennedy wrote: "...the essence of the Westphalian settlement was to acknowledge the religious and political balance within the Holy Roman Empire, and thus to confirm the limitations upon imperial authority." Paul Kennedy, *The Rise and Fall of the Great Powers: Economic Change and Military Conflict from 1500 to 2000* (London, 1989), p. 51.

[20] After the state formations which had disintegrated in the early Middle Ages, only the states that emerged during the sixteenth and seventeenth centuries had those significant territorial obligations and solidity that are suggested by our present day concepts. That is why one generally uses the notion of "territorial state" concerning the Westphalian system of states. Even in the eleventh century "Territorial status and feudal dependence did not necessarily coincide." See Szűcs, op. cit., p. 142.

phalian system, that is, the system of the territorially bound sovereignties, turned out to be remarkably long-lasting and stable until the
end of the twentieth century. However, that system is now unstable
and seems to be changing, and it naturally raises the question: what
was it like before? Whether the new modifications mean a return to
the conditions preceding Westphalia?[21] Whether and in what way reference to the distant past could contribute to the interpretation of new
developments, that is, to the interpretation of the decay of the nation-
states and their sovereignty? All in all, those are open questions.

Thus, when the significance of state sovereignty is diminishing,
or seems to be diminishing—those two things are the same—it is natural to ask what was it like when there were no sovereign states,
when sovereignty had a different meaning, when even the word was
meaningless as far as political entities were concerned.[22]

"All significant concepts of the modern theory of the state are
secularized theological concepts," said a famous antiliberal thinker,[23]
and it is valid in this case too. Before the advent of the word sovereignty, the omnipotent God had all the attributes which later were
encompassed by the secular concept of sovereignty.

In a historical sense, the word sovereignty means supreme
authority. Sovereign is the agent who enacts laws but is not con-

---

[21] G. Gottlieb, *Nation Against State: New Approach to Ethnic Conflicts and
the Decline of Sovereignty* (New York, 1993).

[22] As we have mentioned before, the concept of sovereignty can be used in
connection with medieval conditions retrospectively and in a speculative way.
But in the sense of the modern state of universal significance, there was no
state in the Middle Ages, consequently it makes little sense to speak of sovereign state in that era. The concept of sovereignty had a limited content in
medieval legal theory, as Georg Schwarzenberger noted; practically speaking,
anybody could be referred to as sovereign, since there was no one to appeal
to after a decision in a given social space. Sovereignty and its conceptual
sense were "used in a non-exclusive manner and lacked the awe-inspiring
majesty [they were] to acquire during the era of absolutism." See G.
Schwarzenberger, *Power Politics: A Study of World Society* (London, 1964),
p. 87. We should speak about sovereignties, in the plural, that existed within
a state formation or also penetrated its moving boundaries.

[23] Carl Schmitt, *Political Theology: Four Chapters on the Concept of
Sovereignty* (Cambridge, 1988), p. 36.

strained by laws. A sovereign power is unified, indivisible and is under neither control nor supervision.

According to the history of the idea of sovereignty, for fifteen centuries after Christ the subject of sovereignty in Christian Europe (i.e., who is "sovereign") was not problematic. (By the way, the word sovereignty was not even used during those times though its subject was a category that had undergone diversified conceptual analysis.) The words of the apostle Paul guided the experts writing in Latin on supreme authority. "Everyone must submit himself to the governing authorities, for there is no authority except that which God has established. The authorities that exist have been established by God."[24] According to divine law, the destiny of secular princes is to implement the divine will, and everyone is under obligation to obey and answer to that will. Even today some believe that medieval princes had absolute and unlimited power. Local customs and traditions, but particularly the estates and feudal anarchy limited and fragmented the power of the medieval monarchs effectively and, since according to the recognized doctrine, they ruled only by the grace of God, the Church often interfered in their deeds on legal grounds because it was the only one entitled to interpret Divine Law. The secular prince was obliged to follow the Catholic doctrine. Thus in no sense were the secular princes sovereign.[25] According to prevailing principles, the secular princes were not supposed to see themselves sovereign, neither should others see them as such. In Europe ruled by God, the Church allegedly did not interfere with the internal affairs of a kingdom when it criticized or approved something, it merely fulfilled its own duty, and all that was believed to be obvious.

The Church itself was "the state."[26] The political doctrines, expressed within theology, on the conditions of the Earthly City con-

---

[24] Romans 13:1.

[25] Bertrand de Jouvenel, *On Power* (Boston, 1969), especially the chapter "Theories of Sovereignty," pp. 26–48.

[26] J. N. Figgis, *Political Thought: From Gerson To Grotius: 1314–1625: 7 Studies* (New York, 1960). The seven lectures read by Figgis in Cambridge in 1900 are works of fundamental importance on medieval political thought and on the evolution of the doctrine of sovereignty.

ceived on the model of the Heavenly City, conceptualized the world as a whole, not articulated territorially in a political sense, where the supreme authority was exercised by God, never by mortal beings. And since the Church was "the state," there were no states in the present sense.

The Investiture Controversy, the conflict between ecclesiastic and secular rule, and particularly the Reformation dismembered that unified perspective in which the interpreted world was articulated according to the cosmological spheres arranged along the continuum from family to divine omnipotence. The treatises of the great sixteenth century Jesuit scholars, in which they stretched the doctrine of obedience to the earthly powers from the right of resistance to popular sovereignty, were committed to the flames in Paris and in London.[27] They could not block, however, the unfolding of the new approach that regarded supreme authority as an earthly one. By the seventeenth century, the state as is known today had appeared, and along with it multipolar sovereignty in a world articulated by the dividing lines of politics. Europe became a group of sovereign states.

In our approach, the globe fragmented by political frontiers is taken for granted, as much as the grid of latitudes and longitudes. The boundaries of the medieval state formations, e.g., kingdoms, principalities, dioceses, counties, city-states, were volatile and politically unstable not simply because of continuous warfare but also because of the politically significant Christian Europe principle. In practice, society divided by estates, strengthened the separation of state and society. Consequently, internal and external developments were by no means as clearly isolated from each other as the concepts of foreign and domestic policy would later suggest. The political configuration of territorially separated units, each having separate sovereignty, is a specifically modern development. Its novelty is indicated by the fact that in the sixteenth century only the vernacular languages, could elaborate the phenomenon. Jean Bodin wrote his classic work on sovereignty in French.[28]

---

[27] See Figgis, op. cit., and de Jouvenel, op. cit., as well as Charles Merriam, *History of the Theory of Sovereignty since Rousseau* (New York, 1990). The book by Merriam is one of the best comprehensive works on the subject to date.
[28] N. G. Onuf, "Sovereignty: Outline of a Conceptual History," *Alternatives* 16 (1991), pp. 425–446.

It is important to consider the circumstances under which the classic works on sovereignty were written. When Jean Bodin was writing his volumes wars of religion were being waged in France. When Thomas Hobbes was writing *Leviathan,* England was in the midst of a civil war. Hugo Grotius was jailed because of his involvement in the schism within the Church and went into exile to lay down the moral principles of international law. We should take into account the yearning for order, tranquillity, and civil peace as the main cause of the creation of the treatises on supreme authority that is, the wish for a supreme power within the state what the specialized literature calls internal sovereignty, in order to curb the anarchy that continually threatens the life and property of the individual. Actually this means the establishment of a modern state, whose unity is guaranteed and symbolized by the sovereign. Hobbes wrote:

> ...the Multitude so united in one Person, is called a COM-MON-WEALTH, in latine CIVITAS. This is the Generation of that great LEVIATHAN, or rather (to speak more reverently) of that Mortal God, to which wee owe under the Immortal God, our peace and defense. For by this Authoritie, given him by every particular man in the Common-Wealth, he hath the use of so much Power and Strength conferred on him, that by terror thereof, he is inabled to conforme the wills of them all, at Peace at home, and mutuall ayd against their enemies abroad. And in him consisteth the Essence of the Common-Wealth...[29]

We are concerned here neither with the idea of the state of nature nor with that of the social contract, nor in the political and logical

---

[29] Thomas Hobbes, *Leviathan* (Cambridge, 1991), pp. 120–121. The author of a monograph on C. Schmitt writes: "The Hobbesian relationship of protection and obedience was an integral part of Schmitt's political philosophy. Thus, he later explained, when the Weimar system could no longer protect him, he felt justified in transferring his allegiance to the new regime so long as it granted him this protection." Joseph Bendersky, *Carl Schmitt—Theorist for the Reich* (Princeton, 1983), p. 204.

trends pointing towards absolutism but in the fact that sovereignty seemed to be both the guarantee of internal peace and the promise that the state, organized by the supreme authority, will protect the people against external threats. And for the very reason that the now secular sovereignty was to establish the state and meant an independent state, the difference between the internal and the external, the difference between foreign policy and domestic policy turned to be perceptible in a way which has a lot in common with the way we still perceive it today. And it is since this time that we can apply the difference between these two terms (retrospectively and metaphorically) to ages when Europe was characterized not by territorially articulated modern statehood but, most significantly, by unity in the body of Christ.

The concept of sovereignty elaborated in the sixteenth and seventeenth centuries can be regarded as the fusion of several earlier political discourses. One of them is the ancient category of *maiestas*, which concerns the cosmic chain of being meaning majesty, but often translated afterwards in political contexts as sovereignty. Another part of the conceptual confusion is the word *imperium*, that is, supreme power, which meant governing through rules in the empire that had sprung up from the formerly republican Rome even in the age of the most *erratic* emperors; and it means that the political position of the Roman populus can be said to be one of the sources of popular sovereignty from the aspect of the history of ideas and law. The third component is the manifold interpretation of the concept of the ruling prince, from Niccolò Machiavelli's uncompromisingly direct description to the way Frederick the Great describes the prince as the first servant of the people in *Anti-Machiavel*.[30] The interweaving of various political idioms made a new perspective possible, enabling one to notice a new phenomenon, the modern state. In the era of modernity, the state, the first one that can be referred to as a real state in the present-day sense, had a name derived from the French equivalent of sovereignty. From the sixteenth and seventeenth

---

[30] See the works, already cited, by Onuf and Merriam; and Frederick the Great, *Anti-Machiavel* (Athens, Ohio, 1981).

centuries on, the sovereign state, that is, both state and sovereignty, becomes a new reality, in spite of the long history of the notion of sovereignty in the history of ideas or in political history, extending over more than a thousand years. Various tendencies had prepared the emergence of the sovereign state, but it became a political reality only in the modern age.

The historical subtleties around the idea of sovereignty are similar to the complexity of the theological interpretations of Trinitarianism. It was not enough to understand and explain the state with its sovereign monarch, relatively fixed territory and the loyalty linked to that territory, and its population but, in order to gain and retain loyalty, it was also to be recognized first internally and then externally. Without doubt, recognition needed force and coercion, but brute violence was never enough. Thus, the concept of sovereign state had to be created in a way that Christian faith could be harmonized with the phenomenon of a "mortal God," that is, with the now secular sovereign in power by the grace of God.

Furthermore the accepted Roman law had to be harmonized with the heterogeneous local legal customs, and the concept was supposed to be able to legitimize the reduction or abolition of medieval feudal privileges by absolutist rulers.

Majesty, the secular monarch as an institution and the reception of secular Roman law, authority over a given territory, from the point of view of theology and philosophy of law. Since then, genealogical and religious beliefs have played a fundamental role in the development of communities as did the jurisdiction and the judicial practice characteristic of a territory defined by boundaries, and the latter became more and more important.[31] By the beginning of the seventeenth century, sovereignty pointed to a new perspective, a new reality and a new concept.

Sovereignty has certain attributes without which it does not exist and cannot be perceived. The experts list attributes such as independence, autonomy, integrity, self-government as well as unlimited

---

[31] Roger Scruton, "First Person Plural," in "*Mi a konzervativizmus?*" (Budapest, 1995), pp. 129–147.

nature, exclusiveness, unity, unaccountability as the marks of sovereignty, or they mention categories such as the right to wage war, make peace treaties, give amnesty, etc. In old handbooks such lists take hundreds of pages, and they are mostly no more than a series of circular definitions, leading to a conclusion very similar to Győző Concha's: Sovereignty is "the authority of the state over its own will."[32] It follows that a sovereign does not depend on anybody else, is autonomous, self-governing, etc. Within the framework of a sovereign state, the Hobbesian idea—"autoritas, non veritas, facit legem"—can be seen realized, that is, the laws follow from power and not from truth, and laws can be enacted only by sovereignty ("might makes right," as chapter 26 of *Leviathan* puts it). The question hidden behind the elaboration of the details has always been the same: where on earth does all this comes from? Whether from a kind of divine mission, or just from brute force, and if from the latter, how can it be legitimized, how can the subjects be made to recognize it? Reading the treatises on the theory of sovereignty, one rarely comes across such a clear sentence as that of Carl Schmitt, the founder of decisionism, who begins his analysis with the statement: "Sovereign is he who decides on the exception."[33] The sovereign makes decisions because he is able to do that, that is, he has the power. This "decisionist" statement would hardly have surprised Miklós Zrínyi who, in the classical century of sovereignty wrote the following in his *Az török áfium ellen való orvosság* [Medicine against the Turkish opium]: "And if there were warfare we should arm not only ten or twelve thousand men but the whole of our nation thoroughly, since the Italian saying goes like this: La forza caga alla ragione addosso [force shits on reasoning]: force is to be used against force, and if not in number, but in gallantry and courage, we must leave behind our enemy."[34]

---

32 Győző Concha, *Politika* (Budapest, 1985), vol. 1, p. 255. See also Sándor Krisztics, *Politika* (Budapest, 1931), vol. 1, pp. 351–428; József Szabó, *A szuverenitás*, vol. 1 and *Szuverenitáselméletek*, vol. 2 (Szeged, 1937).
33 Schmitt, op. cit., p. 5.
34 *Zrínyi Miklós hadtudományi munkái* (Budapest, 1976), pp. 339–340.

4. *Sovereignty, Nation-State and Integration*

During the nineteenth century, in real history and in the recent history of ideas, two events took place that marked the ascent of sovereignty to a higher level, similar to the integrative problems of our days. Moreover, in both cases, the ascent of sovereignty was accompanied by diversified theoretical debates. The two events were German unification and the American Civil War, in the process of which one could see the emergence of a state without sovereignty, as part of an empire or a federation.[35] Even the studies on the Third Reich mention Hermann Göring as Prussian prime minister. Prussia as a sovereign state had ceased to exist long ago, though in the unification process Prussia, like the Free State of Bavaria and other provinces, had preserved certain requisites of an independent state: but clearly sovereignty, the internal supreme power, had ascended to the imperial level. A similar process took place in the United States. In the eighteen-thirties, Alexis de Tocqueville appreciated how well the United States functioned under the conditions of "sovereignty fragmented" between the Union and the states, while in reality sovereignty resided with the states.[36] The situation was soon to change, however; time had ripened secessionist aspirations. After the Civil War, after the defeat of the secessionist Southern States, supreme authority ascended to the federal government. Even if one can still see the Confederate flag flying on the top of the state houses of some erstwhile member states, they are not sovereign.

In order to explain, accept and discuss all this and naturally to describe the diversity, sub-categories of sovereignty have been worked out. Some speak about absolute versus relative sovereignty, that is, about indivisible versus double or "two-headed" sovereignty

---

[35] J. C. Calhoun, *A Disquisition on Government and Selection from the Discourse* (Indianapolis, 1953); Merriam, op. cit., pp. 162–172; and Schmitt op. cit.; also the inaugural lecture by Domokos Kosáry and the detailed elaboration of the historical literature on the question in it. See Kosáry, op. cit.

[36] Alexis de Tocqueville, *Democracy in America* (New York, 1988), pp. 163–170. See also Friedrich, op. cit.

(Bodin and Hobbes, versus Grotius and James Madison). One may read essays on legal sovereignty which resides with the parliament, and on political sovereignty that is an attribute of the totality of citizens. A real gem is the invention of British political thinkers: "Queen in Parliament," according to which sovereignty resides not with the monarch who is actually called sovereign, but in her presence at Parliament, which means that the queen reigns but does not rule.[37] In applying the word sovereignty as supreme authority one should use different adjectives depending on whether one speaks about absolutism, a constitutional state or a democratic constitutional state. As far as foreign policy is concerned, we hear of sovereign, semi-sovereign, and non-sovereign countries. As early as 1800, in connection with this classification, it was argued that the acceptance of international law had relativized the external sovereignty of the state from the beginning—in principle at least—hence the category of limited or constrained sovereignty came into general usage.[38]

The developments of the last century completed by the varieties of cumbersome democratic politics combined the concepts of state sovereignty. In the second half of the twentieth century, however, we have been witnessing the multiplication of non-state entities that are eroding the sovereignty of the states day by day. Foreign policy is shaped not only by nation-states but by international organizations as well, of which the states are only members of different standing, and also by international non-governmental organizations, the impact of which is felt beyond any political boundaries.[39] We can analyze and understand those processes with the help of the long history of the concept of sovereignty. It is no accident that the Dutch Johannes Althusius was discovered by German legal scientists precisely in the era of Otto von Bismarck, the age of unification. Althusius lived when the classic concept of sovereignty was worked out. His concepts

---

[37] See the entry "Sovereignty" in Roger Scruton, *A Dictionary of Political Thought* (London, 1983), and see also the entry "Sovereign" in N. Wolding and P. Laundry, *An Encyclopedia of Parliament* (London, 1958).

[38] Merriam, op. cit., and Szabó, op. cit.

[39] Béla Galló, "Ki dönt, ki cselekszik?," in *Szuverenitás—nemzetállam—integráció*, eds. Béla Galló and István Hülvely (Budapest, 1995).

of federalism, corporatism, agreement, and contract, led to a notion of
sovereignty that can be established in the form of federalism and consensus and does not deny that either of the contracting parties could
keep some of their inalienable rights. Althusius built his theory on the
term "consociatio," and considered society a partnership, that is, an
association of associations. The consociation of families, neighbor-
hoods, local communities, urban communes, provinces, etc. makes up
the state which gains its sovereignty by this structure. The idea and
the fact of the sovereign state, however, reached its logical conclusion
in absolutism via a short and historically well-known route, and
Althusius was forgotten for a long time. However, the way of thinking which focused on larger state frameworks instead of small states
made his ideas timely and worth recalling one hundred years ago,
while today he is referred to as a founder of consensual democracy,
and the "consociational" interpretation (based on his concepts) of the
formations of integration may well be promising.[40]

Just because something is promising does not mean that the problem can be solved. The problem of sovereignty as the problem of the
treatment of human conflicts, as the problem of power cannot be
solved, nor be eliminated, nor be filed away indefinitely and disposed
of unsolved. On the contrary, it needs continuous attention and analysis so that the handling of the problems could become more acceptable. In theology considered as the Advent of philosophy,[41] the substantive components of sovereignty were expressed in various ways,
and since the Treaty of Westphalia that notion has been one of the key
issues of secular politics. How can it be worth striving for peace,
tranquillity and security again and again in a political life full of conflicts, embedded in power relations? Is it possible to envisage and to
build a system where the supreme agency may beat the swords of the

---

[40] See Merriam, op. cit. and Figgis, op. cit., as well as A. Lijphart, *Democracy
in Plural Societies: A Comparative Exploration* (New Haven, 1977), which is
built on the category of "consociation"; and see the entry on Johannes
Althusius in *Politikai filozófiák enciklopédiája* (Budapest, 1995). See also
Friedrich, op. cit., pp. 12–13.
[41] Claude Lefort, *Democracy and Political Theory* (Minneapolis, 1988), p.
222.

political factions into ploughshares? With its enforced and legitimized sovereignty, with its supreme authority as state power, the secular state promised and more or less kept that internal tranquillity and provided protection against external threats. At the same time, as far as international conditions are concerned, the so-called Westphalian system, consisting of sovereign states, neither promised nor kept peace. It put a stop to the wars of religion but the task of maintaining international stability was supposed to be handled by the sovereign monarchs, by means of their foreign policy which was unstable, dynastic and lacking in any universal agency. Politics have become irrevocably this-worldly ever since. The network created by dynastic rationality did not seem to be rational later when, after the French Revolution, *raison d'état*, that is, an unshakable and irrevocable value called state interest, came to be determined by the dynamic nation-state. The builders of the nation-state considered the unstable, dynastic foreign policy which had often been generous at the expense of the subjects, to be no more than a caprice of sovereign monarch. Since then, the rationality of international relations was determined by state interest conceived as national interest in the series of bloody conflicts over the past two hundred years. Since the second half of the twentieth century then, that rationality has become questionable because of the processes of integration. The framework of the sovereign, territorial states has proved to be too narrow to handle the new, globally felt media, economic, ecological as well as criminal developments. The various organizations of international integration promise tranquillity and protection within their own boundaries against the confusion located outside the given organization. That can be said to be the denial of the rationality embodied in the sovereign states of the Westphalian system. New rationality means a new perspective. Although there is always talk of global effects and networks, the unifications planned the frameworks of the NATO, European Union, the Pacific Rim or the southern "cone" of Latin America[42] are evidently of a regional (not global) nature. Thus, the new outlook of the world still makes us see the world of politics under the

---

[42] Howard J. Wianda, "The Future of Political Reform in Southern Cone: Can Democracy be Sustained?" *Washington Quarterly* (Summer 1995).

familiar dichotomy of "friend—enemy." What is new is that the right to define the dichotomy is shifting from sovereign nation-states towards the integrating decision-making centers established by the nation-states.

The birth of the European sovereign states in the sixteenth and seventeenth centuries was accompanied by the political demarcation and formalization of space. A sovereign state meant the fixing of a territory and the cementing of the state boundaries as well as the extension of the market, of the legislature and, later, of the official national language too as far as the state boundaries. The system of the sovereign states resulted in a new structure of political space. With the sovereign states becoming nation-states, a new allegorical, anthropomorphic perspective was to prevail, which considered the nation a conscious, autonomous person, a noble genius, which was not just an abstraction but dwelt in the body of the nation as well.[43] At the end of the twentieth century, the post-modern corrections of modernization render both the rigid structure of political space made up by the sovereign states and the anthropomorphic view of the sovereign state questionable. As far as the problem of body is concerned, however, we are witnessing conflicting tendencies, as this personified and collective body is gaining even more significance than it had in the previous era but, in its biopolitical form and contents, it is referred to more in terms of the body of an ethnic state and less as a merely allegorical national body.[44] The sovereign nation-state was oppressive to be sure but those who were newly conquered or accepted were incorporated into society without discrimination. In contrast, the endeavors to establish ethnic states deconstructing and disintegrating the nation-state can be said to be divisive and exclusionary in a biopolitical sense; the state casts out the foreign body.

Nation-state means forcing a culture, a language or a dialect upon those living within the boundaries of the state, whereas ethnic state

---

[43] Benedict Anderson, *Imagined Communities: Reflections on the Origin and Spread of Nationalism* (London, 1983), and Camilleri, op. cit.

[44] Ferenc Fehér and Ágnes Heller, "Biopolitika," *Világosság* (August/ September 1994), and Ferenc Fehér, "Szárszó '93," *Kritika* (April and May 1994), as well as György Poszler, "Nemzeti Sorskérdések—Nemzeti Létfeltételek (Szárszó 1943!—Szárszó 1993?)" *Fényjelek* (Budapest, 1995).

means filling in the idea of state and the institution of state by a distinct ethnic group. The former, which is the older, nationalizes everything in an encompassing and oppressive way within its boundaries, whereas the latter, the new one, etatizes everything in an exclusionary and ostracizing way.

The most important fact is, however, that in the second half of the twentieth century new political configurations were unfolding. Internally, one of them is manifest in the configuration created by the trends in civil society that continuously question the sovereignty of state. Another one is the growth of the importance of the localities and internal regions as well as the trends of their political organization such as decentralization, devolution and autonomy. Externally—also in opposition of the sovereignty of state—there is the configuration of the organizations for international political integration, the supranational, communicative, cultural and economic configuration backed by international law. The sovereignty of the nation-state is wearing away, diminishing, and losing value in our shrinking world. The national meaning of the state is being ground between subnational and supranational millstones. The state as an institutional framework still exists and will be neutral towards national culture, as has already happened to religions and churches in the process of modernization.[45]

Nation, state and sovereignty are three socially-constructed terms which, linked to each other for centuries, have been fixed territorially too. The deconstruction of that conceptual assembly and geographical stability is taking place; it is accompanied by the separation of discrete notions with a different content in a new social configuration. It suggests that neither state, nor nation or sovereignty will cease to exist, having separated and reformed, but each of them will

---

[45] The separation of state and church took place in different ways, and to varying degrees in each European country and we can hardly consider the process complete. There are still debates on the religious indifference of the state and the problems stemming from that are yet to be handled. It is much more emphasized in issues of nationality and ethnicity. None-the-less, by a kind of analogy, the results of the more or less secularized state give rise to the question of the nationally and ethnically indifferent state particularly in a situation where narrow-minded state efforts to ethnicization underlie such thoughts.

take on a new meaning. The great narrative on the European nation-states will give way to minuscule discourses on the smaller but no less interesting dramas in the Europe of regions.[46]

Nowadays when one speaks about integration between or above nations, more often than not we soon realize that the political will behind talk and action is pointing at communities on the defense. The states creating integration steadily produce "social contracts" in order to protect and support one another, in order to be free within their own circle at least from the anarchy threatening again and again on the international scene. That implies both the renounciation of a smaller or larger section of the nation-state sovereignty and the development of a "new sovereignty"[47] on the level of integration in the case

[46] K. Czyzewski, "A határok eszméje az európai hagyományban," *Élet és Irodalom*, October 13, 1995. See also the issue of November 23–29 in *European Voice* 1, no. 8 on the representation of the German provinces and Scotland in Brussels. See as well György Enyedi, "Az átmenet új regionális folyamatai Magyarországon," manuscript, 1995.

[47] We put the notion of "new sovereignty" between quotation marks also because both its reality and recognition is still rather unstable and contingent, we should rather talk about the unfolding of a developing rather than actual, and especially not a finished system of relations. Undoubtedly, however, as far as the European Union is concerned, we are witnessing the evolution of European legislation and legal practice that in many respects bears numerous marks of sovereignty at the level of integration. Robert Schuman puts it this way in his article "Economic Integration is Impossible without Political Integration in the Long Run": "Until 1950, there had been no example of an institution that would have been beyond and above national sovereignty....Thus, the spell had to be broken." "Our policy, declared May 9, 1950, brought about an entirely new turn....The administration of the community is in the hands of the Commission. Within the framework of the Treaty, the Commission has an authority which is not submitted to any national government or legislation. In this sense, we may speak about a supranational authority supported by supranational legislation. It was established by the unanimous vote of the national legislators, whereas since its birth, the community has been living its own life and is not submitted to the contingencies and vagaries of national politics" Robert Schuman, pp. 114–116, originally, *Pour l'Europe* (Geneva, 1990). On the other hand, there is the warning of G. Schwarzenberger: "States cling to their sovereignty if there are values which are more important to them than the well-being of international society or even the maintenance of peace. If, rightly

of really efficient supranational unions. One may be justified in speaking about mutual economic advantages for the member states. Publicly, those benefits are spoken of most of the time and the question of distribution is the most discussed problem among those concerned. We must realize, however, that those organizations of integration are not economic endeavors, but protective and defensive political unions, whatever adjectives are applied to them.

The integration processes at the expense of state sovereignty may not mean the total disappearance of the nation-state as we know it, and it certainly does not bring the essence of sovereignty to an end. Within the integration new forms of ultimate decision-making are being established.[48] We can anticipate that, because of the democratic requirements of the twentieth century, those institutions will not take the form of absolutism nor will they be characterized by the prerogatives of the sovereign princes, whereas the tasks of both internal tranquillity and protection against external threats, which have always been the requirements of a modern state will be the demands expected of present-day organizations of integration. The sovereignty born together with the modern state, with a parallel history, may change so radically at the level of integration as to become unrecognizable. It may even change its name, but the reasons for establishing states and now the integration are very similar. Such reasons are the fear of anarchy, that is, the fear of the lack of authority, on the one hand, and the yearning for peace and security on the other. State sovereignty is on a downward path, organizations of international integration are on the rise. "The king is dead! Long live the king!"

---

or wrongly, a people is convinced of the superiority of its own way of life over that of other nations, it becomes the supreme object of statesmanship to safeguard such cherished values at any price. The doctrine of State sovereignty is then no longer a mere relic of the past. The old bottles have been filled with a new and potent vintage." Schwarzenberger, op. cit., p. 98. At the same time, the two quotations also give evidence that the discussion of the points Europe of the nation states versus a deeply integrated supranation-state Europe has been going on for decades. Although we cannot say that the discussion has been concluded by now, for the past decades the integration process has not only extended geographically but deepened as well at the expense of the nation-states.

[48] Molnár, op. cit.

What is it all about? Is it about the end of sovereignty or are we kicking it "upstairs"? We do see that one cannot speak about global unification, world peace or a world government. More precisely: words along those lines are plenty, whereas one finds mostly no more than regional endeavors for unification in practice, and even within those the sovereign state or the rationality of integration should not be regarded as the guarantee of tranquillity and of the famous "sustainable development."[49] The logic of integration seems to win the competition among the many options. The countries where material and intellectual output as well as quality of life are at a high level are the not so altruistic prime movers for unions. Consequently, the countries that remain outside the framework of integrative organizations may have to face a rather gloomy future or, to put it somewhat rudely, they might shove their useless sovereignty.

Thus, the international organizations of integration do not solve the essential problems of sovereignty: the questions of peace, security, tranquillity cannot be disposed of as resolved. There is no doubt, however, that in the new situation we should still raise all the questions of sovereignty: Whose is it? Where is it? What is it? Does it exist at all? Whose exercise of supreme authority can be justified properly enough to guarantee loyalty? Are the debates about the sovereignty of the state or of the nation? Can those two be separated as were church and state? The end of what are we talking about and what is it that will to survive? Can a nation exist without state, and can a state survive without sovereignty?[50] If we had all the answers to those questions we could feel safe in the political arena and we could enjoy the conditions the idea of sovereignty promised so generously and self-confidently.

---

[49] Kálmán Kulcsár, "Integration and Disintegration in Contemporary Europe," in *Integration and Disintegration in Contemporary Europe*, eds. G. G. Márkus and L. Guba (Budapest, 1995); Galló, op. cit., and Enyedi, op. cit.
[50] See notes no. 14 and 43.

5. *What Should Hungary Do with the Above Questions?*

We have formulated such a title not because we want to give grandiloquent answers for our country, but to show by the very form of the question how deeply our thinking and discourse are determined by a centuries-old tradition of the personification of the sovereign state. "Great Britain regards this question as an insult," "Germany will not delay its answer," "Russia is entering the war," and similar expressions have been used everywhere for long. In our thought, the personage of past sovereign monarchs as well as the supreme authority embodied in their persons survive in the personification of state sovereignty and was even strengthened by the romanticism of the last century, that is, by the allegorical conception of nation-state. We usually refer to a sovereign state as a person who acts in possession of his own rationality, morality, will, freedom, who has a dignity that should be protected always and by any means, and who is not just the sum of its citizens but a higher being. Although in the declaration of *Recrudescunt*, expressions like "renewed are the bleeding wounds of the Hungarian nation" are beautiful and worthy of being taught, they indicate that Hungary could not be a sovereign state even in the age of Ferenc Rákóczi (the ruling prince of Transylvania and the commander of the Hungarian insurgent forces in the eighteenth century); but without an explanation these words can be just plain biologisms and psychologisms that may be a suitable excuse for not thinking. Such images do have their consequences.

As a matter of fact, however, the state is a political institution whose internal sense is made up of different motive forces and conflicting interest groups influenced by various experiences and values, and their coming together is a historical conjuncture. The borders which are but demarcation lines due to the instability of politics, enclose a populated territory, where supreme authority was established traditionally and rationalized variously. This authority may be of different character but hardly anyone considers this to be a personage embodied in the nation any more.

"Does domestic production need help?" "Is there a need for the defense of the homeland?" "Should the domestic film industry or other areas of cultural and academic life be subsidized?" These are familiar questions that are often raised in other forms too. "Should national industry be aided?" "Do we need a national army?" "Are we to save the national film industry?" The concepts of "economic" as well as "cultural sovereignty" emerge in such contexts.[51] Seemingly, it is about the same thing as the questions above. The perception of the tasks to be solved is radically different, though. The questions are put within the narrative of the nation-state. The answers given by the politicians of any persuasion are usually positive. But both the questions and the answers look different if we glance at them with Hungary's European integration in mind. In possession of sovereignty, one may decide that the solutions that satisfy the majority of the citizens can be found only if the country manages to get inside an organization of integration where she can enjoy security. However, a different decision may be taken and Hungary may stay outside international and supranational integration as a matter of moral commandment, since integration would limit sovereignty.

Such a limitation would be an insult. A slur on the body national, on the dignity of the nation-state, etc., etc. And we should see that it is by no means just a lament about some damages conceived allegorically but it assumes factual expressions as well. It may lead to the disappearance of the national film industry or the national army which, within an integrated military organization, must obey even commands that are not linked to national sovereignty. Inside an economic union, the sheer notion of national industry becomes meaningless since both employment and profit-sharing is not constrained

---

[51] The questions raised by everyday practice do not pay attention to the essential nexus. Sovereignty is a political category and it is not worth speaking about economic or cultural sovereignty. If, however, the idea of state is a means of the nation as it is assumed in the concept of nation-state and not that of the actual citizens, then both economy and culture are integral parts of the nation-building, hence of the "national sovereignty" and, furthermore, the national market as well as national culture strive for supremacy within the political boundaries. All this, of course, is no more than a particular outward form of political sovereignty.

by state boundaries except for the accounting of the inherited state debts. Within the framework of integration, the monopolistic position of the state, hence sovereignty itself, remain vulnerable.[52] Moreover, it can disappear, in its strict classic sense, because absolute and indivisible sovereignty either exists or does not exist at all.

As long as three hundred years ago, Hugo Grotius cast doubt upon such a strict concept of sovereignty saying that it is meaningless to speak about absolute sovereignty, about sovereignty that is above law (*legibus solutus*) because the sovereign is actually bound by natural law, by the contracts made either with his/her own subjects or with other sovereigns, hence sovereignty is limited for many reasons and conditions. Grotius's position, on which international law was based, was somewhere between popular sovereignty and monarchic sovereignty and was suitable to a differentiated interpretation of changing reality. It is more difficult to exercise and to understand sovereignty of this kind than to assert seemingly simple absolute sovereignty, but as Grotius wrote "in political affairs nothing is quite free from inconvenience."[53]

With all this we want to suggest that the problem of sovereignty that is limited and restricted to certain functions is not an entirely new one. It was brought forth long before the activities of transnational enterprises and the movement of capital, before the establishment of supranational organizations of our time. The concept of a sovereignty that is monarchic, that is homogeneous and indivisible, still has its influence today, even without absolute monarchs, because of the impetus of a popular sovereignty conceived within the framework of the nation. All the more so as in several parts of Eastern Europe nation-states are being established right now. On the so-called developed side, while there are very strong integrative endeavors aiming at the deconstruction of the nation-state, one sees the interests of the nation-state defended time and again even within the member states of the European Union. All in all, in Europe, since the end of the

---

[52] Rosas, op. cit.
[53] Quoted by Merriam, op. cit., p. 22.

World War II, the perspective beyond the Westphalian system has become widespread as is the institutionalization of that perspective, while there is a strong trend of nation-state building keeping the Westphalian system alive, as well as "Euroskepticism" referring to national interests, or views opposed to the integration process. We could say that there are two views of Europe, and this situation does have its complicated consequences. When both the process of integration and the sovereign nation-state are appreciated, people are suffering from a kind of diplopia. We are prone to think of the same European region as a loose league of sovereign nation-states and as a union above the nation-states at the same time. Because the Romanians or the Moldavians are not the only ones who would like to live within the framework of a nation-state, and look at Europe from such a perspective but, as we know, those inclinations are not alien to the British and French citizens either, whereas the values and benefits of integration are politically definitive factors both here and there. The prevalence of those contradictory perspectives varies locally, of course.

Hungary is in an intermediate position, as is usually the case in other respects too. It is a nation-state and, partly because of its official history, her population looks confidently upon her sovereignty in spite of the many unsuccessful struggles for independence, and in spite of the academically proven lack of sovereignty. Since 1989, it has possessed the formal marks of sovereignty too. Neither the citizens on the whole nor the elites feel any obligation to prove that Hungary is a nation-state. Yet the possible circumstances of getting into a dependent position and the vague nature of the benefits and disadvantages of being within an integration, that is, simple uncertainty, create much doubt and anguish. In return for the benefits of integration, either the population of the country or the politicians in their place may decide to renounce the sovereignty that has become mostly fictive and anachronistic, but they may also decide to insist on the country staying outside a particular or all unions.

By taking a sovereign decision concerning a union—has a widespread view holds—we keep and preserve our sovereignty. In many cases,however, the depth and the nature of integration are such that it becomes generally hopeless to try to loosen the bonds once they have been accepted.[54] Sovereignty is fictive and anachronistic as a result of both internal and external factors. Those focusing on the nation-state should see that the unified and indivisible sovereignty of the nation-state is limited by at least four factors: political pluralism and democratic parliament; the private sector independent of the state and influential also outside the economy; local and regional governments and the new configuration of the European cities; the development and impact of international integration. The order of those factors suggests the hierarchy of their power, the last one being the strongest.[55] With regard to legal formalities, one may say that the state does no more than delegate some decision making to external, internal, higher and lower authorities. It keeps its sovereignty, however, as far as being able to annul the results. In case of the institutionalization of the delegation of power, the efforts at withdrawal are mostly in vain. Thus local governments may recognize that property can be used independently of the state, and political pluralism is protected by law. The international organizations of integration, on the other hand, function on the basis of international law, whose stipulations the domestic legal practice is obliged to accept in several cases.[56] Many "external decisions" on security policy, human rights, economy and the protection of the environment and nature demand acquiescence by Hungary. To put it bluntly: those decisions have to be obeyed!

That obedience is, however, only an outcome of the will to join an organization of integration. And one may also renounce one's obedience. If one considers the enforcement of international law (which depends to an increasing extent on the activities of the international organizations of integration as well as on the activity of the states within the organizations) as an infringement on the idea of nation,

---

[54] It can be said that after the decision of joining an organization of integration it is possible to make another—withdrawal. In the supranational European Union the practice of expulsion and withdrawal, hence their consequences are unknown

[55] A description of the four agents impinging upon sovereignty can be found in Rosas, op. cit. and Enyedi, op. cit.

[56] And this is particularly true concerning so-called European law. See Rosas, op. cit.

one will be prone to oppose it in order to defend the sovereignty of the nation-state. The questions are open: what is such an agent actually defending then, and does the people, whose name is evoked so often, really need that defense. Just like it is generally possible to fight for the autocratic centralization of the state in opposition to democracy, that is, for the restoration of the old internal sovereignty, it is also possible to hinder, slow down, delay, even block for a long time the integration of a country into a given international organization. Everything is imaginable in policy and, if the collective imagination is strong enough, almost everything can be implemented as well. Luckily, however, certain fantasies are rather far-fetched.

In Hungary today it is impossible to implement an anti-democratic policy passionately addicted to a certain past, and which would try to restore the internal sovereignty of the nation-state. However, the case is not so simple if we consider sovereignty in the international sense, which is based on the equal rights of states.

As we have already mentioned, Hungary is a confident nation-state. That makes it easier to join a strong organization of integration because Hungary does not need to prove its nation-statehood. On the other hand, the experience and the awareness of that quality have been historically conditioned by a continuous lack of independence, that is, with limitations on sovereignty leading to a state of insecurity. That can be regarded as a handicap in an integration process since the multidimensional unification is apt to foment emotions of independence anytime. Besides, there is another burden to be carried: the various political interpretations of the difficult circumstances under which Hungarian minorities live beyond the political boundaries of Hungary.

In Hungary, many would prefer integration into a developed international organization because they focus on its supposed economic benefits. According to others, integration threatens national values that can be preserved only within the framework of an independent nation-state. Others claim that joining an international organization of integration would mean giving up on the Hungarian population living abroad since, they presume, a sovereign Hungary is able to do more along these lines than a member state bound by the rules of the community. The opinions vary also on the issue as some think that the problem can be solved satisfactorily only within and by an organization of integration. All these opinions are articulated within the context of party politics. The distribution of opinions can be measured more or less by public opinion polls, but we can state outright that the questions to be raised in such research concern the problems of the nation-state. In everyday politics the sovereignty of the nation-state is going to be the main issue.

The reason why the problems of the nation-state are going to be steadily on the agenda of international politics in the foreseeable future is not that the politicians and the citizens interested in politics are unable to rise intellectually to the level of the specialized literature declaring the twilight of the European nation-state with a fairly consistent logic. One reason for this resistance is that the existing organizations of integration curtail the sovereignty of the member states whereas they are supposed to yield only benefits, and they cannot become objects of loyalty.[57] Moreover, the benefits are sometimes rather questionable.

Let us take a look at the debates on the unified currency to be introduced in the European Union. The decision taken to collectively and unanimously by the member states in 1991, stating that a monetary union should be established by 1999, was an essentially political one. The common money may be referred to as a clear symbol of the political union, of turning the page on a past of warfare between sovereign states. The use of common currency would also be, of course, more profitable. But the criterion for membership in the monetary union is that the deficit of the current balance of payment should not exceed three percent of the gross national product. In order to meet this requirement social expenditures have to be cut, several welfare programs must be withdrawn from the recipients. The population of the member countries is worried, afraid, and disturbed. Indeed, why three percent, why not two or five? Who knows? The leading politicians of the member states, guided by political aims, in an enthusiastic and excited mood, agreed to set a number, and that number has come to a

---

[57] S. Hoffmann, "Thoughts on French Nation Today," *Daedalus* (Summer 1993).

life of its own since then.[58] The decision was made by the appropriate European forum; the "new sovereign" expressed its existence through the decision. No one else has the right to decide. Thus, benefits can be questioned from different point of view, and the issue of loyalty is not raised at all, but the existence and the influence of a "new sovereign," which makes state sovereignty impossible in several respects, can be clearly felt. Hungary would only like to join the union, yet she is forced to comply with that mysterious number even without actual membership.

The power of international institutions is increasing while that of the nation-states is decreasing. Moreover, the states that remain outside the integrated states live amidst insecurity. The values of profitability and security are set against the values of national independence and dignity. Is it reality or appearance?—one may raise the still hopeful question, trying to establish harmony between the values in conflict. The values, making up a world of non-existing yet valid essences, do not tolerate such questions. It is only human to perceive appearances linked to values as facts.

In Hungary, five percent of the population claimed being very much concerned by the national question, while thirty-one percent confessed some concern, forty percent little concern, and twenty-three denied any concern for it.[59] It is up to the analysis whether one

---

[58] See the features in the December 13, 1995 issue of *Newsweek*. The setting of the above-mentioned three percent, just like the invention of other criteria, must have been prepared by thorough calculation and speculation, yet those were carried out within the framework of a definite political conception. That concept was to serve the acceleration of integration, thus it was a political standpoint. That view was accepted by the representatives of the member states unanimously and has become official at the institutional level of the European Union. If we want to see convincing evidence that, above the nation-state, there does exist a level of integration invested with power, it is enough to take into account that a considerable part of the population and of the politicians in the countries concerned fight against something. That something in turn is neither their own government nor simply the bureaucracy in Brussels but an integration movement that lives its own life, a separate agent of authority at the level of the European Union.

[59] Mária Vásárhelyi, "A nemzet és a területi kérdés a közgondolkodásban," *Jel-Kép*, no. 1 (1994) and Ildikó Kováts, "Közszolgálati műsorszórás és nemzetállam," in *Közszolgálatiság a médiában, ábránd vagy realitás?,* ed. Tamás Terestyéni (Budapest, 1995).

sees evidence of national nihilism in that statistical distribution or, on the contrary, that the majority still harbors a national loyalty of sorts, even if to different degrees. That uncertainty makes the diplopia mentioned above, that is, the paradoxical evaluation of the integration process, more understandable. It is strengthened by the double talk of political spokespersons of the different international organizations emphasizing the benefits and the inviolability of national dignity in the field of culture while tactfully ignoring the curtailing of authority, the decrease of the sovereignty of member states. Is it tact, tactics, or ignorance? Or is it because the sovereignty of the nation-state is withering away while no new sovereign evolves?

As even at the core of political integration they do not have answers to those questions that would be clear and relatively definite from a political point of view, it is easy to see why such questions are raised only tentatively in Hungary. What are the definite statements we can make at this point?

6. Summary

Sovereignty as it evolved historically and the fact that Hungary was never sovereign historically are the complex consequences of several circumstances. Because of different interest and diversified, conflicting values, the sovereignty of Hungary is simultaneously sacred, an empty political slogan, a determined aspiration, a commonplace, a flattering platitude, a misleading conceit and a fact recognized by international law.

The constitution and practice of the United Nations are in many respects the modern application of the Westphalian system. Apart from the internal political conditions, the United Nations includes more and more sovereign members, in the traditional sense of the word. The evolution of the Westphalian system was the revolution of norms in Christian Europe. Today, the European Union is a qualitatively new alteration which came into existence after the Westphalian system had expanded globally.[60] And in international politics it is not

---

[60] Daniel Philpott, "Sovereignty: An Introduction and Brief History," *Journal of International Affairs* (Winter 1995).

the United Nations, a world forum of the old type, that represents the new trends but strong regional organizations like NATO or the European Union. Those are the "new sovereigns." They are sovereign in the sense that in selected functions they are entitled to make decisions that are mandatory for the member states. Those decisions do have an impact beyond the borders of the communities; the sovereign states outside the organizations have to put up with them in a rather passive way. The boundaries of the organizations of integration in turn coincide with the borders of tranquillity promised and protected by the military, the communication and economic forces of the given union. The place of indivisible sovereignty associated with the idea of the territorial state is being taken by functionally articulated sovereignty, and that means that certain functions are to remain with the state while others, undoubtedly the more important ones, are to shift to the centers of integration.[61] Outside the regional organizations of integration, the tranquillity among the proliferating large and small—increasingly smaller—sovereign states is neither guaranteed nor promised by anyone; it may only be enforced by regional integrational authorities if it is in their interest. Outside the supranational organizations, neither tranquillity nor welfare are to be expected. Thus, Hungary is interested in joining.

There is no sign to indicate that a global, unbiased or even unequal unification encompassing the whole world is likely take place in the foreseeable future.[62] The countries that are sovereign traditionally and the proliferating ethnic states aspiring to sovereignty would like to take part in a developed organization of integration in competition with one another. In most cases, their plea goes unheeded. Hungary may have the opportunity to join such an organization if she is both lucky and resolved to do so. It is questionable, however, if there is, or will be such determination in domestic politics.

---

[61] See the works, already quoted, by Camilleri and Gottlieb.

[62] István Bibó details the problems including the legitimization of central authority and the political elite on a world scale. At the time he wrote his book, he could refer only to the pattern of the United Nations organization. See his *The Paralysis of International Institutions and the Remedies* (New York, 1976).

As we know in Hungary the moderate political authorities, the political parties in Parliament, the ruling as well as the opposition parties are all in favor of integration. We should not, however, avoid the question: how important are the political parties in the present situation, when the gap between politicians and public opinion is widening all over the world? In the global economy, national governments and domestic politics have to face rather strong constraints, the "political market" frozen in the first half of this century is thawing, the democratic political parties are viewed with growing skepticism. The main reason is that only a few can sell themselves easily and on advantageous terms as workers by making use of their knowledge of the new information technology, while many are afflicted by growing worries and by a feeling of superfluousness in the information age.[63] And those who are not capable or are little capable of "cognitive mobilization," that is of mobilizing their marketable knowledge, may not want to listen to moderate politicians and can easily be mobilized against international integration. We must also take into account extensive resistance; the resistance of those who cling to the slogans of autonomy, since the desire for independence resists all promises and opportunities of security. And one must be aware of the resistance of the politically articulated groups who may become the economic losers of the integration. Thus in Hungary we must also consider that not only will the externally set preconditions hinder joining any regional organization, but the internal democratic acceptance will prove difficult to attain as well.

In Hungary, those with a voice in politics use the narrative of the nation-state independently of the feelings of the citizens. The spoken agenda of politics is filled mostly with the national issues: the unchangeability of the boundaries of the nation-state, the guarantees and doubts about that principle; the relationship of the ethnic minorities vis-à-vis the nation-state within and beyond the borders; signing the so-called bilateral treaties with the neighboring nation-states, as

---

[63] Hans-Georg Betz, "The Confidence Gap Between Citizens and Politicians in Advanced Western Democracies: How Serious Is the Problem?" in *Tackling the Credibility Gap Between Politicians and the General Public in Europe* (Brussels, 1994).

well as the debates on the use of such treaties, etc. The political discourse on nation and ethnic identity, carried on within the conceptual framework of the nation-state, suits the modern configuration of the Westphalian system, in which territory demarcated by state boundaries is given sovereignty which is to be regarded as sacred. When, however, not only theoretically but also because of the existence of international regional organizations, sovereignty is actually being deconstructed, when the unity of the authority over a definite territory and population is dissolving into institutional configurations, then the endless discourse on nation-state, on its sovereignty, seem to be rather outdated.

Economy-based reasoning cannot outweigh those factors which many people consider "soft" or insignificant; which can be used as arguments both for and against integration; but if they are ignored by the adherents of integration, they can be used entirely as counter-arguments. We are thinking of the elements of political culture: of feeling, of ideas, of attitudes that have a political impact. That concerns the possible association with the European Union or with the NATO. Because of the level and content of its education, the population of Hungary belongs to Europe intellectually. It should not be overlooked, however, that this population is characterized by an ethnic perspective, that is, by an inclination to approach things with the help of emotionally based ethnic categories. That is mostly unconscious, but reinforced through political means by the state. This characteristic mix of ethnic thought and national pride works more against integration than for it. Consequently, the appreciation of the practical benefits of integration may result in remorse, even for the individuals. To put it symbolically: the conflict between the European super-ego and the ethnic id, might cause confusion for some egos.

The functionally articulated delegation of state sovereignty is not directed only upward. Although not independently of the internal decisions of integration, the regionalism that develops autonomously inside borders, and often transcends the borders too, erodes nation-state sovereignty and state-centered politics from below as well. The theory and practice called the "Europe of regions" means the decentralization of familiar state politics, even in the form of transferring certain items of legislation; namely, a new kind of decentralization that concerns even foreign policy, which is supposed to be the prerogative of the central government. We may also say that the difference between internal and external policies is vanishing in that area too and, because of the efficient regulation and economic distribution carried out by the "new sovereign," the external one is becoming more decisive. Although the present administrative county structure of Hungary does not suit regional cooperation because of the degree of its particularism and lack of authority, the regional networks beyond the borders, particularly the metropolitan belt of the Vienna-Budapest axis, can be said to be widening dynamically even today.[64] Those systems help Hungary work her way into European integration, promoting the internal political acceptance of the process of integration as well.

We cannot foresee the results of the internal political and democratic procedures and particularly the results of a referendum, which would make everybody face the question of integration. Much work can be done towards an assessment of the "pros" and "cons," for the political articulation of the benefits and drawbacks, but the "social unconscious" cannot be influenced by words. It should be taken into account that our political culture is premodern, our political institutions are newly modernized ones, while our intellectual atmosphere is saturated with postmodern elements.[65] Some would protect the independence of the nation-state at any price, or want a Hungarian ethnic state. For the advocates of the latter, European integration is threatening or at least a suspicious strategy and, like the West European "new right," they may organize themselves as a political movement in opposition to integration.[66] Others regard the European Union as a loose alliance of sovereign nation-states and support a union of that kind in the interest of modernization. Their wishful thinking coincides with the opinions expressed by some government

---

[64] György Enyedi, "Kettészakadt ország? A területi egyenlőtlenségek és a területfejlesztési politika," in *Kérdőjelek: a magyar kormány 1994–1995* (Budapest, 1995).

[65] See the discussion on ethnopolitics in *Politikatudományi Szemle*, no. 4 (1994); nos. 1–3 (1995); Enyedi, op. cit.

[66] See the August 21, 1995 issue of *Time*.

politicians of certain countries already inside the Union, while it is in essential contradiction with the principles and practice of unification. Finally, there are some who (beyond good and evil, that is, beyond the virtues and vices of the nation-state) fascinated by multiculturalism, thinking in terms of a multiethnic and multinational state, and suppose that smaller or larger cultures can be preserved and maintained intact only within a wider framework.

People are neither wise nor stupid, they are fallible mortals influenced by their own imagination. If, instead of the insistence on the integrity of the "body national," an approach which focuses on security and quality of life is gaining strength, there will be greater emphasis on the practical issues of integration. If there is less room on the political agenda for the "bilateral treaties" with neighboring countries, which are to guarantee the permanence of state boundaries (so crucial for some politicians), and there is more talk of improving the quality of life, then we can afford moderate optimism, for these perspectives are beyond our narrow political limits. The lack of vision, so often mentioned, the lack of perspective, so characteristic of party and government programs, can be partly explained by the fact that, stuck within a territory of ninety-two thousand square kilometers, they are unable to visualize the perspectives of integration. Hungary will always be where she is. But it makes a difference whether she will be here within the continually contracting framework of nation-state sovereignty or within a far-reaching unification. The former, that is, the withdrawal behind "the borders," would be an understandable historical reflex. The latter would be an open ended adventure. Let us hope that we will be given the opportunity to choose.

László Valki

SOVEREIGNTY, INTERNATIONAL LAW AND INTERNATIONAL ORGANIZATIONS

> A customs union is not a homeland and
> mutual interest in the price of milk is not a
> constituent element of a state.
> *Le Monde, January 24, 1966*

International law, of course, always protects sovereignty, which is under constant threat. Barely has "in-between Europe" freed itself of socialist internationalism or of the friendship, cooperation, and mutual assistance agreements with the Soviet Union, when many began to ponder ways of letting loose foreign predator capital and uniform European milk prices upon it, with masses of GI Joes descending from the sky. Under these circumstances it is difficult to defend sovereignty.

International law itself is not always clear on the subject. It protected sovereignty even at a time when the Soviets first stepped on the soil of "in-between Europe." The United Nation's Charter, signed in 1945, declared the "sovereign equality" of member states, furthermore, the first friendship, cooperation, and mutual assistance pacts with Moscow, signed in 1948, also specified the obligation to respect state sovereignty, though only with regard to the development of economic and cultural relations.[1] A second series of such agreements twenty years later already mentioned sovereignty in the proper place, namely, in the article on "Socialist Internationalism and Fraternal Assistance." A 1957 bilateral treaty expressly stated: "The temporary

---

[1] Article 5 of the Hungarian-Soviet friendship, cooperation, and mutual assistance agreement signed on February 18, 1948.

stationing of Soviet troops on the territory of the Hungarian People's Republic does not in any way affect the sovereignty of the Hungarian state; the Soviet troops shall not interfere in the domestic affairs of the Hungarian People's Republic."[2]

Characteristically enough, the agreement referred to the legal status of armed forces already stationed in Hungary without reference to any previous agreement authorizing the presence of these troops. Subsequently, the notion gained broad currency. There were hardly any "progressive" Asian or African country with which Hungary did not sign a friendship agreement with the almost ritualistic affirmation of respect for sovereignty. In the sixties and seventies, United Nations General Assembly resolutions were literally sprinkled with the notion. This was the period when a large number of colonies acquired independence which, understandably, laid emphasis on their sovereign status at every opportunity. On the other hand, it would be futile to look for the notion of sovereignty in the documents of the Potsdam Conference, in the peace treaties of Versailles and Paris, in the North Atlantic Treaty, or the Warsaw Pact. In case of the first three documents, this may be considered a natural omission as their primary aim was not the declaration of sovereignty of the defeated states. In the case of the Washington Treaty, the omission may have been inadvertent, which cannot be said for the authors of the Warsaw document. Not wanting to do much paperwork, its authors simply copied, almost verbatim, passages of the North Atlantic Treaty. The situation was no less ambiguous in other regions and in other eras. The term "sovereignty" was used in some treaties, giving rise to conceptual contradictions, while it was omitted in others where it should have been mentioned.

––––––––––––––––––

[2] Article 1 of the "Agreement between the Government of the Hungarian People's Republic and the Government of the Union of the Soviet Socialist Republics on the legal status of the Soviet troops temporarily stationed on the territory of the Hungarian People's Republic, signed in Budapest, on May 27, 1957." The agreement regulated questions such as criminal procedure in the event a Soviet soldier commits a crime, or answerability for damages caused by Soviet troops.

How Does International Law Interpret Sovereignty?

There is no precise answer to this question, since written international law has never defined the notion of sovereignty in any form. Nor, for that matter, has it defined the notions of non-intervention or the right to self-determination, nor a whole list of other terms used time and again, as if their meaning were clearly understood by all. None of this is surprising, however. Legislators do not usually undertake impossible and/or needless tasks. Often they consider it sufficient to include a notion into domestic law, leaving interpretation to judicial practice. Penal codes, for example, usually do not contain a definition of manslaughter.

In any case, international law, by nature, does not favor such definitions. Written norms demand consensus on the part of the community of states. This is near impossible as long as the sovereign statehood—of, say, Taiwan—is a matter of debate, or as long as there is no acceptable definition equally applicable to the People's Republic of China and Lesotho in the middle of the South African Republic, or to such mini-states as Saint Lucia or Vanuatu. The latter are long-standing members of the United Nations, but only experienced skippers are reputed to know their exact geographical location.

Definition of the notion would have been the task of international legal experts, but they do not particularly excel as far as definitions are concerned. An entry in the Hungarian *Encyclopedia of Diplomacy and International Law*, published in the sixties, gives the commonly accepted view, according to which sovereignty means "the unlimited and indivisible supremacy of the state domestically, and independence in relation to foreign powers....A state is sovereign if it is independent in every sphere of its activity, in every aspect of its decision-making."[3] To this day, many start from this definition when they seek to answer whether Hungary would stay sovereign if admitted into the European Union or NATO. But is there a single state in the world with unlimit-

---

3   Gyula Hajdu, ed., *Diplomáciai és nemzetközi jogi lexikon* (Budapest, 1967), p. 802.

ed and indivisible supremacy? Is there a single state which is independent in every sphere of activity, in every aspect of decision-making, which can make decisions regardless of the interests, goals, and aspirations of other—also sovereign—states? Is it impossible to reconcile the sovereignty of two states under such conditions? Can we speak of independence in an age when states are becoming increasingly interdependent, particularly within the framework of economic or military-political integrations? The answer is obviously negative, inferring that the sovereignty not only of Hungary, but of all states which have joined these organizations may be questioned. Since this inference is meaningless, another solution should be sought. The evident solution would be to discard the notion itself, but it has become so much a part of political usage as to preclude this possibility.

Searching its historical roots would not help much either. Although the concept was known in ancient times (for Aristotle, for instance, the highest authority in a community was the sovereign),[4] the category of sovereignty became important only toward the end of the Middle Ages. In the struggle against the imperial ambitions of the pope and the emperor, feudal lords and princes aimed to establish their own sovereignty. For them, sovereignty was not a notion for social science to define, but a militant slogan intolerant of exceptions or precise description. Those lords and princes who gained their independence from papal and imperial rule and, at the same time, vanquished the suzerains on their own territories, subsequently became absolute monarchs. They claimed unlimited power, unrestrained by anything on their territories. As it happened, their interests eventually coincided with the interests of the growing bourgeoisie which wanted to create a unified (national) market to replace the divided feudal market and supported a strong, stable, central, that is, state power against the unstable feudal hierarchy and its chaotically interwoven power structure.

Concerning the external aspect of sovereignty, the Peace of Westphalia also defined internationally meaningful restrictions on

---

[4] Helmut Steinberger, "Sovereignty," in *Encyclopaedia of Public International Law* 10, ed. Rudolf Bernhardt (1987), p. 399.

sovereignty, inasmuch as each cosignatory had to respect the territorial integrity of the others. The restriction, however, did not extend to those not party to this peace treaty system. The European Christian powers did not recognize the sovereignty of countries of the non-Christian world, which they thus felt free to conquer. However, they could not take control of the seas, because it contravened the merchants' interest in free shipping and that of their respective states.

Actually, at that time, the absolute monarch was considered sovereign, not the state. According to Jean Bodin—the first to write a comprehensive essay to discuss the meaning of sovereignty (1576)—sovereignty is the right of the nation as a whole, which it confers on the monarch who, given this right, becomes the sovereign of the country. In Bodin's interpretation, however, sovereignty itself is not an absolute category and, therefore, not unrestricted, being limited by natural law, Divine law, private property, and international law. In other respects, the sovereign is invested with unlimited legislative powers, wherefore sovereignty is tantamount to absolute power over the subjects. Grotius professed the same view in his work published in 1625. He wrote that supreme power is the power the exercise of which is not subject to the rights of others. According to him, a monarch has unrestricted power, but he must obey Divine law and natural law.

Once the bourgeoisie turned against the feudal system the interpretations no longer identified sovereignty with a single person. John Locke, for instance, wrote about the idea of parliamentary sovereignty and recognized the right to rebel against the absolute monarch on the basis of natural law. Charles-Louis de Montesquieu, and later Jean-Jacques Rousseau, talked about the sovereignty of the people, and not their representatives, as the embodiment of sovereignty.

In the evolution of the notion of sovereignty, different aspects were alternately stressed. Although Bodin believed that a sovereign is bound by existing international law, and the common law of non-intervention also became widely accepted, several authors began to discuss the unlimited nature of sovereignty. This interpretation was closely related to the expansionist ambitions of feudal empires and, eventually, of capitalist nation-states. The jurists of the age rushed to meet expectations by proclaiming the complete independence of the state, arguing that no one may violate the sovereignty of the state which may, however, bring decisions without regard for other states. Their argument received an unexpected boost from Hegel, who called international law an "external state law" that can be changed similarly to domestic law, consequently, a state may take a unilateral decision to withdraw from international agreements. Without necessarily referring to Hegel, the idea persisted that in case of "injury" a state— if it served its interests—had the right to do anything in international relations, thus, it had the "sacred" right to start a war, hence the right of conquest, of territorial acquisition.

However, the unlimited national supremacy and complete external independence of the state—that is, sovereignty in the absolute sense—was irreconcilable with expanding international relations. Legal regulation of the latter made sense only if unilateral changes were backed by sanctions. Permanent reciprocal commitments meant that in the future a state pledged to act in accordance with, or refrain from acting, some specified policy. In other words, the state consented to curtail its sphere of activity in foreign relations. Generally, this limitation was self-imposed, yet it brought forth a contradiction hard to resolve: namely, it limited the unrestricted supremacy of the state. The untenability of this notion had to be corrected and an attempt to do so was made by the German scholar Georg Jellinek. He wrote that contractual limitation approved and decided by the state is, in fact, a self-limitation which does not affect the totality of sovereignty, while limitation imposed by an external power (or another state) curtails it. Supremacy of a sovereign state is unlimited, but not absolute, since it may be self-limited.

This explanation however, left yet another basic contradiction: a state was sovereign in terms of international law, but its sovereignty could be voided by force at any time. Not even the devastation of World War I motivated the international community to ban waging war. The Covenant of the League of Nations banned only wars of conquest thus it became simply a matter of deciding what the government press release should say to explain why it crossed the borders of a neighboring state. Consequently, a sovereign state could still be attacked if the attack was "justified." The formal, but total ban was pronounced only a few years later as a result of an incidental diplomatic interlude. Amidst the European foreign policy skirmishes of the twenties, French Foreign Minister Aristide Briand proposed to his American counterpart, Frank Kellogg, a bilateral treaty declaring their eternal friendship and the renunciation of war. Briand was seeking United States backing for the preservation of the post-war status quo. Kellogg agreed, but suggested a multilateral treaty instead. The French had no choice but to concur, and within a short period nearly every state involved agreed to sign. In 1928, the document known as the Kellogg-Briand Pact virtually declared a ban on war.

This represented a turning point in international law and, specifically, in the evolution of the notion of sovereignty. After 1928, it could no longer be said that although every state is sovereign, its sovereignty can be voided by war. It is an entirely different question that there was still no precise definition of the concept of sovereignty and practical efforts to have sovereignty respected were even less successful.

The whole problem of unrestricted national supremacy and other aspects of external independence remained unsolved. The category of "self-limitation" did not become generally accepted, mainly for reasons of logic. Originally, the term meant restriction on the state's general freedom of action. It was applied to cases when a state pledged not to attack another state, as well as to cases when it committed itself to positive action—such as providing assistance to a state under attack. However, the suggestion that the state was free to provide assistance, until a commitment was made, was an etymological fallacy. In addition, the term allowed for the conclusion that a state is free to withdraw from its international commitments, since it can abrogate its own "self-limitation" at will. The fact is that commitments are never unilateral: they create a legal relationship between two or more parties which, theoretically, may end only by the common consent of the respective parties.

Hans Kelsen tried to solve this dilemma—and that of the interpretation of sovereignty in general—by attempting to create a "pure legal doctrine," in which sovereignty is given as a notion "cleansed" of its sociological, psychological, and political elements.[5] We do not know

---

[5] Hans Kelsen, *Das Problem der Souveränität und die Theorie des Völkerrechts: Beitrag zu einem reinen Rechtslehre* (Tübingen, 1920).

his reasons for the cleansing, especially since very few contributed as much as he did to the sociological aspects of international law.

According to Kelsen, sovereignty can only be used in an exclusively legal sense, since this term does not originate from nature. The purely legal abstraction can only be reached by conceiving of the state as a legal system rather than as an actual institution. This is characterized by the fact that it allows for no further logical or legal deductions, and is not subject to any other legal system. Everyone in the country is subject to the legal system embodied in the state which, in turn, is not subject to any superior power with jurisdiction. In other words, in Kelsen's interpretation, sovereignty is the further irreducible quality of the legal system constituting the state. Kelsen disagreed with the traditional view which recognized two different notions of sovereignty, one pertaining to internal or national law, the other to external or international law. According to him, a sovereign legal system occupies the supreme position and, therefore, it is independent of every other legal system, including international law. In his view, the former, together with other sovereign legal systems, creates the latter. The legal system embodied in the state is not independent of other legal (state) systems, but is equal to them that is, *gleichgeordnet..*

Essentially, what Kelsen did was to go one step further in theoretical abstraction by identifying the state with the legal system, saying that sovereignty is the latter's attribute. If we placed the state back into his conceptual system, the result would be the same: sovereignty of the state lies in the fact that in terms of law and logic its supremacy may not be further reduced, and it is not subordinate to any other institution, not even to the international law it helped create. Although it is very closely associated with the latter, the supremacy of the state is—to use the nice German expression—*völkerrechtsunmittelbar.*[6]

International organizations were just taking their first hesitant steps at the time, having coordinated their functions (thus they caused no special legal problems. Traditional thinking still allowed for the fact that while the Council of the League of Nations was entitled to take

---

[6] Hanspeter Neuhold, Waldemar Hummer and Christoph Schreuer, eds, *Österreichisches Handbuch für Völkerrecht* (Vienna, 1991), pp. 138–139.

mandatory measures against a state waging a war of conquest, no resolutions imposing sanctions were passed, since every member state—not only the permanent members—had the right of veto. (The sole exception was the resolution in the thirties to impose an embargo on Italy for attacking Abyssinia which, due to the conflicting interests of the members of the League of Nations, failed.) The situation changed fundamentally after World War II. The Security Council was empowered to bring binding decisions, including military measures, and only the Great Powers retained the right of veto. The European Community could bring majority decisions directly binding on states as well as on the individuals residing in these states. This meant that Brussels could issue decrees that had the same force as domestic law. These fundamental structural changes will be discussed below, but this may suffice to indicate that the traditional notion of sovereignty is no longer applicable to such institutions. In fact, the exemption from external instructions (*Anweisungsunabhängigkeit*, to use another nice German term) ceased in the case of states joining the United Nations or the European Community. Taking the above literally, we have to conclude that these states cannot be regarded sovereign in the traditional sense of the concept, which would hardly correspond to actual relations among members of the international community.

This means that the traditional notion of sovereignty cannot be adequately applied to a modern international organization, particularly in the case of integration. The notion may have been adequate in a historical period when the idea of sovereignty was used as a militant slogan and, perhaps, while an international community was still unorganized. The stabilization of modern states and the subsequent increasingly organized relations in international affairs made a new approach indispensable.

As mentioned in the introduction, written international law has merely buttressed state sovereignty with legal obligations specified in the United Nations Charter and elsewhere.[7] It stated that states a) must

---

[7] See, in particular, United Nations General Assembly declaration no. 2625, accepted in 1970, on the "principles of international law governing the friend ly relations and cooperation" of states, also the Final Act of the European Conference on Security and Cooperation signed in 1975, and the document called the Paris Charta for a New Europe signed in November 1990.

respect the legal equality of every other state, as well as b) their territorial integrity and political independence, furthermore, c) cannot use force or the threat of force against other states, d) must find a peaceful solution to their international conflicts, and e) must not interfere in the internal affairs of other states.

As we can see, these principles—most of which written international law has yet to clearly define[8]—are a negative approach to sovereignty, that is, they stipulate what cannot be done in international relations. They do not specify in positive terms what constitute the actual sovereignty of a state.

This is not surprising. By the nature of international law, only one condition is taken into consideration, namely, does a state act independently in international relations or not. There is not a single forum in the world which could examine whether a state declaring itself independent is in fact sovereign. Not even the United Nations can fill this role in the absence of an agency suited and authorized to perform such examinations. The founding states of the United Nations authorized the organization to decide only on whether or not to admit, say, Vanuatu or the Turkish Republic of Northern Cyprus. (It admitted the former, but not the latter.) In this respect, the United Nations is the totality of its member states. For this reason, the decision on admission means nothing more than an individual statement by the member states whether or not they recognize the applying state as sovereign. Herein lies the essential element: every state makes its own decision as to which political formation—declaring itself an independent state—it wants to enter into relations with, or reject. Should a member state find such a formation to be not sovereign, it simply does not establish relations with it.[9]

Admission to the United Nations does not mean the international community declared a state sovereign, nor does it mean that the states opposing admission must recognize the new member state as

---

[8] In 1974, the United Nations General Assembly defined the concept of aggression in Resolution 3314, but almost nothing was accomplished in defining non-armed intervention.

[9] Diplomatic relations, however, may be established with a formation that does not constitute a state (e.g., the Vatican or an international organization).

sovereign. And, vice versa, rejection of an application does not mean that the state concerned is not sovereign. For instance, it is common knowledge that for many decades after Israel—whose sovereignty could hardly be doubted—gained admission to the United Nations, the Arab states refused to recognize it and some still reject its recognition. Or, although the two German states existed side by side for a long time, the German Democratic Republic recognized the sovereignty of the Federal Republic of Germany, but was not recognized in return. The split into two states entailed that one half of the world maintained diplomatic relations with Bonn, the other half with East Berlin. When West Germany did recognize East Germany, both states were admitted into the United Nations. For ten years after World War II, Hungary was not a member of the United Nations while, at the same time, it maintained diplomatic relations with all the important states. Or, today, only thirty-two smaller states have embassies in Taipei which, until 1971, represented China in the United Nations, yet its sovereignty is indisputable.

Legally dependent countries are a different matter. Dependence may arise from domestic law (the constitution) or international law. Member states of federations are not sovereign according to domestic law, because they lack supremacy, which is usually stated in the constitution of the federation. The 1944 amendment of the Soviet Constitution is the only one containing the noteworthy item according to which the federation is sovereign, as are its member states. Earlier socialist textbooks on international law took this fact to be a sign of the indisputable superiority of socialist federations. The reason for the amendment was simple: Moscow wanted both the Soviet Union and its member states to be among the founding states of the United Nations. (It succeeded only in the cases of Belorussia and the Ukraine.) In accordance with international legal regulations, occupied Austria did not regain its sovereignty after the World War II, but was placed under the supremacy of the Allies' military commanders. Lastly, colonies were not sovereign in terms of either national or international law, irrespective of the circumstances under which they lost their independence, if indeed they ever had it.

All in all, international law is content with the fiction that a state not legally subordinate is sovereign. This means that states with politically nominal independence or which have lost their independence, are regarded as sovereign until their status is legally defined by law. In general terms, law is blind to *de facto* restrictions on sovereignty— at most, it protests against violations of sovereignty—but reacts immediately to *de jure* threats. International law recognizes only two categories: a country is either sovereign or not. It knows nothing of semi-sovereign states.

It derives from the above that sovereignty is not definable in exact legal terms. It is a political and legal category closely related to the notion of statehood and is one of its fundamental elements. In essence, sovereignty means that the state constitutes the highest level in the hierarchy of political institutions created by human society. Using Weber's terminology, the legitimate monopoly of force, or supremacy, belongs to the state. No political institution may be established above this level with a monopoly of force or supremacy of its own, independently of the state, or if one were to be established, that would have to be called the state. Theoretically, therefore the state is always sovereign, and sovereignty belongs exclusively to the state.

Sovereignty within the state means that the parliamentary power and state administration embodying supremacy occupy the highest position in the internal institutional hierarchy.[10] In international relations sovereignty denotes the social phenomenon when relatively separate centralized powers exist side by side. In this sense sovereignty is a special relationship between the state and other members of the international community. This is an adjunctive relationship in terms of authority and politics, as opposed to the sub- and superordinate relations within the state—empire, federation, colonial system.

As for the international community, it is characterized by a decentralized power structure and—anticipating one of my final conclusions—will continue to be so despite attempts at integration. The international community of independent states has presumably assumed its final form; in this respect, it seems that history has truly come to an end. Of course, this will not in the least placate states in

---

[10] The organs that constitute the formation known as the "state" cannot be defined. One of the reasons being that the regulation of the sphere of authority and the role of the individual organs differs from one country to the next.

some regions of the world which lack the assurance of permanence concerning the size of their population, territory, and even in their sheer existence. Nowhere in the world, not even on a continent, has a stable central power ever evolved. There were plenty of attempts at creating empires, but the larger units thus established either disintegrated or were forced to halt expansion at some point. The remaining empires (China and India) face the danger of disintegration. Today, as the end of the twentieth century draws near, stable state boundaries have finally been drawn in the two regions, which became integrated into a larger unit in the course of the past two centuries (like the United States), or is on the way to becoming integrated (like Western Europe with the possible inclusion of Central Europe without, however, turning into some United States of Europe.)

The states were never completely independent in the political sense. They maintained sporadic and incidental relations, with geographic distance often precluding contact. Nevertheless, interdependence was inevitable, since states had to consider the interests of their neighbors and take their political goals into account. With social and economic development this mutual dependence continued to increase. The industrial revolution and establishment of the global market were the "great leap" whereby a far more complex system of interdependence evolved among countries leaving the autarchic era behind. The full realization of the process known as the scientific-technological revolution represented the other qualitative change. This was followed by the rapid acceleration of the development of the international division of labor. Everywhere in the developed world, trade grew faster than production. National money markets were linked, important development took place in the spheres of financial and capital movements and there was a rapid growth in foreign capital investment. Relations among the participants in economic life became stable. Increasingly, production turnover involved the same sellers and buyers, and the same was true of the participants in production cooperation; they did not change partners unduly. Relations became stable particularly in the transportation of raw materials, and also in certain areas of infrastructure.

A situation evolved in which the individual national economic-policy decisions (on the use of production subsidies, the modification of the parity of currencies and customs rates, the determination of the conditions of capital turnover or the rights of foreigners in establishing companies) exerted an immediate effect on the position of other national economies and their internal balance. In theory, these decisions could be made at any time, under any circumstances, yet they were made with circumspection, since other states could, in turn, make similar decisions. Consequently, the state had no interest in exercising its "free" and "unrestricted" rights to achieve temporary goals, because it was immediately confronted with the similarly "free" and "unrestricted" decisions of its partners. The state was relatively quick to recognize that due to the above-mentioned processes it was irreversibly enmeshed in the world-wide system of interdependence. Yet, it took the Great Depression of 1929 and the devastations of World War II for the international community to call the conference at Bretton Woods, and create the system of economic organizations for global coordination.[11] The states recognized the fact that the possibility for making optimal national economic-policy decisions had passed and hence such decisions could only be made on the international level. The operation of such organizations as the International Monetary Fund, the World Bank, the GATT and, later, the OEEC had no bearing on sovereignty, because they lacked the right to make mandatory majority decisions.[12]

The development of military technology also played a role. World War II led many to the conclusion that the mass production of arms and the enormous increase in their destructive power made traditional offensive warfare obsolete. It became clear—even if not to all—that the state launching a war has little chance of winning and will, in fact, put the country in grave danger. This consideration, among others, led the Allied Powers to create a new global security organization within the framework of the United Nations instead of reviving the League of Nations. The founders made it clear that, given

---

[11] The goal of globality was not achieved. The Soviet Union was represented at the Bretton Woods Conference, but later neither the Soviet Union, nor the East European countries joined the organizations created there.

[12] The IMF and the IBRD could pass majority decisions, but these concerned the granting of loans and other issues unrelated to state competence.

the system of interdependence, states must rely on one another, at least those that are part of the coalition or are asked to join. The development of nuclear weapons and long-range missiles represented another qualitative change. In the early sixties, every country—including the greatest military power, the United States—became fatally vulnerable. The superpowers became capable of the total annihilation of one another, which made their mutual dependence unequivocally clear.

Thus, a worldwide system of interdependence came into being. Of course, this dependence became mutual and balanced only in the global sense. Obviously, states with greater economic capacity and military potential possessed more efficient means of asserting their interests and achieving their goals than smaller ones. For this reason, in some relations one may speak of the dominance of unilateral, rather than mutual, dependence. It would be a mistake, however, to evaluate a bilateral relationship in every case, out of the context of the complex system of multilateral interstate relations extending over the whole world. A country may become relatively dependent on another, which may be offset in many respects by the fact that both are embedded in the global system of economic and political relations. Whatever course a state's relation to the outside world takes, it will not in itself affect its sovereignty as its statehood remains.

The state is sovereign as long as it is a state. Once statehood ends, so does sovereignty. The state loses its supremacy, the legitimate monopoly of force, either when the state joins a federation (voluntarily or by coercion), or through the subjugation, military occupation of the state, which often also means disintegration of the state administration. Even if there remains a formal government, the occupying power may force its will upon it.

Returning to the basic question, it has to be examined whether the activity of international organizations, invested with broad powers, affected the sovereignty of their member states: specifically, how the United Nations—more exactly, the Security Council—and the two integrations, NATO and the European Union, affected the independent decision-making powers of their members, that is, which spheres of national power were transferred to international bodies, and the extent to which these organizations became separate from their member states.

The Security Council and Its Binding Decisions

The founders of the United Nations set ambitious goals. They strove to give an international legal definition to the idea of collective security, on the one hand, and—learning from the shortcomings of the League of Nations—facilitated decision-making and invested the Security Council with broad powers, on the other.

They set out from the assumption that the Allied Powers would be able to continue the cooperation worked out during World War II and face would-be aggressors jointly. They presumed that after 1945 the states would continue to regard war as the foremost evil and, on the principle of "all for one and one for all," would even take up arms to prevent war. They planned that—at the authorization of and in accordance with specific agreements with the Security Council—the member states will make available specified contingents of their armed forces to the United Nations. The founders also conceived sanctions not involving the use of military force: thus, the introduction of economic sanctions against the aggressor state, the suspension of land, sea, and air traffic, as well as breaking off communication and diplomatic relations. They stipulated that only the permanent members of the Security Council have the right of veto and included the provision requiring a qualified majority vote to adopt resolutions. The latter could even be made legally binding. Thus, theoretically, the Security Council was empowered to adopt truly effective measures.

The collective security system however, was based on false assumptions from the start. At that time, the states did not at all regard acts of aggression as the prime evil, unless directed against them. Not only did they not view the aggressor with aversion, but sometimes showed a distinct preference for and even supported that state if it served their interests. Another false assumption was that, after 1945, the member states would begin work toward establishing a multinational military force to fight the unknown aggressor. Virtually none of the states wanted such a military force, especially not against an unknown state, consequently, the Security Council did not at any time conclude agreements to this effect with any of the member states. Thus, the United Nations military forces were never established.

Finally, the assumption also proved false according to which, in case of a specific armed conflict, members of the Security Council would agree which state was the aggressor and which the victim. Since the states that won World War II were also the permanent members of the Security Council, in the evolving Cold War a consensus could only be reached if one of the defeated countries were to embark on a revanchist course. This, however, was quite unlikely, because every defeated state was occupied by the victors, their armies disbanded and dominant political parties dissolved.

Hence, the actual powers of the Security Council were less broad than outlined in the United Nations Charter. Although the Council could adopt legally binding resolutions against states that entered into armed conflict or posed a threat to peace in any other way, it meant nothing more than condemning the act in a legal sense. Even if an agreement was reached, the United Nations was powerless to enforce its resolutions in the absence of a military force. The Security Council had only two means at its disposal: it could either call on certain member states to take part in an ad hoc armed operation (which the states are not obliged to comply with) or oblige member states to employ coercive measures not involving armed force against the transgressor. However, the chances for making such decisions were slim, because it was unlikely the great powers could reach an agreement even concerning the simple act of denunciation.

Between 1945 and 1990, the Security Council exercised its special powers only four times: in the Korean war, the civil war in the Congo, and against the apartheid regimes in Rhodesia and South Africa. The absence of the Soviet Union from the sessions of the Council enabled the latter to pass a resolution on the Korean question in 1950.[13] The Western powers promptly passed a resolution to defend South Korea. The resolution, however, did not have a binding effect. It merely recommended that member states take armed measures—under US command—for the restoration of peace. In this

---

[13] By its absence the Soviet Union protested representation of China by Taipei on the assumption that it would obstruct Security Council procedure; however, the other members of the Council considered the absence of the Soviet Union an abstention.

case, naming the state in command of military operations was not accidental: at the time in the West only the United States had the military capability to deploy armed forces on other continents. The only surprising element was the continued absence of the Soviet delegate even after the resolution was passed. As a result, China was also declared an aggressor by the Council when it entered the war. Thereafter, the Soviet Union ceased to boycott meetings of the Council. After 1950, it vetoed the draft proposals of the Western powers one after the other.[14] Concerning the Congo question, in 1961, the Security Council authorized the use of arms by the peacekeeping forces sent there earlier. Subsequently, this decision led to serious debates between the Soviet Union and the Western powers.[15]

Only in the case of Rhodesia and the Republic of South Africa was an agreement reached with Moscow. As a result, the Security Council resolution, backed by sanctions for the second time, ordered an economic embargo against the Smith regime. It was not a smooth process. In 1965, only a resolution of condemnation was passed, followed three years later, in 1968, by the imposition of a total embargo on Rhodesia. Another twelve years had to pass before the independent state of Zimbabwe was established, which was not due entirely to the embargo. The third Security Council resolution implemented an em-bargo on supplying armaments to Johannesburg. This proved a failure. What it did accomplish, unintentionally as it were, was the development of the South African war industry. The Security Council made no effort to enforce the embargo. The states which continued to maintain trade relations with the two apartheid regimes were not sanctioned.

In addition to the above, the Security Council adopted several

---

[14] The majority of the 279 vetoes prior to 1990 were by Soviet delegates. For more detail, see Theodor Schilling, "Die 'neue Weltordnung' und die Souveränität der Mitglieder der Vereinten Nationen," *Archiv des Völkerrechts* 33, nos. 1–2 (May 1995).

[15] The ONUC carried out peacekeeping tasks in the Congo between 1960 and 1964. The Soviet Union charged that the reason for the presence of forces acting under the command of the United Nations Secretary General in the Congo was not so much the keeping of the peace as the ousting of Patrice Lumumba and his adherents from power.

other binding resolutions, most of which did not name the aggressor states, but only called on the states concerned to cease hostilities and withdraw their troops. There were only three cases (the Palestinian war in 1948, the Falkland war in 1982, and the Gulf War in 1987), when the Security Council designated the states guilty of the "breach of peace," to use the wording of the Charter. Condemnation of the acts of aggression against Hungary in 1956 and Czechoslovakia in 1968 was, of course, vetoed by the Soviet Union. Other serious armed conflicts or wars (for instance, in Vietnam) either were never brought up before the Security Council, or the Council issued only a recommendation with no binding force whatsoever.

Has this situation changed since 1990? The answer to this question is partly affirmative. Although the idea of collective security remained unrealizable, the fact that the antagonistic rivalry between the two superpowers had ended brought about an important change at least, in the first years, the effectiveness of the Council increased significantly. Of the number of resolutions adopted by the Council since, only those will be discussed which concern the two most serious armed conflicts: the Gulf War and the war in former Yugoslavia.

The Security Council was prompt to react to Iraqi aggression against Kuwait. In its first resolution, adopted in August 1990, it condemned the aggression and called on the aggressor to withdraw troops from the territory of Kuwait.[16] This resolution—as opposed to the Korean—was legally binding. The November resolution, however, set the deadline, whereafter it authorized the beginning of the Operation Desert Storm, but contained nothing about the command of the international forces assembled in Saudi Arabia and at sea. According to the resolution, the Security Council "authorizes Member States co-operating with the Government of Kuwait...to use all necessary means to...restore peace and security in the area."[17] It was left to the member states to decide to what extent they wished to "cooperate" with the Kuwait government, whose command they intended to accept, and how far—even in the literal sense of the

---

[16] Security Council Resolution 660 (1990), of August 2, 1990.
[17] Security Council Resolution 678 (1990), of November 29, 1990.

word—they wanted to go in the course of counterattack. An *ad hoc* coalition was formed under American command with the participation of NATO members and many other states, including Arab countries.

It is noteworthy that—based on additional Security Council authorizations—the cessation of military operations was followed by an all-out series of actions in Iraq, for which the case of occupied Germany and Austria at the end of World War II offers the only precedent. Although these operations were conducted under the auspices of the United Nations, the decision was made by the ad hoc coalition. The committees, established for the supervision of the demilitarized zone, the search for and destruction of chemical and biological weapons, as well as of missiles, the observance of the ban on oil shipment, and the protection of the Kurdish population, were free to move about in Iraq. They imposed rather strict limits on the country's sovereignty, without otherwise affecting Saddam Hussein's authority. Legal considerations are only part of the explanation for the latter.[18]

Similar decisions were made in the Yugoslav war. The October 1992 Security Council resolution banning overflights in Bosnia was not really intended to have a binding force (UNPROFOR was assigned merely to "observe" any violation of the ban).[19] However, in March 1993, the Security Council—in the usual terms—"authorized member states" to carry out the "necessary measures" against violators of the ban.[20] The resolution contains a fundamentally new element whereby the authority to carry out coercive measures is invested not only in member states in general, but their "regional organizations and institutions" as well. In view of the fact that by this time NATO was virtually the only regional security organization in the

---

[18] The coalition could not assume the political responsibility for the occupation of the capital of an Arab state and for replacing the government in power.

[19] Security Council Resolution 781 (1992), October 9, 1992. This resolution contains no reference to articles of the United Nations Charter, which allow for the adoption of a legally binding resolution.

[20] Security Council Resolution 816 (1993), March 30, 1993. This resolution already refers to those articles of the United Nations Charter, which allow for the adoption of a legally binding resolution.

world, it received, practically speaking, direct authorization to influence ensuing events. (Although the general headquarters of the European NATO forces—making use of facilities in Mons—provided important logistic assistance to its member states during the Gulf War, the Council's resolutions made no reference to it whatsoever, nor did NATO regard it as participation in the war.)

The adoption of the resolution providing for the current IFOR operation has an interesting history. First, in April 1993, the Security Council established safe areas in Bosnia then, in June, it authorized UNPROFOR to deploy armed forces—specifically, air force—if necessary for their defense.[21] It is noteworthy that the June resolution promptly went a step further by authorizing the use of weapons by NATO to, so to speak, "support" UNPROFOR. Thus, the authors of the resolution gave the North Atlantic Alliance what was in effect a blank check for action.[22] Few would have thought that two years later NATO would use this resolution to deploy its war machinery for restoring peace in the former Yugoslavia, especially since the interlude of the American-Russian "honeymoon," which made efficient work by the Council possible during the first years of the new era, had already come to an end. It became increasingly likely that Moscow would veto further coercive measures.

To be sure, the prompt actions taken in February 1994 alarmed Russia. On February 6, 1994, the United Nations Secretary General called on NATO to initiate an air strike, if necessary, against Serb artillery deployed around the "safe area" of Sarajevo. On the 9th of the same month NATO already issued its ultimatum calling on Serb forces to withdraw heavy armaments from within a twenty-kilometer radius. On the 10th, Russia expressed its misgivings concerning the lawfulness of NATO's planned air strikes and asked that the Security Council be convened. However, no decisions were taken at

---

[21] Security Council Resolution 836 (1993), June 4, 1993. Two weeks after the discussion of the General Secretary's report on the first measures taken to carry out the resolution, the Security Council confirmed its earlier decision in Resolution 844 (1993) adopted on June 18.

[22] Robert Uerpmann, "Grenzen zentraler Rechtsdurchsetzung im Rahmen der Vereinten Nationen," *Archiv des Völkerrechts* 33, nos 1–2 (May 1995), p. 123.

the sessions held on February 14 and 15.[23] A few days later, Russia called for another meeting of the Security Council, where it became clear that Moscow wanted to prevent large-scale intervention by NATO. An informal agreement was reached according to which, since the ultimatum achieved its goal, the air strikes would be cancelled. Notwithstanding, in February 1994 the Russians virtually lost their chance to substantially influence the course of events and had to yield to NATO.[24] To change the June 1993 resolution would have involved making a new decision requiring the consent of the three Western powers. However, since all three also represented NATO in the Security Council, no change in the decisive June resolution could be expected. In consequence of the foregoing, the Security Council adopted no further substantive resolutions on the Bosnian question; henceforth all relevant decisions were made by NATO.

In the ensuing period, Western powers kept postponing the implementation of decisive measures. The United States and NATO began preparations for large-scale military intervention only in the spring of 1995.[25] By the time extensive deployment of the air force began in August, Moscow could only express its disapproval of the NATO action. The Bosnian bombing raids showed what NATO is capable of, Boris Yeltsin observed in September. The Russian president was not exactly referring to the successful use of smart weapons. "NATO tends to bomb first and count civilian casualties after" he added.[26] Deputy Foreign Minister Nikolai Afanasevsky complained that NATO did not discuss with Moscow the bombing of Serbian

---

[23] An unusually high number of delegates, fifty-eight to be specific, addressed the meeting. The overwhelming majority called the measure lawful. See in detail: *The United Nations and the Situation in the Former Yugoslavia*, Reference Paper (New York: United Nations), March 15, 1994.

[24] This was one of the reasons for Moscow's growing protest against NATO expansion.

[25] The May 1995 resolution of NATO's top command does not contain explicit reference to preparations, but it does indicate that its troops "stand ready" to carry out earlier decisions. (*Statement on the Situation in Former Yugoslavia*, Issued by the North Atlantic Council in ministerial session at Noordwijk, The Netherlands, May 30, 1995.)

[26] *Frankfurter Allgemeine Zeitung*, September 9, 1995, p. 2.

positions nor the subsequent deployment of its armed forces. According to him, NATO should have consulted with Russia as a member of the Security Council.[27] Later, following the Dayton Peace Accords, to keep their face, the Russians did send units to IFOR, but the initiative and command remained permanently with NATO and the United States.[28]

As concerns the war-related embargo, at first it banned only the shipment of arms into former Yugoslavia; (later, in the case of Serbia and Montenegro, it was extended to all consumer goods and even to civilian air traffic, as well as cultural, scientific, and sport relations.[29] These resolutions differed from the ones adopted in the case of Rhodesia insofar as they allowed the use of armed force against the violators of the ban—though only in the Adriatic and on the Danube. They were insufficient to prevent supplies from reaching the warring parties but, from the legal point of view, they represented a modest step forward. Besides, with the setting up of IFOR, the embargo was suspended.

During the Yugoslav war two resolutions were passed for which the United Nations Charter does not have explicit authorization for the Security Council. One concerns calling to account perpetrators of war crimes in former Yugoslavia, the other, those in Rwanda, including the establishment of the International Tribunal in The Hague. The Security Council did not make such decisions before.

For years a draft treaty has been under discussion at the United Nations on calling to account perpetrators of war crimes in any part of the world. The deepening of the Bosnian conflict made this imperative. The Western powers believed that there was no time for a detailed discussion of every article of the draft, then wait until each of the states decides to sign, then for ratification by their parliaments.[30]

---

[27] Cited by Michael Mihalka, "Continued Resistance to NATO Expansion," *Transition*, August 11, 1995, p. 41.

[28] Security Council Resolution 1031 (1995) passed on December 15, 1995, saluted the Paris and Dayton agreements authorizing the member states to set up and participate in NATO organized IFOR, as well as to enforce by every available means provisions of the resolution.

[29] Security Council Resolution 757 (1992), May 30, 1992.

[30] See, *Report of the Secretary General pursuant to paragraph 2 of the Security Council Resolution 808 (1993)*, Security Council, S/25704, May 3, 1993, p. 7.

For this reason, in February 1993, the Security Council ordered the calling to account of everyone guilty of violation of humanitarian law during the Yugoslav war.[31] Thus, the Security Council forestalled that the states most involved be exempt from their obligations concerning prosecution for war crimes. The Council's resolution ordered that every state extradite war criminals to the Tribunal (even if they be citizens), as well as assist the investigation in every way and search for war criminals.[32] Similar rules were formulated in the case of Rwanda.[33]

The decision gave rise to a lively debate among international lawyers. Some believed that an international treaty must rule on the establishment of this type of judicial forum,[34] while others argued—correctly—that, in this case too, the broader decision incorporates the lesser one. If it is possible to wage war on violators of international peace and security under the auspices of the United Nations, then there is no reason why an independent tribunal could not be authorized to convict war criminals.[35] Although the Tribunal has only a modest chance of apprehending the perpetrators, the possibility that it may order any state to extradite suspects became a new element in international law.

Security Council decisions concerning Somalia and Haiti also provoked debates. The overthrow of Siad Barre in 1991 led to serious armed conflict among the various clans in the East African country with many casualties, and rendered state administration impossible.

---

[31] Security Council Resolution 808 (1993), February 22, 1993. Prior to this, the Security Council issued several resolutions calling on the warring parties in Yugoslavia to observe these norms.

[32] The Security Council set up the International Tribunal in accordance with Article 29 and the instructions contained in chapter VII of the United Nations Charter. The former provides for the establishment of subsidiary organs, the latter contains compulsory coercive measures if so decreed.

[33] Security Council Resolution 955 (1994), November 8, 1994.

[34] For instance, Frederic Kirgis, Jr., "The Security Council's First Fifty Years," *American Journal of International Law* 89, no. 3 (1995), pp. 522–525.

[35] Article 42 of the United Nations Charter on the cases when the Security Council is empowered to pass binding decisions does not contain an itemized enumeration.

At first, the United Nations provided aid to the starving population, then attempted to mediate between the hostile parties. Later it ordered an embargo on arms supplies into Somalia and sent in observers.[36] Its efforts were unsuccessful; the situation deteriorated and mass starvation was threatening.[37] At this stage, Washington offered to place troops at the disposal of the United Nations in order to get humanitarian assistance through to the needy. Consequently, in December 1992, the Security Council—indirectly, but in unequivocal terms—authorized the United States to send armed forces into the region and also extended the authorization to other member states of the United Nations. The Council justified its decision by saying that the Somalian situation threatened the security of other countries in the region.[38] After many months of unsuccessful attempts to restore order and incidents which led to American casualties, the United States withdrew its troops. A year later, United Nations forces left Somalia. The American failure in Somalia is the reason why the Security Council did not even attempt the use of force to prevent the unprecedentedly brutal massacre in Rwanda.[39] In May 1994, President Bill Clinton issued a directive to the effect that the United States will participate in similar United Nations missions only if they serve American interests, set realistic goals, and do not unduly expose American lives.[40]

Yet, soon after, Washington decided on firm measures against the military regime in Haiti which had overthrown President Jean Bertrand Aristide in 1991. The administration grew weary of the regime and of the flood of refugees. Since unilateral economic sanctions proved ineffective, in July 1994, at the request of the United States, the Security Council authorized its member states to establish

---

[36] Security Council Resolutions 733 and 751 (1992), January 23 and April 24, 1992.

[37] According to some estimates, three thousand people starved to death daily, on the average. *The United Nations and the Situation in Somalia*, Reference Paper, UN Department of Public Information, New York, December 15, 1992.

[38] Security Council Resolution 794 (1992), December 3, 1992.

[39] The estimated number of victims is between five hundred thousand and one million.

[40] Presidential Decision Directive 25.

a multinational army for the removal of the junta and to create the conditions for the return to power of the democratically elected president. Again, the Security Council gave the reason that the Haitian situation threatened security in the region.[41] The military pressure achieved its goal. At the last minute the junta ceded power to President Aristide. Nevertheless, the United Nations-backed armed forces did land on the island, but only to maintain order.

The Security Council resolutions concerning Somalia and Haiti were criticized because the situation did not pose an immediate threat to international peace and security. In both countries it was an internal conflict which probably would not have spilled over the borders, unlike the case of the Yugoslav war and Rwanda.[42] Furthermore, events in Haiti resulted in few casualties, therefore, humanitarian considerations could not have played a role. In consequence, the question was raised: does the Security Council have the right to pass judgment over the almost daily military takeovers in the developing countries of the world? Furthermore, does it have the right to choose among the various military takeovers and intervene in one case, but not the other? The United States was also much criticized for its arbitrary decision to send armed forces to a nearby country (Panama) without United Nations authorization and for persuading the Security Council to authorize armed intervention in others (as in the above cases). Politicians and others were asking whether it is up to the United States to act as the armed guardian of democracy and human rights? They added that America had no real cause to intervene in Somalia and Haiti.[43]

---

[41] Security Council Resolution 940 (1994), July 31, 1994.

[42] After disintegration of Yugoslavia and the recognition of the successor states, the Yugoslav war was classified as an international conflict.

[43] See, for instance, Michael Mandelbaum, "Foreign Policy as a Social Work," *Foreign Affairs* 75, no. 1 (January-February 1996), p. 22. According to others, in today's interdependent world, conflicts like the one in the Yugoslav region, or in Somalia, or in Haiti, may lead to events, the outcome of which could damage the United States, therefore, intervention serves the latter's interest. See Stanley Hoffmann's response to the above-cited article ["In Defense of Mother Teresa: Morality in Foreign Policy," *Foreign Affairs* 75, no. 2 (1996), p. 175].

The scope of the present study does not allow for a detailed discussion of ongoing debates in the literature and elsewhere concerning the question of humanitarian intervention. It has to be pointed out only that prior to 1990 the question hardly ever arose whether the Security Council's powers and voting procedure affected the sovereignty of the member states. As we have seen, the Security Council adopted binding resolutions only in the case of one aggressor state and of the two states pursuing the policy of apartheid. Its influence on international relations was negligible.[44] It is important from the point of view of international law that the resolutions involved states that violated the fundamental norms of international law, threatening the security of the international community.[45] Indisputably, the Security Council resolutions wanted to impose a behavior that the respective states would not adopt on their own. However, the states which signed the Charter—and did not possess the right of veto—were well aware of the consequences an act of breach of peace would entail. It could be said that by signing they gave their prior consent to sanctions that the Security Council would, given cause, adopt even against themselves.[46]

Characteristically, the same applies to the "innocent" states that apply the sanctions, since Security Council resolutions are as legally binding on them as on the states sanctioned. An embargo is, in general, against the economic interests of every state involved, because the suspension of trade and monetary relations may incur heavy losses for all concerned. In joining the United Nations however, they accepted the broad authority invested in the Security Council, including the fact that this body has the right to make decisions contrary to the

---

[44] Undoubtedly, the United States would have come to the aid of South Korea even if the Soviet Union had vetoed the draft proposal in the Security Council.

[45] During the period when the colonies, achieved independence one after the other, there was general consensus in the United Nations that the continuance of apartheid threatened international peace and security.

[46] Non-member states are an exception, but under Paragraph 6, Article 2 of the Charter, the resolutions of the Security Council apply to them as well. At the time the Charter was drafted, its authors had in mind primarily the formerly hostile states, those that remained outside the organization.

immediate interests of the member states.[47] Undeniably, the independent decision-making powers of the members of the international community were restricted.

Since 1990 the Council's activity acquired greater scope, yet—discounting intervention in Somalia and Haiti—it never extended the interpretation of the instructions laid down in the Charter and, more importantly, it never issued an order for the compulsory use of force by member states against an aggressor state. What the Council was primarily assumed to do was to legitimize a group of member states, specifically, the joint action of the *ad hoc* coalition under United States command against the aggressor state, or against one that threatened international peace.

Although the Security Council is further removed from its member states than other international bodies, and is a nearly independent decision-making body, it has not become " supranational" and, therefore, has not encroached upon the sovereignty of the member states of the UN.

NATO and Its Integrated Military Organization

From the point of view of sovereignty, NATO presents a simpler picture despite the fact that there exists a close military and political integration within the framework of the North Atlantic Alliance. The main reason being that, while in the United Nations a small governing body with real decision-making capability had to be established which, by the nature of things, was distinct from its membership of more than one hundred and eighty states, the small membership of NATO did not call for the creation of such body.

---

[47] It is another matter that it would make the embargo truly effective if the organization were to compensate the states for their losses. This occurred only once, during the Gulf War when the states involved received some compensation from Iraq's proceeds from oil. The perennial budget problems of the United Nations make regular payment of compensation impossible. It is not surprising, therefore, that some of the states concerned often took no notice of evasions, as a result of which the embargo could not become the effective coercive measure it was intended to be.

The primary question in this case, too, concerns the obligations imposed on members by the instructions of the Treaty. In accordance with the North Atlantic Treaty, an attack against any one of the member states is regarded as an attack against all, and they are obliged to assist the state attacked, using force, if necessary. In addition, the Treaty stipulates unanimity of decision in every case, as well as on the means of assistance.[48]

This means that in case of external aggression, unanimity in the respective body of the Alliance is necessary for deciding which states will take action, by what means, and contingency plans to defend the state under attack. There is no question of an automatic obligation to provide assistance, as many suppose. The founders did not wish to assume responsibility in advance for implementing military and political steps with regard to unforeseeable situations. In 1949, none of the member states could foretell when, under what conditions, and which member state would be attacked, and they could only surmise who the aggressor would be.[49]

Fortunately, before 1990 no one "tested" the validity of the collective security NATO provided. During the Cold War years, Moscow had every reason to expect that the member states would implement collective measures. In case of external aggression, every member state—probably including France, which withdrew from the integrated military structure—would have been ready to assist the state under attack.[50] In other words, NATO deterrence was credible. This deterrence, among others, explains why the immediate threat of an armed conflict between the two military blocs did not arise even when relations were most strained.

This is why it is surprising that on the issue of NATO expansion several politicians and experts hold the opinion that the situation has

---

[48] Article 5 of the North Atlantic Treaty.

[49] It was clear to all which power posed the main threat to NATO, but provocation of incidents, armed conflicts by other states could not be excluded either.

[50] According to a well-known expert, the instructions concerning collective defense could be regarded virtually as "quasi-automatic." See Uwe Nerlich, "NATO at the Crossroads, Once Again," *Stiftung Wissenschaft und Politik* (Ebenhausen, 1995), p. 24.

changed since the Cold War and, therefore, the stipulations of the Treaty should be reassessed. Some even find the above cited not very strict obligations excessive, and assert that if NATO were expanded, the new Central and Eastern European states should not be granted the same defense guarantees enjoyed by present members. Many question whether NATO would be willing to defend the security of the newly admitted states with every available means. In any event, it is reassuring that a NATO study, published in September 1995, containing the first authentic outline of the conditions of admission, does not question the extension of these obligations, but clearly states: "the new member states will enjoy all the rights and assure all obligations of members under the Washington Treaty."[51]

Whatever interpretation the articles of the Treaty are given, in no way do they involve obligations affecting the sovereignty of member states. In view of this, the question arises: How is NATO's role in the Bosnian peacemaking mission to be seen?[52]

The North Atlantic Treaty contains no provisions in this regard. In 1949, the founders signed only a collective defense agreement; they could not foresee that the organization would later be used for other purposes. However, the extension of its powers with common consent is not contrary to law. Should the member states decide to go beyond the provisions of the Treaty—in compliance with the norms of general international law, and the goals and functions of the organization—they can do so.[53] In such cases, the same rules apply to decision-making as defined in the Treaty, namely, the decisions must be unanimous. The Bosnian question was such a case.[54] In all other respects, the principle

---

[51] *Study on NATO Enlargement.* para. 4, September 1995.

[52] As mentioned earlier, in discussing Security Council resolutions on Bosnia, NATO as such did not participate in the Gulf War.

[53] All the same, the instructions specified in the Treaty have restrictive power. However, international law recognizes the principle of so-called implied powers which, in this case, means that member states may extend the jurisdiction of the organization when the matter at hand concurs with the goals and functions of the organization.

[54] See *Statement on the Situation in Former Yugoslavia,* issued by the North Atlantic Council in ministerial session at Noordwijk, The Netherlands, May 30, 1995. NATO Press Communiqué.

of voluntary participation applied; every state declared the extent to which it wished to partake in the operation and contingency plans were prepared accordingly. It is noteworthy that half of the member states had less than one thousand troops each in the international force of sixty thousand. According to the NATO study, the organization expects new members to take part in future joint operations falling outside the sphere of collective defense. In these cases, however, the military capability of the new member states shall be taken into account.

Unanimity is the guiding principle in the operation of every NATO civilian and military body. The right of veto is not exercised; representatives of member states continue discussions until they reach *consensus*. The sole exception concerns the composition of the individual organs and not decision-making. All sixteen member states are represented in the top-level civilian (political) body of the North Atlantic Council and the Defense Planning Committee, but not in the Nuclear Planning Group where Iceland, having no army, is present only as an observer.[55] Iceland and Spain have no delegates in the Military Committee, the latter having left NATO's military organization as a result of a 1986 referendum.[56] In practical terms this means that the foreign policy decisions of NATO and the definition of its strategic concept requires the consensus of all sixteen members, while strictly military decisions require the consensus of only fourteen countries.

The supreme commanders of the European and North Atlantic

---

[55] The permanent delegates of the member states accredited to NATO are the members of the Council, who usually meet weekly. Foreign and defense ministers, sometimes the prime ministers and heads of state of the member states convene at least twice a year. Defense ministers attend the meetings of the Defense Planning Committee and the Nuclear Planning Group.

[56] In 1966, France, too, withdrew from NATO's military organization, but remained a member of the North Atlantic Treaty. The election of Jacques Chirac brought about a change in policy: France rejoined the Defense Planning Committee and the Military Committee, albeit it continues to remain outside the military organization. (The chiefs of staff of the member states constitute the membership of the Military Committee.)

regions are responsible for execution of military decisions.[57] Due to the nature of the tasks, plenary decisions are not made at this level, the strict hierarchical relations of the army apply instead. The European supreme command (SHAPE) and the other commands have international staffs. Even during the Cold War years NATO did not duplicate the usual Warsaw Pact practice of appointing only Soviet generals to the highest positions. Notwithstanding, the supreme commander of the European NATO forces is, customarily, an American general, which is offset by the fact that the Secretary General is always a European politician.

Military organs are subordinate to civilian organs. The Military Committee cannot pass decisions without authorization from the North Atlantic Council and the other two civilian organs. Nor can the supreme commanders make any decisions without instructions from the civilian bodies or the Military Committee. The fact that in crisis situations the Council can be convoked without delay virtually excludes the possibility of independent decision-making by military leaders.[58]

NATO military integration is represented primarily in the integration of high commands. A general staff was established under the command of and to assist the supreme commander. In peacetime the national armies are not integrated and are not under the command of the SHAPE in Mons. The units serving under the direct command of the Mons headquarters in peacetime are insignificant in number. These are:

1. joint air-defense, also comprising a small aircraft fleet, including the AWACS, established for the purpose of early warning;

---

[57] Commonly known as SACEUR and SACLANT. The United States and Canada have set up the Regional Planning Group at this decision-making level. There are three further regional commands subordinate to SACEUR in Northern, Central, and Southern Europe.

[58] The permanent missions of the member states have their offices in NATO headquarters in the same building as the general secretary. Similar permanent cells have also been established in Mons. If, for some reason, the representatives are unable to convene, the respective ambassadors to Washington assume their jurisdiction.

2. permanent naval forces, including a few destroyers, mine-detector and auxiliary vessels;

3. the so-called rapid reaction force which, today, comprises only two multinational divisions;

4. specific parts of the national communication units.

In addition to the above, national armies are required to keep in readiness rapid reaction forces which can be deployed in crisis situations.[59] In such an event, the general headquarters assumes command.

The foregoing indicate that the independent decision-making powers of member states is diminished only slightly in peacetime. At the same time, members of the organization agreed to develop their national armies in harmony and with regard for one another. A considerable number of agencies and committees were established to work out the ways of linking national armies, creating uniform military standards, etc. They developed a common infrastructure in a number of areas, primarily in the field of communication, data-base technology, fuel supply.

According to the NATO study, the newly admitted states will have to become part of the integrated military structure, which means they will have to join the agencies in Brussels and Mons, the joint system of military command, as well as the peacetime units at the disposal of the Supreme Commander.

The NATO study raised the issue of the possible permanent stationing of foreign troops on the territory of the newly admitted states. The study does not explicitly preclude this possibility for the future, neither does it consider it as an a priori requirement. However, it does consider it important that other Allies' forces can be deployed, "when and if appropriate" on the territory of new members.[60] How this will be achieved may require, according to the study, further examination. New members may develop specially-trained units capable of reinforcing NATO forces or of being reinforced by ally units. Storing of material in critical areas could also be a solution to the problem.[61] In other words, there is a wide range of possibilities; both NATO and the

---

[59] This involves ten divisions and a few smaller units.
[60] *Study On NATO Enlargement*, para. 45/e.
[61] *Study On NATO Enlargement*, para. 45/e.

applicants would be able to reach arrangements which would satisfy the interests of all parties concerned.

The study does not *a priori* exclude deployment of nuclear weapons either, but states:

> In the light of both the current international environment and the potential threats facing the Alliance, NATO's current nuclear posture will, for the foreseeable future, continue to meet the requirement of an enlarged Alliance. There is, therefore, no need now to change or modify any aspect of NATO's nuclear posture or policy but the longer term implications of enlargement for both will continue to be evaluated.

According to the study, NATO retains "its right to modify its nuclear posture as circumstances warrant."[62] The new member states must join the Nuclear Planning Committee and its subordinate organs, furthermore, they must attend consultations on nuclear questions during military exercises or in crisis situations. Furthermore, decisions on these questions will be made on the basis of consultation and agreement among the allies. This means that any modification in NATO nuclear policy requires that they be made only after the admission and with the participation of the new member states. If a new member state does not wish to have nuclear weapons deployed on its territory, it is not required to do so. This is not unusual in NATO practice: there are no nuclear warheads, nor is there a plan to deploy any, in six and a half of the fourteen member states (Spain, Portugal, Norway, Denmark, Luxemburg, Iceland, and the territory of the former GDR).[63] It is an important fact that although there are ongoing strategic discussions in the Nuclear Planning Group on questions concerning nuclear weapons, and even guidelines are formulated, the ultimate decision on their use—with the exception of missiles carried

---

[62] *Study On NATO Enlargement*, para. 58.

[63] National law prohibits deployment of nuclear weapons on the territory of Norway, Denmark, and Spain. Concerning the former GDR, an international agreement to this effect was signed at the 2+4 negotiations. The necessity of deployment did not arise in the case of the other member states.

by aircraft used for both civilian and military purposes—lies with NATO's three nuclear powers: the United States, Great Britain, and France, individually.

To be sure, the need for deployment of nuclear weapons on the territory of new member states will not arise later either. Short-range nuclear weapons proved useless from the military point of view, and the superpowers renounced deployment of land-based intermediate-range missiles during Mikhail Gorbachev's time. As regards the strategic nuclear weapons, they served a single purpose: to deter the other side from the use of such weapons. The question of the deployment of the latter in Central Europe does not even arise, since their presence on the territory of the current nuclear powers and on the seas is more than sufficient. It follows that a future deployment of nuclear weapons in the new member states is quite unlikely. Thus, the danger that deployment would lead to countermeasure by some future enemy of NATO has also been eliminated.

As the foregoing show, in peacetime the decision making procedure of the leading organs of NATO has not become separated from the governments of the member states. They participate in every substantive decision making, therefore, their sovereignty remains intact. Theoretically, the above also characterize a situation of war but, obviously, the role of central military bodies would increase considerably, while the number of actual participants in decision-making would decrease. Naturally, no one knows what course the relationship between civilian bodies and the SHAPE would take in a world war. In the foreseeable future, however, we have no reason to envisage a conflict of such magnitude. Presumably, NATO efforts will be less directed at collective defense and more at carrying out peacemaking operations similar to the one in Bosnia. Voluntary participation and obligations will play a greater role than defined in the Washington Treaty, which means that it will not affect the sovereignty of old or new member states.

By nature of the foregoing, the question of sovereignty is even less likely to arise in the period preceding admission. As regards the IFOR base in Hungary and the Hungarian IFOR contingent in Croatia, in possession of the Dayton Accords and the appropriate Security Council authorization, the NATO turned to the Hungarian government with a request for establishing a military base for

American troops on Hungarian soil and for participation in some form by the Hungarian army. The Hungarian government was ready to comply with both. It wanted to contribute to the peaceful settlement of the Yugoslav conflict, on the one hand, and it was aware of its geostrategically important position of carrying out the IFOR operation, on the other. The Alliance needed a peaceful region lying outside, but with easy access to the earlier theaters of operations in order to be able to deploy its troops, ensure supplies, etc. Naturally, the Hungarian government also took into consideration the fact that close cooperation with the organization would enhance its chances of admission to NATO, in addition to the experience the army may thus acquire.

The request was followed by negotiations. As NATO accepted the standpoint that—for well-known historical reasons—it would be imprudent for Hungary to send armed units into former Yugoslavia, they agreed that Hungary would send an army engineer corps unit of no more than five hundred personnel. In accordance with the Dayton Accords, every participant covers the costs of its own participation. Thus, the United States pays for establishing and operating the base in Hungary, while the latter pays the deployment and maintenance costs of the engineer corps unit. An agreement to this effect was signed. Furthermore, Hungary joined one of the multilateral treaties of NATO, which regulates the legal status of armed forces in foreign countries.[64] The treaty states that troops serving abroad shall not interfere in the internal affairs of the receiving state, they shall obey its laws, they shall be subject to the jurisprudence—including criminal and civil jurisprudence—of the host state, furthermore, they shall not carry out any military operations without the consent of the latter. In accordance with the provisions of the Hungarian Constitution, Parliament authorized the sending of troops abroad, as well as the presence of NATO forces in Hungary.

American NATO troops will remain in Hungary as long as there are IFOR troops in former Yugoslavia. The Dayton Accords set a term of one year, which—if the signatories agree—may be prolonged. In other words, should Hungary decide to close the IFOR base upon expiration of the one year term, the agreement in question becomes void.

---

[64] Status Of Forces Agreement (SOFA).

However, according to the rules of general international law, the Hungarian government may annul the agreement prior to the expiration of the term, if the other party commits a serious breach of the said treaty.

All this indicates that Hungary's participation in the Bosnian peacemaking mission does not affect the country's sovereignty. Hungary would make the same decision if admitted into NATO. Following the bilateral consultations on admissions that began in 1996, the Alliance is expected to decide in early 1997 with which states to begin negotiations regarding membership. Should Hungary be in the first round, these negotiations would serve to clarify the conditions of joining. If, as a result of negotiations, an understanding between the two parties is reached, the conditions will be set down in a treaty. When this happens, NATO will issue an official invitation to join.[65] Following this, the Hungarian Parliament will set a date for a plebiscite on the question of joining. In case of an affirmative decision, the Hungarian Parliament, as well as the parliaments of the sixteen member states will have to ratify the treaty. Upon ratification by the respective parliaments, Hungary becomes a member of the organization. This somewhat lengthy procedure precludes violation of Hungary's sovereignty.

The European Union and the Question of Supranationality

It is a widespread view that the European Union had long ago moved beyond the bounds of nation-states and, in its present form, may already be considered virtually supranational. Many say that it will become even more so once the resolutions outlined in the Maastricht Treaty are adopted at the Intergovernmental Conference (IGC) begun in April 1995 which have the establishment of the European Monetary Union as their focal point. Yet, few have reached the conclusion that the development of integration does not necessitate the burial of the notion of sovereignty.[66]

---

[65] See Article 10 of the North Atlantic Treaty.

[66] See, for instance, Michael Mann, "Nation-States in Europe and Other Continents: Diversifying, Developing, Not Dying," *Deadalus* (Summer 1993), pp. 115–139.

The results of the IGC and the realization of the ideas set forth in the Maastricht Treaty cannot be predicted.[67] Therefore, the present situation has to be examined with the consequences the Maastricht plan entails. The following organizational and decision-making elements are primarily mentioned in relation to sovereignty:

1. Some of the binding resolutions require a two-thirds majority vote in the Council; in these cases, large states have more votes than small ones.[68]

2. The Council may adopt binding resolutions on a number of issues. These become immediately binding on the member states, as well as on the natural and legal persons residing in these states.

3. The Commission and its apparatus, drafting and proposing the decisions, act independently of the governments of the member states.

4. The Commission may adopt immediately binding resolutions by a majority vote, in the interest of carrying out Council resolutions.[69]

5. In the European Parliament, which is elected directly, large states have more, small states have fewer votes. The Parliament has the right of decision-making in an increasing number of areas.

6. With the creation of the Monetary Union, member states will void their national currencies. The single currency, called euro, will be issued by the independent central bank of the Union.

7. Member states will continue to increase the range of those economic policy powers, of which they will relinquish independent decision-making and agree on the obligation of joint decision-making.

Voting by qualified majority in the Council does not formally affect the sovereignty of member states in view of the fact that they

---

[67] Nevertheless, several attempts have been made, thus, for instance, by Stephan Breitenmoser, "Die Europäische Union zwischen Völkerrecht und Staatrecht," *Zeitschrift für ausländisches öffentliches Recht und Völkerrecht* 58, no. 4 (1995), p. 961.

[68] The four large member states have 10 votes each, Spain has 8, the rest have 5, 4, 3, or 2. Ministers decide recommendations of the Commission, and at least 62 affirmative votes of the maximum 87 are required for passing a decision. (If it falls short, a further restriction applies, namely, at least 10 member states must support the draft proposal.) If the Council does not concur with the recommendation of the Commission, the decision must be unanimous.

[69] Large states have two seats each, the rest have one seat each in the Committee.

consented to this when they founded—or subsequently joined—the European Union. The basic assumption of the founders was that they will have to make administrative decisions in the Council, often without delay. They thought they had to create an expeditious and efficient system of decision-making and believed that the majority vote will, in certain cases, serve this purpose.

In practice, however, they discovered that majority voting can become a highly sensitive issue. Under ideal circumstances it causes no problems if one state or the other is voted down. Actually, the decision in an individual case may conflict with the interests of a member state, but this may be counterbalanced by the expeditious adoption of the decision and the fact that the state voted down will continue to have a fundamental interest in being part of the integration process. On the other hand, a state may be voted down time and again, which could lead to serious consequences, since such a state could easily turn against its partners. It may then not carry out resolutions conflicting with its own interests, or may withdraw from the process. The majority may attempt, and may even have the means, to apply enforcement. But due to the close economic ties among the participants of the process, enforcement does not lie in their interest; an economic confrontation would damage the interests of all concerned. The maintenance of the integration process takes priority. For this reason, the majority strives to make compromises and gain the consent of the minority.

The history of European integration shows that the member states have been aware of the advantages and disadvantages of majority voting. Initially, the founders foresaw a unanimous decision on every important issue. The idea at the time was to gradually enlarge the sphere of questions that would require a qualified majority vote. Before this could be implemented, however, Charles de Gaulle's obstructionist, nationalistic policy made it necessary that member states assent to the Luxemburg Compromise in 1966. Accordingly, if a member of the organization announces that the decision in a specific case affects vital interests, negotiations will be continued until agreement is reached.[70]

---

[70] The compromise also mentioned an "appropriate deadline," but this, as it turned out, bore no significance. It has been noted that some members actually approved de Gaulle's policy, but were reluctant to take France's side in the debate.

Hence, consensus became a permanent feature of decision-making and majority decisions were few and far between.

This method of decision-making characterized the ensuing two decades. With few exceptions, the right of veto was not exercised, and no state was voted down. Usually, during the preparatory procedure, the president in office of the Council made inquiries as to which state disagreed with the draft proposal at hand, and endeavored to compile a package deal which contained some form of compensation for the state concerned. If there were several opponent states, a so-called blocking minority could easily form. (This meant that holding twenty-five of the total of eighty-seven votes would prevent acceptance of the draft proposal.) In this event, the only course left open to the president—and the members of the Council, of course—was to find a compromise acceptable to all member states. It is noteworthy that never once during the past decades did a majority group form that voted down, time and again, the few member states constituting the minority. On the contrary, there was a tendency for states with conflicting interests on certain issues to form *ad hoc* alliances which—if they had the votes necessary to make a blocking minority—could firmly assert these interests. In these cases, any reference to the Luxemburg Compromise was extremely rare.

Introduction of the immediately binding decisions adopted by the Council was an important development in the history of the integration. In traditional international relations cooperation was always impeded by endless delays in putting into force the treaties concluded and in their ensuing incorporation in national legislation. A system was finally created as part of the integration process whereby decisions adopted in the form of decrees would become binding, without intermediate steps and immediately upon publication in the Union's official journal, on the member states, as well as state administrative organs, and private persons. If such a decision contradicts domestic legislation, the Union law takes priority, regardless of whether it was enacted before or after the domestic law. The members of the organization endeavored to have decision-making and execution resemble national legislative procedure as much as possible.

This solution does not affect the sovereignty of member states. At most, it contradicts the conventional notion of sovereignty, because it is irreconcilable with the absolute supremacy of the member states.

However, as we have seen, this supremacy was never really all that absolute. Within the European Union the problem was merely a technical question of implementation. In the long run, the question whether the decisions of an international organization are immediately binding or become binding only after the respective state organ incorporates them into national law, was a matter of indifference to the addressees, the natural and legal persons residing in the respective state. Decisions of the international body are binding on the state, and if such a decision is not immediately binding, enactment by the state should make it so. Immediately binding decisions skip one stage, but only one. (True, this "leap" means that after an intergovernmental decision is made in Brussels, the national parliaments no longer have a say. However, this problem belongs to the sphere of democracy, and not to the realization of sovereignty.) The crux of the matter is that decisions in the Union are not made by some outside institution but by the member states themselves which regulate their own relations to one another in a way that the decisions, in the making of which they participated, become immediately binding in their respective countries.

Due to its independence and important role in decision-making, the Commission is considered a supranational institution. It is the responsibility of this body to represent the common interests of the member states—as distinct from narrow national interests—in opposition to the Council, in other words, to confront common interests with national interests. The Commission was authorized to propose the majority of resolutions, to draft and elaborate them for adoption. (The decisions proposed by the member states are brought before the Commission first, then before the Council for discussion.) All this provided the Council—relying on the biggest international staff in the world—with considerable informal power within the Union. From the point of view of sovereignty, this does not change the fact that the right to reach fundamental decisions remains with the Council. For this reason, it is of no consequence that large states have two seats in the Commission and that, theoretically, decisions require a simple majority vote (in practice, however, the body aims at consensus).[71]

---

[71] A body of independent persons, by its very nature, can only adopt majority decisions, since the commissioners are not backed by any—state or business—power, whose interests need to be protected by exercising the right of veto.

The independent decision-making powers of the Commission concern primarily the application and enforcement of law, that is, it pertains to administration, albeit the Commission also has legislative powers in several areas. Essentially, these decisions are founded on the Treaty of Rome or international agreements ratified by the member states since, and on the acts of the Council. They do not determine the national economic processes and cannot be contrary to the long-term interests of the member states.

The former also apply, in part, to the increasingly important role played by the European Parliament. This independent body, originally invested exclusively with the authority to make recommendations, has become increasingly capable of asserting its authority. Nevertheless, it does not play a decisive role in the European Union's decision-making procedure and has not become a legislative body in the strict sense. Depending on the powers involved, the Council

1. must conduct preliminary consultations or negotiations with the Parliament (at which time, the Parliament can get its amendment proposal accepted on urgent issues by the Council);[72]

2. needs the cooperation of the Parliament (if the Council decides in contravention of the Parliament, it can carry such decisions only by a unanimity of votes, instead of the usual qualified majority);[73]

3. must obtain the consent of the Parliament (it cannot decide without it);[74] and

4. must make its decisions together with the Parliament (otherwise the Parliament may subsequently reject Council decisions).[75]

The latter elements allow the Parliament to have a considerable say in decision-making.[76] The organization wanted to end the fre-

---

[72] The Council gave its assurance that—discounting technical matters—it will hear the Parliament's views on every issue.

[73] In questions related to the internal market of the Union.

[74] The Parliament has the right of veto on questions concerning the admission of new member states, international agreements, structural and cohesion funds, specified spheres of authority of the central bank, etc.

[75] On specific questions concerning the freedom of movement and settlement of individuals, the development of internal markets, education, research, culture, public health, and consumer protection.

[76] It also deserves mention that the Parliament may set up investigative com-

quently mentioned democratic deficit characterizing the first two decades of its existence. The only question is whether enlarging the sphere of authority of the Parliament affects the decisive role of the member states. The answer is affirmative, of course, but the Parliament does not thereby take over the Council's function, nor does it make decisions instead of the Council, and the Council is not required to take into consideration the Parliament's opinion. What the Parliament can do is to delay the decision-making process or block adoption of a resolution. This means that the Parliament has broad powers, but does not mean that it is a "supranational" body.

This is particularly true, if we consider that two radically different series of events took place within the organization concurrently, as a result of which national interests gained prominence. In every area committees with representatives of the governments were set up, which asserted the national interests of the member states with increasing vigor in the preliminary stages of decision-making. The Committee of Permanent Representatives (COREPER), where every draft proposal passes through several rounds of discussion, was invested with increasing authority.[77] In every committee the procedure is based on consensus of opinion, that is, proposals are forwarded to the Council or other organs only after approval by all members present.

The introduction of a new procedural element, called opt-out, allowing member states to abstain from carrying out some joint program, also served to strengthen the "national" aspect of decision-making. The establishment of the European Social Charter was the first spectacular manifestation of opting-out, when the member states acquiesced in Britain's decision not to participate. Later, during the negotiations of the Maastricht Treaty, Great Britain and Denmark were given the choice to opt-out of the last phase of the monetary union, creating the single currency, should they deem it irreconcilable

---

mittees with the right to summon even the ministers of member states; furthermore, it has appointed an ombudsman to deal with civic complaints.

[77] Ambassadors of the member states accredited to the European Union are seated on this Committee. Much like conventional diplomatic missions, they have a staff to assist their work.

with their capabilities or interests. Subsequently, upon joining the organization, the Swedish prime minister announced that Sweden's participation in the last phase is contingent on approval by the country's parliament. Thus, an approach was recognized whereby the deepening of the integration may hinge upon the interests and capabilities of the member states, that is, a differential integration process may evolve which is characterized by the participation of different sets of member states in the different programs, and at a varying pace. It is conceivable that some states will not participate in some program in the foreseeable future, or will join in only after a specified period.

Lastly, the introduction of the principle of subsidiarity also strengthens the national aspect of the European Union. The aim is to have decisions made at the lowest possible level, at a national, local, or regional level as the case may be. This means that citizens would come into closer proximity with decisions and decision-making would be referred to the European Union only if it becomes unavoidable. For this reason, in the near future, the European Union intends to review earlier legislations, because it believes that too much authority has been concentrated in the Council and the Commission.

A still more important question concerns those areas wherein the independent decision-making right of the member states has been annulled, or is in the process of being annulled, as a result of the Intergovernmental Conference. Even a few examples give the impression that the member states have given up—or will give up—their powers in all the important economic policy spheres. In public opinion, beginning with the joining of GATT, through signing the Treaty of Rome to the course leading to Maastricht, the member states "have lost" or are about to "lose" their powers as follows:

1. they cannot prescribe customs and quantitative restrictions,

2. they cannot impose restrictions on the freedom of movement of services, capital and labor,

3. they cannot apply other protectionist measures (such as subsidies, tax breaks, standards, etc.) in the above areas,

4. they cannot regulate the national market of agricultural products,

5. they cannot restrict the freedom of movement and settlement of citizens, and must recognize qualifications and university degrees

received elsewhere,

6. presently, they have the right to modify national currency rates within limits, however, their national currency may become void in the future,

7. presumably, they cannot carry on an independent monetary policy, nor an independent economic policy for that matter,

8. they lose their right to sign international agreements concerning these questions.

However, the question is: Is it correct to speak, in all respects, of a "loss" of national powers? The answer is negative. It is not a question of "relinquishing" the right of decision-making and "delegating" it to a separate, independent supranational body. Actually, in each and every case the member states agree that with regard to the above-mentioned economic policies, they will make decisions together, respecting each other's interests, and not independently, at least until such time as the Council becomes the final decision-making forum. As seen above, the Council has not become separate from the member states and the fundamental decision-making powers have not been delegated to that body (the Commission) of the European Union which is composed of legally independent personalities and in whose activity the member states do not have a say even today.

It is not by accident that the first part of our study discussed at some length the powers and decision-making procedure of the Security Council. Under the present conditions of international relations, the Security Council is the only international body in the world which has become almost completely separate from its member states and which has been invested with specific powers, including the right to adopt binding resolutions. At the same time, this body—virtually, the sole example of what may be called supranational—has not in fact deprived the member states of the United Nations of their sovereignty. Aside from the two disputed resolutions, it took care not to extend its jurisdiction and to remain within the bounds specified in the Charter, that is, to exercise its authority only in questions concerning peace and security. It does not disregard the right of veto of the great powers, furthermore, it authorizes the use of armed force by member states, but does not make it obligatory. Although, in every other respect it has become independent of and separate in its activity from the rest of the "ordinary" member states, it left their sovereignty intact.

If the activity of the in many ways supranational Security Council has not affected the sovereignty of member states, then it is even truer of the Council of Ministers in which every member state is represented and which is therefore not supranational. This is precisely the reason why the allegation cannot be accepted according to which the member states of the European Union would have lost their sovereignty within a system founded on a decision-making body like the Council. The history of integration to date has proved that the nation-states of our time must be treated as subjects of integration, without whose consent and active cooperation on substantive issues the process could not develop in the future, rather than as objects of integration.

This will hold even if the Intergovernmental Conference reaches an agreement to introduce the single European currency, to establish the central bank of the European Union, and to entrust the organization with the conduct of a joint monetary policy and, perhaps, economic policy as well. At least, it would hold if the Council would continue to supervise the central bank, as well as regulate the monetary and economic policy of the European Union. This would ensure continuation of the process and broaden further the sphere of joint decisions. It does not follow that the national flags displayed on the respective parliaments would have to be lowered. The parties would remain national and continue their contest for mandates in parliament, for the right to form a government, and also for delegating more of their representatives to the European Parliament. (This would also prevent the formation of European Christian and Social Democratic parties, predictions to the contrary notwithstanding.) Questions, such as who is going to be appointed to the post of industrial or agricultural minister, or elected to hold a high position in local administration, would not become indifferent.

It is particularly important that the European Union relies and will continue to rely on national administrative agencies to carry out central decisions, because it has no "local" executive organs. Although decrees of the Council and the Commission are immediately binding on the member states and private persons, their enforcement usually requires further decisions and measures. These fall within the exclusive competence of national agencies, and it also lies with them to supervise compliance. If those concerned fail to carry out the resolutions of the European Union, implementation of coercive measures becomes the responsibility of the national administration.

As far as the admission of Hungary is concerned, the procedure is similar to the one outlined with respect to NATO. In April 1996, the European Union presented a detailed questionnaire to the governments of associated countries inquiring into their economic situation, the present state of law harmonization, and other issues. After evaluating the answers provided, the European Union will decide with which states it will begin negotiations on admission. Should Hungary be considered in the first round, negotiations would start concerning the conditions of joining and membership. These largely depend on the decisions the present member states will make at the Intergovernmental Conference on the future of the European Union. The conditions would be set forth in a treaty to be ratified in Budapest and the respective parliaments of the fifteen member states; furthermore, the European Parliament would also put it to a vote. Presumably, a plebiscite would also be held in Hungary preceding ratification by Parliament.

The conclusion to be drawn from the foregoing is that the blue flag with the circle of white stars would not have to be hoisted on public buildings in the respective capitals of member states, nor of the newly admitted states. Sovereign states, instead of supranational institutions, will play, as they have in the past, the leading role in organizing the activity and cooperation of the community. Thus, joining the European Union, just as accession to NATO, would not restrict Hungary's sovereignty.

For the time being, Hungary awaits the invitation by both organizations to start negotiations.

László Lengyel

COURSE OF CONSTRAINT AND SCOPE OF MOBILITY
Distress or Glory of Small States

The Evolution of a Small State Is Shaped by Its Ability to Maneuver within a Set Course

We have to define no less than three notions in the first sentence: small state, course of constraint and scope of mobility. The characteristics of a small state were given by Kosáry as follows: modest physical power, feeble international position, international perspective constrained to the state's own region, narrow internal market, limited economic resources, a structure highly dependent on external markets, and a high exposure to the impact of external economic cycles.

And, finally...in the mentality of a small state, even in that of the more developed ones, an awareness of vulnerability, the tendency for identity crises as well as a keen endeavor to justify her existence and her will to survive by emphasizing her historical "merits" or, perhaps more skillfully, her services rendered to humanity.[1]

Kosáry's words are entirely valid, but only until the sixties. For the last two decades, we have been witnessing the great economic successes of some small states in Asia, where Singapore, Taiwan, South Korea, Hong Kong, Malaysia, that is, the "little tigers," have produced an extraordinary export-oriented growth without having much power, large internal markets, or domestic resources. All this

---

[1] Domokos Kosáry, *Az európai kis államok fejlődési típusai* (Budapest, 1990), p. 18.

suggests that economic growth does not necessarily need either abundant domestic resources or large internal markets. The large countries of Latin America have hardly stepped forward whereas Chile, a "small country" has managed to close up. In the Middle East, small Israel, even if with American help, has built a new country, won every war against countries much bigger than itself.

In Western Europe, we find small countries like Luxemburg, Switzerland, Austria, Denmark, the Netherlands, Belgium among the richest and the most able to develop. None of them has a large internal market or abundant domestic resources. Although they often face identity problems, those are by no means more serious than the ones that confront Great Britain, Germany, France or Spain. Finally, even in East Central Europe, it was not the larger, coercively created federations like the Soviet Union or Yugoslavia but the smaller ones, first of all Hungary, that have achieved considerable economic and social successes.

The European small states, having been created by the peace treaties in Versailles and the Paris suburbs, proved to be powerless victims because the settlement had cut them from their natural markets, without compensating them with other markets, and because, between the two world wars, the only economic opportunity for the states squeezed in between Germany and Soviet Russia was to produce and export raw materials for a larger market. In the economic space altered after World War II and particularly since the sixties, a small state has not been constrained to link to the world economy only by selling either raw materials or the crops grown on her territory on a large market. In the global and regional network of world economic relations, the investors look for "free ports," small islands able to export, from where they can cover huge regional markets rather than cover a whole territory and population of imperial size where the risks of marketing are considerably higher.[2]

---

[2] Malaysia with seventeen million people attracts more capital yearly than East (including Russia) and Central Europe with four hundred million. With a base in Malaysia it is easier to net the huge Pacific markets. The greater part of the capital in East Europe was invested in Hungary, because it was easier to cover Eastern Europe from Hungary. It also seemed to be most suitable to fit into regional trade.

After 1989, it became evident that the specific integrations which had been created at the time of the Versailles settlement, such as Yugoslavia, Czechoslovakia, and the Soviet Union, all pushed to the margins of Europe, were fragile; they proved to be too large and too small at the same time. They were too large because richer and more "European" countries had to share the cake with poorer and more Balkanized countries and regions, the latter dragging down the more developed ones. On the other hand, they were too small as integrations since they did not make it possible to get into the world market, did not let the population of the developed areas achieve the level of expected consumption. At the same time, the phenomenon of "free ports" also presupposes that the given harbor should not have nationality problems, that is, it is supposed to be not only small but possibly homogeneous as well, as far as nationality and culture are concerned, or if they contain more than one nation and culture, the state and the society are supposed to be able to achieve cooperation among them.

The possibility of so-called voluntary integration, the constraining of sovereign states inside large organizations of integration have not decreased the wave of secessions, or even, the wave of shrinkages. The more affluent parts of the country, regions, provinces do not want to share the wealth with the poorer nationalities and regions: the small and richer Catalonia with Spain, Flanders with Walloon Belgium, Lombardy with Italy,[3] Slovenia with Yugoslavia, and Moravia with Czechoslovakia, the Baltic states with the Soviet Union, or Russia, Kwantung and Fukien provinces with China.[4] Some disintegrate, some stay more or less together but realize their

---

[3] The Northern League demands the secession of the Northern Italian provinces: Lombardy, the Veneto, Piedmont and Emilia-Romagna under the name of *Padania*.

[4] Kwantung, a province in South China, has been closely linked to Hong Kong, like Fukien to Taiwan. These two provinces are incomparably more affluent than the rest of China. The two provinces are continuously bargaining with Beijing on the share "imperial" China is willing to leave in the special belts and the provinces around them. The threat to Taiwan concerns not only Taiwan but Fukien as well, the democratic or dictatorial way the transfer of Hong Kong to China is carried out concerns both Hong Kong and Kwantung.

economic autonomy as much as possible. Paradoxically, as a tiny and rich economy not compelled to partition revenues, a small state does have a scope of movement, whereas if she stays inside a larger and more unequal organization, she gets on preordained tracks.[5]

On achieving national self-determination, areas or provinces are more capable of developing hope for a better position in the global and regional spaces of world economy, that is, they hope to replace a forced integration with a voluntary "large market" integration. Since they do not have to share with others either their tax revenues or the external investments, since they do not have to plant industry, infrastructure in the less developed parts, since they can get rid of the rustbelts of industrialization and the institutions of social care, since they do not have to drag an unemployed mass that is unable to meet international requirements of productivity the new small self-determined states and provinces are neither victims nor midgets unfit for life; on the contrary, "small is beautiful."[6]

If we observe the small states within the framework of their ability to maneuver within courses of constraint, we will note that only those small states will have to follow a course of constraint which develops into a single and unipolar dependency or those that drop out of the global or regional economy. Those who have elbowroom to maneuver are

---

[5] "There is no proof that larger units make a better starting point for greater integration than small ones, and there are indications that nations need to be clearly formed if they are to be able to merge into a viable supra-national form. And nations may have to reject federations which are unable to offer the perspective of nation-formation and social progress together" István Bibó, *The Paralysis of International Institutions and the Remedies. A Study of Self-Determination, Concord among the Major Powers, and Political Arbitration* (New York, 1976), p. 61.

[6] Social selfishness defeats the imperial or great power dreams and patriotism, and since the status of a great power is more costly, and implies more sharing and responsibility, the population of certain areas are ready to create even new nations just to escape from a larger integration. Although the "Padanian" inhabitants of the Northern League do not have an ethnic identity, they have an economically, socially and culturally unified space instead, and they would prefer to secede or to federate themselves in that "small space" rather than within the "large space" of a single Italy. I guess that the "Pannonian" citizens of Western Hungary and of Budapest could also imagine federating with the "Hun" Eastern Hungary.

states that are multipolar dependencies and have joined the world and regional economy.[7] They never have total freedom of action, total sovereignty, however, for generally these are the rewards in the purview of empires.[8] Meanwhile, the empires and the great powers of the modern age do not have total sovereignty and freedom of action either.

---

[7] The Baltic states, for example, did not have a scope of movement inside the Soviet Union, they moved along a preordained course. Since their independence, they have had a scope of movement as now they depend on the global economic space, on the prescriptions of IMF and the World Bank, on a regional organization of integration: the European Union and, parallel to that, on Russia as a great power as well as on the United States, who assures their self-determination indirectly. The more diversified the dependencies, the wider the scope of movement. As soon as the IMF and the European Union renounced them, the international capital would not flow into those countries, that is, they would fall out of the world economic circulation, the United States would not consider it necessary to guarantee their independence directly or indirectly, consequently they would land in the sphere of Russian power; the Latvian, Estonian or Lithuanian scopes of mobility would diminish, they would turn up on a preordained course again (as did Belorussia). In the meantime, Malaysia, being a member of the ASEAN, of a closed and more confined region, defends herself from the influence of the more developed countries by insisting on the consultative status of the APEC (Asian and Pacific Economic Cooperation) that she herself has also joined and in which the two mountain-like figures of the United States and Japan cast shadows over the rest, as well as insisting on the liberalization of the APEC within the framework of the liberalization of the WTO, the former by no means faster than the latter. Thus, in opposition to the "institutionalist" United States, who wants to apply compulsory resolutions in the administration, the "evolutionist" Malaysia achieved that the liberalization of trade to be realized by 2020 should not be compulsory. Moreover, by Malay proposal, a new organization was established: the East Asian Economic Council (EAEC) consisting of China, South Korea and six members of the ASEAN, in order to protect the interests of the developing countries against the United States and Australia. Whatever the final results may be, the scope of movement of Malaysia or Singapore is based on their success in sticking to a balanced position among the giants: the United States, Japan, and China.

[8] In his well-known book, Paul Kennedy gives evidence that historically even empires can only temporarily have "total" freedom of action, and even they follow a set course in the long run. See, Paul Kennedy, *The Rise and Fall of the Great Powers: Economic Change and Military Conflict from 1500 to 2000* (London, 1989).

The small Hungarian state at times moves on a course of constraint but at times is able to maneuver. Hungary has to acknowledge that its fate is determined, first of all, by a global configuration and, secondly, by the great powers, or rather by the balance of power system. By her choice depending on her political and economic system and social mentality, she can modify that fate to a certain extent by adjusting the relationship between the a course of constraint and the space within which it can maneuver.

The collective mentality of Hungarian society is presently undergoing transformation. That process involves the alteration of values, conventions, traditions concerning independence and dependence, national self-determination and submission, sovereignty and the lack of it, the largeness and smallness of the country. That change of mentality would take place even if Hungary stayed outside the Euro-Atlantic organizations, if she had to build her future on her own resources or become a dependency of an East European country. We ought to deal with the question of independence and dependence even if we did not want to, if we wanted to postpone their thorough examination to a remote future never to come.

Hungary, Hungarian society has fallen out of a relationship of dependence, and gained, willy-nilly, a mini-sovereignty. In the Hungarian mentality, the sovereignty achieved is based on many previous dependencies, on many curtailed or limited sovereignties. The sovereignty of the state, of the nation as well as of the individual is the kind of new sentiment, towards which national and individual historical experiences and traditions may harbor suspicion, uncertainty, fear, and bad presentiments.

Punishment and Reward

The twentieth century attitude built into the mentality of Hungarian society is that the world, the great powers, punish independence, reward dependence; they promote the self-determination of the peoples and of the nations, but do not realize that idea in the case of Hungary. Hungarian independence and sovereignty, achieved in 1918 when the Monarchy disintegrated, was followed by the punishing Vix Ultimatum from the victorious Great Powers leading to the rise of the short lived Soviet Republic. Then the brief Romanian occupation and the Peace Treaty of Trianon. Hungarian society experienced sovereignty as a failure of its democratic attempts, and in exchange for the mirage of sovereignty it lost half the territory and one-third of the population of the country.[9] All that had a traumatic effect on political consciousness.[10]

From 1867 on, Hungary lived the dilemma of "small nation in a large state," that is, it was the Monarchy within which she realized her relative sovereignty, security, and her primacy over other small nations. After 1918 and 1919, Hungary had to experience the uncertainty and vulnerability of a "small nation in a small state," moreover, she did it under conditions of isolation, as she was surrounded by hostile small states without possibility of compromise.[11]

In the early twenties, Hungary proved unable to stabilize its economy based on its own resources alone, consequently the government initiated negotiations for a loan from the League of Nations. The great powers linked the loan to Hungarian recognition of Trianon and it is obvious that the Hungarian political elite perceived that as a violation of Hungarian sovereignty. Hungary's dependence was rewarded with the loan and, through that, with an opportunity for economic stabilization. These developments resulted in a two-faced and hypocritical Hungarian political behavior which could justify undemocratic policies on the grounds that the country was surrounded by enemies, so a self-confident patriotic policy was not realistic. That was how the ethics of a twofold policy unfolded: a policy emphasizing the symbols of the Hungarian mythical past internally, and another one painted in European colors externally.[12] The politicians strove to resolve the dilemma of "small

---

[9]   "With the disintegration of the Habsburg monarchy, the country gained sovereignty, but...that fact had no more than symbolic significance." See Domokos Kosáry "Magyarország kultúrpolitikája az első világháború után," *Európai Utas* 28, no. 4 (1995).

[10]   Bibó called it the "Trianon complex." In István Bibó, *Democracy, Revolution, Self-Determination. Selected Writings* (New York, 1991), p. 28.

[11]   Neither the French nor the English wanted to draw Hungary into their spheres of interest or to let her into their security systems, whereas Weimar Germany and Soviet Russia were still unable to do that.

[12]   Bibó, op. cit., pp. 34–35.

nation in a small state" for themselves by declaring that Hungary and the Hungarians were still the leading country and nation of East Central Europe, differentiating her from the rest as a "cultured nation" and as a "nation with a mission."

By the second half of the thirties Hungary had become a dependency of Germany. The "reward" for dependence was the territorial growth of Hungary between 1938 and 1941.[13] The feeble and hesitant Hungarian attempts towards independence were punished by Hungary's occupation by the Germans in 1944. And Hungarian sovereignty in 1945 was accompanied by Soviet occupation.

The right to national self-determination briefly won in 1956 for a few days was followed by immediate retaliation. It was clear to Hungarian society that Soviet tanks trampled down the Hungarian struggle for independence with the tacit agreement of the United States and the European great powers.[14] The experiences of Czechoslovakia in 1968 and of Poland in 1981 reinforced the isolation Hungarian society had felt in 1956. This helps explain the popular mentality of the Kádár period: the complacent renunciation of sovereignty and self-determination in exchange for relative well-being.

Hungarian society of the Kádár period attached less importance to state and national sovereignties than to the sovereignty of the family and the individual. Sovereignty in private life seemed more essential than public sovereignty. The image and the interpretation of the direct political, military, and economic dependence on the Soviet Union changed. Political dependence was considered bearable as long as the economy felt the benefits rather than the direct harm of

---

[13] From 1938 to 1941, Hungary reincorporated territories in four steps and grew by 79,100 square kilometers and 4,576,000 inhabitants. By the First Vienna Award (November 2, 1938), she was given the southern strip of Slovakia and the south-western part of Ruthenia. In March 1939, she took the other half of Ruthenia. By the Second Vienna Award (August 30, 1940), she obtained North Transylvania and the Máramaros-Körös Area (Maramureş-Crişu). In April 1941, she was granted Bácska (Bačka), the Baranya triangle and the area beyond the river Mura (Mur).

[14] Henry Kissinger, *Diplomacy* (London, 1994), pp. 559 and 563; John Lukacs, *The End of the Twentieth Century and the End of the Modern Age* (New York, 1993), p. 28.

this dependence, as long as society simply did not attach any importance to the military dependence. The "small nation in a small state" situation did not really appear to be a dilemma any more. On the suggestion of the masters of the system as well as by its own pragmatic principles, society accepted that the Kádár system above other East European countries and nations in one respect: "though those (socialist) states and nations may be larger, more national, more socialist, we small-Hungary and small-Hungarians live better."[15]

The events after 1989, the achievement of independence were not associated in the minds of people either with any significant amelioration of the economy or with the resounding success of the democratic experiment. Sovereignty did not gain its "European reward." On the contrary, Hungary that had been the "success story of the East," became a country "lagging behind" and begging from the West.[16]

A paradox of Hungarian history is that the idea of independence was perhaps the most important factor in shaping Hungarian mentality until the ideals of 1956 withered away during the Kádár era.[17] Because of the

---

[15] The Kádárian "small nation in a small state" looked down upon the rest of the "socialist camp" with an unprecedented awareness of economic superiority. For the first time in this century, society felt that the people in the surrounding small states envied its products, its currency, its freedom of consumption.

[16] It is not by chance that various political forces and their voters feel that the West was interested in Hungary as long as it was under Soviet control but wanted to separate. Once independent, the West lost all interest.

[17] During the Kádár period, the ideals of 1848, and 1956 focusing on independence were replaced by the cautious compromise ideals of the 1867 as well as of the post-1968 reforms. Even more important than the changes that took place in Hungarian historiography, was a withering away of the appeal of independence as successive new generations appeared on the scene; this was the result of everyday deals and making of compromises. The breakdown of the "revolutionary idea," the end of the "age of revolutions" throughout Eastern Europe played an important role in the transformation of attitudes after 1989. As the Russian socialist revolution of 1917 regarded itself as the heir of 1789 as well as of the revolutions of the nineteenth century, and as it divided the world into revolutionary and non-revolutionary nations, it brought a "revolutionary idea" into the societies of Eastern Europe. The collapse of the heritage of 1917 took with it the revolutionary heritage of both 1918–1919 and 1956. On the end of the "revolutionary era" see Tony Judt, "Europa am Ende des Jahrhunderts," *Transit* 1 (Fall 1995).

tragic perspective on history, the punishment for independence and the reward for dependence brought about a dignified aura of sovereignty. A Hungary bleeding for independence and for sovereignty became the symbol of the historical mission of the Hungarians. It was a matter of course that Hungarian independence was punished because the Hungarians always strove for aims no one would recognize, and which were unattainable. On the other hand, the acceptance of dependence, the resignation to the lack of sovereignty was identified with the deformation of the Hungarian national character, with a "cul-de-sac mentality."

The generations growing up in the Kádár era took dependence for granted and clearly realized that the "small nation in a small state" is only allowed to choose from among the roles imposed on her by the great powers. Consequently, they referred to the history of the country and the nation not as a series of disasters but as the history of possible (successful or unsuccessful) adaptations. The ideas of "total independence," "national liberation" or the ideals of 1848 and 1956 did not and could not have as much influence as they had been expected to have by a part of the elite participating in the change of regime.

The Prestige of State Sovereignty

Since 1918, Hungary could not have the illusion that she was part of an empire, of a large state that has sovereign prestige.[18] The states of the two revolutions—the one of October 1918, and the other one of March 1919—lost their prestige very quickly. Even the post-Trianon counterrevolutionary small state, "the kingdom without a king" did not expect identification from its citizens. It sought a historical identity in a Greater Hungary stretching beyond the borders

---

[18] The Hungarian part of the Dual Monarchy after 1867 had an ambivalent sovereignty, the prestige of which originated from the sovereignty of the empire. In the second half of the nineteenth century and in the early twentieth century the Monarchy was counted among the six great powers that determined the situation in Europe, and Hungary shared in that authority to a limited degree. See, Kosáry, op. cit.

and in the sovereignty of a large state. It tried to base its prestige on assuming the role of the agent who will reestablish Greater Hungary.

It accepted small state sovereignty as an international obligation, but did not appreciate it.[19] Hungary did not regard its small state boundaries, its symbols, its army as its own, but built the constitutional order, the boundaries, the symbols and the army of an envisioned large state. It did not expect its citizens to accept the sovereignty, the prestige, the boundaries of a small state but, as "good Hungarians," to identify themselves with "Hungarianness," with the nation independent of the borders. To accept the borders, to accept a sovereignty constrained to the "Hungary of Trianon," the "truncated Hungary," was considered to be a sin as serious as high treason. (No political or intellectual agent would have recognized the existing boundaries voluntarily.) Consequently, the prestige of the Hungarian small state was made questionable and temporary by the very political parties, the administration and the system of education that dominated the state.[20]

The formal independence of small states has different contents in the different systems of great powers. The peace settlement based on French hegemony, which established buffer states against Russia and Germany, was built on a French illusion according to which France

---

[19] We can speak of a double consciousness in this respect too. The political realism of Prime Minister István Bethlen made most people accept that Hungary was a little state with small physical force, moderate international influence, a narrow and truncated market, whose possibilities were determined by great power coercion. On the other hand, there was always the ideologically-based hope that all this was just temporary, sooner or later Hungary would play the role of a middle power among the small countries. See, György Ránki, *Economy and Foreign Policy: The Struggle of the Great Powers for Hegemony in the Danube Valley: 1919–1939* (Boulder, 1983),

[20] Austria vegetated as a similar temporary state without prestige after 1918. Most of its political forces were convinced that a self-contained Austria could not be maintained economically and politically, and sooner or later an *Anschluss* would take place. The attempts in the thirties, carried out by some political parties, to incite Austrian patriotism and sympathy towards the institutions of the republic in opposition to German National Socialism were hardly successful.

would be able to fill the economic gap in the region and enforce security there.

> French power politics did not threaten the independence of the countries directly for reasons of geography, since her hegemony was based on a policy in which the East European countries played but a marginal role, while precisely because of their independence, they could gain value with their politics of confrontation. It was one of the tragic contradictions of Hun-garian foreign policy that it endeavored to undermine an international constellation that fettered Hungary on the one hand yet, on the other, still allowed it some movement.[21]

The main goal of the competition among the small states in the power vacuum which developed after 1918–1919 was not to join an empire but to achieve the leading role, the status of middle power among the small states. That was the aim of Poland, Czechoslovakia, Yugoslavia and Romania. Hungary was so deeply shaken by Trianon, however, that she could not expect to undertake such a role.

While Hungary's neighbors did their best to vest their temporary, not yet prestigious states—boundaries, symbols, armies, etc.—with prestige and to "make them permanent," the Hungarian small state did the opposite. In the new countries—in Romania, Czechoslovakia, Yugoslavia, Poland—the establishment and recognition of the prestige of the state was made a national goal. To be a "good" Romanian, Yugoslav, Pole was the same as to recognize and to accept state sovereignty, prestige and, particularly, borders. They made their citizens realize that their everyday well-being as Romanians, Serbs, Poles depended on the state, on the maintenance of the state's prestige, on the permanence of the borders. They were supposed to identify themselves not with "the Romanians of the world," not with "the Poles living anywhere," but with the Romanian, or the Polish nation-state. In the Hungarian state, people had to confess their faith in the visionary

---

[21] György Ránki, "Mozgástér és kényszerpálya," in György Ránki, *A harmadik birodalom árnyékában* (Budapest, 1988), p. 12.

kingdom of Greater Hungary day in and day out.[22]

Since the mid-thirties, since the end of the power vacuum, the Hungarian state was queuing up for the prestige of the best intermediary, the best lieutenant on the market of the German great power. The exchange rate of Hungarian state prestige depended on the German market because Nazi Germany took active advantage of the rivalry. The German National Socialist system of power did not expect the small states to play a balancing or buffer role, rather it needed only their raw materials and human resources.[23]

In the Soviet system the small states could only play the role of dependencies and satellites again. The Soviet Union did not want a buffer zone between the West and itself, just the opposite, it rejected initiatives for the integration of smaller states. Not only its negative experiences with the interwar regimes of the buffer states but also its doctrine of direct intervention led to the conclusion that wherever the power vacuum created a non-aligned state, the Soviet Union would have to draw it into her sphere of influence at once.[24]

After 1948–1949, the Hungarian state once again derived prestige from external Soviet "prestige." The lack of state sovereignty was adumbrated again by the leadership tracing its "greatness," its "power" its "influence" back to Soviet imperial sovereignty instead of the Hungarian

---

[22] The populist writer László Németh saw Hungary treated as a conquered state by its own leaders: "The slogan of 'No, no, never' holds true of all. We do not recognize the new boundaries, we reject the plebeian utopias, we do not appreciate the great artists, we do not let Jews into the universities. No, no, never! But us: Yes, yes, and at once? Yes, yes, and at once: many new desk jobs, many new loans, many new university professorships and as a matter of course many new taxes." See László Németh, *Magyarság és Európa (1935), Sorskérdések* (Budapest, 1989), pp. 302–303.

[23] Ránki, op. cit., p. 14.

[24] The Soviet Union simply annexed some of the small states, and kept others under direct control. She did not recognize any new states in the buffer zone, and let no integration of any kind develop—Neither a Balkan confederation nor any kind of customs union or a Danubian economic community. It is also the consequence of traditional Soviet-Russian foreign policy that after the Soviet withdrawal initiated by Gorbachev, Yeltsin is protesting more and more forcefully against an East Central European buffer zone.

state institutions and symbols. The omnipotent party-state installed itself everywhere, while it was still lacking the sovereignty-based prestige of its own. Most of its citizens were convinced that, without Soviet backing, the state would lose its power. The prestige of the state was built on brute force, the vulnerability of which became evident at once in 1956.[25]

In the Kádár era, the prestige of the sovereign state was at a nadir at first. The state of Kádár had neither internal nor external sovereignty, being forced to draw close to Soviet empire. After the repression, one of the means for Kádárism to gain state prestige was the declaration of the new, sovereign nation-state. That could have been the "national communist" kind of relative increase of sovereignty. But the system, as opposed to the Romanian, Yugoslav, Albanian, Asian attempts, carefully avoided the risk of such an increase of prestige.[26]

---

[25] The lack of state prestige does not mean that the state does not preserve its sometimes unmerciful power over its citizens. The Hungarian state between the two world wars was authoritarian with a low level of authority. The state of Rákosi was totalitarian, but the Hungarian state, its organizations and institutions did not have any prestige in the eyes of the citizens: "These organizations are not ours, these institutions are not ours."

[26] After 1956, Albania or Yugoslavia were in the position of nation-states with sovereign prestige. Since the end of the sixties, Romania ventured on the "national communist" path in order to increase her prestige as a sovereign nation-state. The Hungarian position was far less strong than those of Poland, of East Germany or of the recalcitrant Romania in negotiations with the Soviet Union, in either the COMECON or the Warsaw Pact. Contrasting with Romania, whose politicians counterbalanced their domestic problems with a spectacular drawing away from the Soviet foreign and military policies, and increased their political prestige both in the West and at home, Hungary made no similar attempts. On the contrary, until as late as the collapse of the Kádár regime, Hungary insisted on emphasizing its loyalty to the Soviet Union, on not questioning any decisions of the Warsaw Pact. On the other hand, it did its best to decrease secretly Hungary's burdens caused by membership in the Warsaw Pact and to achieve a favorable position in the COMECON. In 1982, precisely in the midst of a period when the will to independence and sovereignty had broken down, "behind the Soviets' back," Hungary joined the World Bank and the IMF, linking the country to an opposite dependency system. Dual dependence meant greater independence. That was the Kádár regime's concession. This policy was due to pragmatism: on the one hand there was the Soviet presence in Hungary, on the other, the financial indebtedness and the opening towards the West.

It did its best to replace the sentiment for independence and political neutrality with tolerable dependence and economic compensations, and so to place the prestige of the state on solid foundations. It excluded the wish for a great state and for independence, without establishing Hungary's political prestige as a small state.

Kádárian limited sovereignty was based less and less on the possibility of violent Soviet intervention, and increasingly on the willing acceptance of Hungarian state institutions. The prestige of the redistributive state derived more from the social security it established as well as from the rising standard of living. Enjoying these "blessings," the citizens forgave and took for granted not only the authoritarian, hierarchical operations of the state but also the lack of democracy and sovereignty. By the early eighties, the regime attained a position where most of its citizens would have presumably accepted it even if the Soviets left. By the time this could have happened, however, the state lost its resources for compensation with which it obtained the citizens' acquiescence and even identification with its institutions.

The state that emerged in the 1990 transformation is this century's first Hungarian state that has sovereign prestige. This state is granted an unquestionable prestige by its external independence. The right of the center coalition of 1990–1994 could identify which kind of sovereignty would be accepted by society: the sovereignty of a small state, or the sovereignty of a visionary large state. Contemporary Hungary is surrounded by ethnically self-confident societies that are imbued with the doctrines of "national communism," for whom sovereignty is a fresh experience, whereas Hungarian society lacks a similar self-confidence and feeling of independence. Hungarian society has already accepted the consciousness of being ruled by a small state, it has reconciled itself to being in a small state and ceased to dream about becoming a great power and a dominant nation.

The power of the post-1990 state is limited by both parliamentary democracy itself and private (frequently multinational) capital. Its internal constraints on it are the so-called constitutional institutions: the Constitutional Court, the Supreme Court, the National Bank, the State Auditing Board. It is also limited by local democracy, by the municipal democracy of the cities, by the network of international institutions and, finally, by international and domestic media. At the same time, state prestige is whittled down by the deeply rooted political mentality of Hungarian citizens: they look suspiciously upon all references to independence, they do not recognize state prestige just because it embodies Hungarian sovereignty.[27]

The governments established during the transition have to create a new state prestige and face a situation in which that prestige cannot be built above other powers but alongside them, in cooperation with them.

The Effects of Globalization

> The state has become too small concerning
> the big problems of life, and too big in the
> small things of life
> *Ronald Inglehart*

The prestige crisis of the Hungarian state coincides with the general prestige crisis of nation-states. The states of the European democracies are losing their leading and decisive role in the nineties, and the techniques of the New Deal and those of the postwar welfare state are breaking down. The welfare state and the nation-state playing the main role of mobilization have become obsolescent at the very same time. In post-industrial societies, the state has been losing its nation[28] and the authoritarian regimes have also been subjected to

---

[27] Those who accept the ideas of republican patriotism condemn that mentality as a feature of "Homo Kadaricus," and the politicians believe that the most important task of the intellectuals is to elicit positive sentiments towards the institutions of the Hungarian republic. They trace the corrosion of state prestige back to the recalcitrant behavior of the intelligentsia, which propagated the liberal and reformist values of "the smallest possible state," to that behavior which is suspicious even of the now "properly" sovereign state, or its attacks against the prestige of the democratic state, initiating anarchy and discrediting democratic institutions.

[28] See, Bernard Paqueteau, "De la nation armée à la société défendue," *Commentaire* (Spring 1996). One of the subtitles given by the author is: "L'État à la recherche de la nation," that is, "The state in search of the nation."

the global economic and cultural configuration.[29]

Globalization means that state sovereignty is generally permeated by internationalization in the developed part of the world, and those not participating in that process lose all their opportunity to keep up or catch up with the developed countries. The yawning and ever-widening gap between developed and underdeveloped countries clearly demonstrates that the poor countries not participating in the world-wide division of labor, in the redistribution of revenues, in the investment of working capital, have no chance to narrow that gap (even in a relative sense) in the present world system.[30]

Table 1

Global Income Disparities between Rich and Poor Countries
Percentage of Global Income, 1960–1989

Year	Poorest 20%	Richest 20%	Richest to Poorest (Poorest=1)
1960	2,3	70,2	30 to 1
1970	2,3	73,9	32 to 1
1980	1,7	76,3	45 to 1
1989	1,4	82,7	59 to 1

Source: *UNDP, 1992:36*

Can we speak of a global political and economic configuration and structure? Or should we rather speak about a tripartite division of the globe, into economic regions and integrations by a triad consisting of North America (the United States), Western Europe (Germany) and the Far East (Japan). And will not the previous organizations of integration

---

[29] "Whether we like it or not, at the end of our century, we control not through social, political or ideological agents like in the late nineteenth century, but through the structural proposals of the IMF and the World Bank; that is to say, the political and social control over economy has diminished, while the influence of the world market and that of the countries' comparative benefits has increased." Alain Touraine, *Lettre à Lionel...* (Paris, 1995), pp. 11–12.

[30] On the gap between the rich and the poor countries see tables 1 and 2.

disintegrate into their components, into fragmented nation-state sovereignties? We can find the three trends of globalization, regionalization and nation-state secessions going on together and in competition, enhancing as well as destroying one another.[31]

There exists a global configuration that influences and partly constrains sovereignties. Since 1945 the global configuration includes the United Nations and its institutions;[32] world economic institutions; international financial institutions such as the IMF and the World Bank,[33] as well as the organizations for trade policy and labor, such as GATT/WTO, ILO.[34] The OECD is also a global insti-

---

[31] The global configuration, the universal structures and organizations are above the great powers in a certain sense; they are only partly controlled by the great powers. Thus, without returning to the period before the sixteenth century, when popes and emperors laid claim to universal authority, structures of universal powers are emerging. On the other hand, the sovereign and contending great powers still determine the place and the role of the not entirely sovereign small states by either drawing them into their spheres of interest or ignoring and pushing those unimportant to them into isolation.

[32] The United Nations is the community of sovereign states, which exercises rights turned over to it by the sovereign states.

[33] From the early eighties, because of the radical rearrangements of the financial "positions, the IMF and the World Bank, unimportant until the mid-seventies, broke through by having their short and long term crisis management programs accepted globally. The abundant supply of capital until the end of the seventies postponed the need of managing the crises. The debt crisis of the post-1982 period, however, trusted forward the rigorous liberal financial policies of the international financial organizations. Since then, the IMF has represented the corporate conditions set by the cartel of the creditors. Béla Greskovits "Lehetséges-e más, mint a neoliberális stratégia?" *Beszélő*, no. 2 (1996).

[34] The ILO (International Labor Organization) has been once again gaining importance among the institutions of United Nations.

The Clinton administration wants to use ILO to influence the global configuration; that is one of the reasons why the importance of ILO has increased by the mid-nineties. On the one hand, the ILO is ready to initiate an international labor standard that would regulate the rights of the labor force, the freedom of association, the conditions of collective organization and intervention, the limitations on child labor and dangerous jobs. The acceptance of the ILO convention would have a strong impact on the Asian labor market, on labor costs.

The United States has been claiming more and more vehemently that the

tution.[35] In its special way the G-7, that is, the summits of leaders of the most developed countries, are also components of the global configuration mentioned above.[36]

Table 2

Economic Disparities between Rich and Poor Countries
Percentage of Total, 1989

Quintile	Income	Trade	Domestic Investment
Poorest 20%	1,40	0,95	1,20
Second 20%	1,80	1,40	2,60
Third 20%	2,30	2,55	2,90
Fourth 20%	11,80	13,90	12,70
Richest 20%	82,70	81,20	80,60
Total:	100,00	100,00	100,00

Source: *UNDP, 1992:36,* reprinted from Werner Kamppeter, "The Wealth of Nations, the Market and the Modern Rentier State," *Internationale Politik und Gesellschaft,* no. 3 (1995), p. 229.

European Union should also accept the international labor standard, that is, a lower minimum wage structure tied to its productivity. It was the first occasion in the history of the ILO that the organization was allowed to participate in the professional conference of G-7 in Lille in the Spring of 1996, and to express its opinion on the management of employment problems. See, Steve Charnovitz, "Promoting Higher Labor Standards," *The Washington Quarterly* (Summer 1995).

[35] In 1995 and 1996, the integration into OECD became an important question for the East Central European countries. The Czech Republic and Hungary were admitted, Poland was put on a waiting list. The Paris Center of OECD drew up very clear criteria for admission. The close interrelations of the global configuration are clearly shown by the fact that although Hungary had met all the requirements of the OECD by the end of 1995, the admission was linked to Hungary's agreement with IMF. Hungary was expected to obtain a stand-by credit from the IMF first. The agreement was signed in March 1996.

[36] W. R. Smyser, "Goodbye G-7," *The Washington Quarterly* (Winter 1993); W. E. Whyman, "We Can't Go On Meeting Like This: Revitalizing the G-7 Process," *The Washington Quarterly* (Summer 1995); G. J. Ihenberry, "Salvaging the G-7," *Foreign Affairs* (Spring 1993).

NATO as a quasi-global security organization extends over North America and Europe; it can be used in peacemaking outside the sphere the original treaty covers: in the Middle East, in the Persian Gulf War and in Southeast Europe.

Multinational industrial investment companies make transactions also on a global scale. These side step or rearrange organizations of integration as well as nation-states, they rearticulate them. The circulation of goods and services as well as the flow of working capital would be nowhere without the multinational corporations.[37] Today, one finds the networks and the competition of the multinational corporations in the background of the processes of regionalization and globalization.[38] That is why one may have the impression that there are no United States or Germany, rather there are General Motors and IBM or Siemens and Volkswagen.

Multinational portfolio investors (pension funds, insurance companies, investment and hedge funds) can be regarded as an even greater challenge to nation-states and organizations of integration.[39]

---

[37] In 1993, still 60 % of foreign investments was realized in the developed countries, but already 40 % went to the developing countries including the Asian 26 %. The share of the Visegrád countries increased from 0.6 % in 1990 to 2.7 % in 1993. China alone attracts three times more capital per year than Eastern Europe. Germany, the country most interested in the East, directs 48 % of its foreign investments to the European Union, 24 % to the US, whereas only 2 % to Eastern Europe. See, W. Kamppeter, "The Wealth of Nations, the Market and the Modern Rentier State," *Politik und Gesellschaft,* no. 3, (1995).

[38] The globalization strategy of the multinational corporations demands the type of institution which controls the affiliated companies from a single center, harmonizes their production, resources, and services. In such cases, the sovereign states as well as the organizations of integration have to face the fact that all strategic decisions and the activities of the enterprises are determined from abroad. On the other hand, a regional strategy means that the affiliated companies, are being adjusted to the market of the given region, and production, services, and employment are controlled from a single regional center. Moreover, upon entering the region, the affiliated companies are "nationalized," in marketing and in employing local managers. The world is covered with a network of 200, 000 affiliated companies of 37, 000 multinational corporations.

[39] The value of the financial assets circulating on financial markets had amount-

Since the seventies, those have been the largest investors in the United States. The privatization of social insurance in the European states will take place in the near future, giving birth to further mobile portfolio investors sensitive to foreign investments and rearranging the markets and their rules. The international stock exchange is the institutional framework of global capital flow; the stock exchanges are supermarkets, chains of money and capital markets that are able to limit sovereign great powers in their everyday decisions.[40]

One of the characteristics of globalization at the turn of the millennium is that the competition takes place among megapolises, giant cities, rather than among states. The capital and information chains are chains of cities. The capital moves via megapolises or rather along the networks linking them. Today, cities attach countries to themselves and not the other way round. In the European developed area it is not only Germany, the Netherlands, Belgium, France that can be regarded as networks but Frankfurt-Cologne-Düsseldorf, Amsterdam-Rotterdam, Brussels, or Paris as well. Because of that boom of big cities, we should rather speak about a Budapest-Hungary than about a sovereign Hungary with a Budapest inside.

---

ed to five trillion dollars in 1980, growing to thirty-five trillion dollars in 1992, which is twice the total GNP of the developed industrialized countries. Thus, in 1992, the hedge funds supported by portfolio investors, undermined the ERS (Exchange Rate System), tearing Great Britain and Italy away from it, in spite of all the efforts of the central banks of the countries concerned. The Halifax G-7 of June 1995 proposed that the IMF might keep a closer check on the financial policies and financial markets of the poorer countries. Erik R. Peterson, "Surrendering to Markets," *The Washington Quarterly* (Autumn 1995); Pam Woodall, "Who's in the driving seat? A survey of the world economy," *Economist*, October 7–13, 1995.

[40] "Instead of superpowers there are supermarkets. There's the Tokyo stock exchange and the Frankfurt stock exchange and the Singapore stock exchange and the Wall Street stock exchange. These stock exchanges are actually more powerful than many governments today." See Thomas Friedmann, "Yesterday's Man," *The New York Times*, March 19, 1995. He thinks that there is a "global investment highway" where the countries having the most stable governments, the most efficient economies, the most westernized legal systems, the most educated labor forces, the most convertible currencies can obtain capital from the supermarkets.

The new global communities (NGC), that is, the world-wide organizations of the civic, nonprofit sector, are such important organizations of globalization that overstep boundaries.[41] The NGCs publish reports on the basis of certain values. Those reports evaluate and classify the countries, and their conclusions are regarded by the given countries as pressure exerted by a special "world public opinion."[42]

The global media powers have an influence that is inescapable. The contending cameras and voices which see and make visible the whole world, influence the fate of all countries no less than the global transactions on the stock exchanges or the international financial institutions. They show, what's more, they shed light on the countries, the events—events exist only as media events—the political, economic and cultural traditions along definite values and interests and

---

[41] Both the sovereign states and the transnational companies have to learn that the new global communities have remarkable strength to constrain their sphere of action. Greenpeace forced Shell and Great Britain to retreat in the case of a drilling tower in the North Sea, and exercised relentless pressure on France against the renewal of nuclear experiments in 1995. Amnesty International, the World Wildlife Fund or the Open Society Foundation of George Soros, with widespread activities in the former socialist countries, and the new churches have money, international influence, global strategies. Those organizations take direct part in the management of several crises in the East European countries, they build local networks, they hoard specific local knowledge, shape local policies concerning human rights, education, culture, environment etc. See, Lester M. Salamon, "The Rise of the Nonprofit Sector," *Foreign Affairs* (July/August 1994); Peter J. Spiro, "New Global Communities," *The Washington Quarterly* (Winter 1995).

[42] We should note that the socialist countries were " attacked" by the reports of the very human rights organizations which, referring to the Helsinki Final Act, did not resign themselves to the argument used by the Soviet Union and the socialist countries according to which the cases of the human rights were internal affairs not questionable without questioning their sovereignties. By accepting continuously the reports of Amnesty International, of the Helsinki Commission and other civic organizations, President Jimmy Carter exercised that kind of constraining of sovereignty. It is characteristic that the Carter Center and the former president have been efficiently taking part in peace-making in Ethiopia, Haiti, North Korea and other places. See, Douglas Brinkley, "Jimmy Carter's Modest Quest for Global Peaces," *Foreign Affairs* (November/ December 1995).

wrap them in those values and interests.

State sovereignty is also limited by transnational criminal organizations. With the collapse of the Soviet Union and with Eastern Europe opening up and undergoing crisis, global mafias and *mafiyas* spring up, divide the world and the spheres of interest in different products and services among themselves.[43]

Global diasporas exert a world-wide influence on the transformation of the world economy. Global migrations result in the creation of successful or not so successful local or global systems of relations.[44] A great part of the material capital and the "human capital," of the information and the services, many of the techniques of civilization and innovation, move within the diasporas of the Chinese, the Russians, the Vietnamese, the Jews, the Koreans, the Italians, the Irish, the Armenians, etc.[45] The Hungarian, Polish, Croatian,

---

[43] On the influence of the transnational criminal organizations and particularly on the Russian *mafiya* see, "Russia's Mafia," *Economist*, July 9, 1994; Vladimir Ivanidze, "Perspectives radieuses pour la mafia russe," *La Nouvelle Alternative* (March 1995). Phil Williams recalls the Prague Italo-Russian mafia meeting of October 1992, where the Czech spheres of interest were divided. Williams, "Transnational Criminal Organizations: Strategic Alliances," The *Washington Quarterly* (Winter 1995). On East European and Chinese transnational criminal organizations see, Szilveszter Póczik, "Maffió-zók internacionalizmusa," *Kritika*, no. 11 (1995).

[44] Thomas Sowell, *Migrations and Cultures: A World View* (New York, 1995).

[45] "In his book *Megatrends Asia* (New York, 1996), John Naisbitt refers to the Overseas Chinese," the Chinese network without a nation-state, as an economic great power. In his opinion, the "Overseas Chinese" show the future of the new global economy: "Today's global economy is dominated by inter-company trade and person-to-person communications. Countries do not trade; people and businesses do. Networks are at the core of the new global economy. The Overseas Chinese are a network of networks" (p. 15). Recently the largest amount of such capital can be found in the Chinese diasporas located in mainland China, Taiwan, Hong Kong, Singapore, Malaysia, Thailand, in the countries of the former Soviet Union, in East Europe, in the United States and Europe. As far as the flow of "human capital" and the brain drain is concerned, it is also the Chinese who take the prime. "Within" the Russian diaspora, one can see capital, labor force, professionals move to Eastern Europe, Israel, Western Europe and the United States.

Romanian diasporas play important roles in the East European transformation. The Hungarian diaspora has the specific advantage that it embraces both the Hungarian and the Jewish world diasporas at the same time. In addition, it can take advantage of the Swabian-Hungarian diaspora in Germany.[46]

The global diasporas and networks have much influence on the policy of the sovereign states and the organizations of integration among them. The churches and religious communities independent of the nation-states function partly parallel to, partly separately from the diasporas; they also move enormous real and cultural capital.[47] The expansion and conflicts of those global networks produce both clashes and compromises time and again.

Global linguistic and semiotic discourse accompanies the global configuration as a binder as well as a principle of power. The "newspeak" shaped by the developed countries and by the international organizations, the special United Nations-American-English, IMF-American-English, NATO-American-English, Wall Street-American-English, CNN-American-English, McDonald's-American-English mean understanding, interpretation as well as exclusion. The global linguistic and semiotic discourse has a decisive influence not only on international parleys but on everyday life as well since by

---

[46] Hungary gained immeasurable benefits from the role of the Hungarian Jewish/Jewish-Hungarian diaspora as lobbyists in the United States, first of all. A process of similar importance both in macro- and micro-relationships, was the gradual ethnic German-Magyar compromise in the Kádár era, from which Hungary obtained economic ties and a cultural pattern that exerted important influence on the image of villages, and on the behavior of entrepreneurs.

[47] For example, the American Roman Catholic Church with its community of 67 million people, its 20,000 parishes, 8,300 schools, 231 universities, 900 hospitals and 1,400 organizations of charity is the greatest nongovernmental organization in the United States, its material effects can be felt not only inside the United States but throughout both Americas. And when the Vatican made an autonomous and independent declaration on the women issue during the United Nations world conference of 1995, the cultural effect also became visible. The movement of capital and values is similar in the Islamic or the Protestant communities.

that discourse things that are unknown/ or desired are made familiar.[48] No wonder that even "anti-language" has become global. Those raising objections against IMF-newspeak may talk in French, Hungarian, or Russian, sound the same in "translation": national sovereignty, protectionism, the defense of the nation, "people-betrayed-by-evil-elite," "international conspiracy," etc.[49]

The conditions on which the emerging markets (countries like Hungary) are allowed to join the global theater are determined by the developed economies, the international financial institutions, the multinational investors who possess that theater. The competition among the countries in the global and regional theaters is regulated by the developed ones. The respect for the interrelated preconditions and compliance with the rules will decide where and on which rung of the ladder Hungary can get a foothold. The only choice the sovereign Hungarian governments have is whether they are willing to pre-

---

[48] The negotiator of a given country has to be able to carry on talks or draft proposals not simply in English but in the language of the International Monetary Fund, or in that of the European Union, or the NATO. Just like in the Middle Ages, when discourses used not simply Latin, but the Latins of the different monastic orders, universities, present-day talks use the American-English political, economic, technical, etc. languages. But compared to the Latin that could be secularized in spite of its fastidiousness, or compared to the diplomatic French that clung to the logical formulas of the eighteenth and nineteenth centuries, the loose American-English is characteristically polysemantic. And that linguistic-symbolic discourse shapes the mother tongue too making it come closer to the international version (mondializes it). Thus, East Central Europeans have to get accustomed to the fact that they are participants, users or, on the contrary, the embarrassed and vulnerable victims, of the global discourse in the production, in the services as well as in their leisure time.

[49] Thus, the dominant discourses are not the discourses of left versus right, national versus antinational, but rather the discourses of the political forces conforming to or rejecting the globalized system of values (accepting the Washington consensus). In Europe, the transnational, IMF, OECD, NATO, pro-Maastricht way of thinking ("pensée unique") clashes with the discourse that is anti-Maastricht, national, and rejects the interrelated system of conditions elaborated by the multinational institutions. Consequently, leftist governments and voters may propagate and represent global discourses in spite of their traditional culture and political background, whereas rightist political forces and voters may use anti-global, anti-Maastricht discourse and symbols.

pare for the tests adjusting to their merciless, often unjust conditions, whether they are willing to fill in the questionnaires, to climb higher on the steps, or whether they prefer exclusion, prefer to stay outside, choose the lower status. Neither Hungary nor Eastern Europe has a chance to change the rules radically or "erase them by a revolution."[50]

The organization, the values, the civilization of the global configuration is undoubtedly in crisis. The organizations described above have not become more suitable to manage the global crises after the end of the Cold War. The tensions between the rich and the poor regions and countries, between the integrated (those inside) and the excluded (those outside) of the world have been increasing. It concerns Hungary and Eastern Europe too that a new tension has unfolded in the competition of wages between the poor of the developed countries and the labor force of the emerging markets. The sovereign decision of the states has ceased to exist or has at least been limited, and the social contract, the institutional system of agreements shaped after World War II have reached a state of crisis.[51]

The process of globalization is limited internally also by the three great, more or less integrated economic communities: the North

---

[50] The national or communist revolutions, revolts or resistances in East Europe do not threaten the powers and systems that rule the global configuration. For example, the "Washington consensus" (the principles of liberalization and stabilization to be applied to every economy) followed by the international financial institutions may be questionable and disputable, but under the present circumstances it cannot be changed radically either by convincing the politicians of the developed world, or by a coordinated revolt of the poor countries against IMF, or by some maverick East European menace. The "anticolonialist" and "anti-imperialist" struggle for the defense of national sovereignty have lost their ideals and means.

[51] From the point of sovereignty, what is most basic is that countries are under great pressure towards global and/or regional integration.Thus the French voter is fully aware that the Juppé plan is not simply a project elaborated by the sovereign French government in order to stabilize the country and improve French competitiveness, but also a consequence of the system of values propagated by the European Union as well as of its economic and political pressures. Consequently, not only the French government and the French trade unions were confronted in the long strike of November-December 1995, but strict Germany and Maastricht Europe also cast their shadows on the strikers.

American, the European and the Far Eastern. The economic, political and, in some respects, cultural competition among them end in crises. In principle, a country may be able to keep in balance her own system of relations, increase her scope of action by winning over the organizations of integration in order to counterbalance the pressure and influence of the global institutions or by creating links with many partners.[52] But that kind of balancing act also has its limits.[53]

Such signs of crisis are evident in Europe, whose sphere of influence includes Hungary, too. The European Union does take part in the competition in the global configuration described above, and its perspectives are not bright. Countries yearning to be full members of these regions may be justified in having fresh doubts in the light of global crisis and the crisis of integrations. For a group of countries whose citizens have been reared for decades in the spirit that it is possible and even inevitable to attain a world that is going to provide them with solutions to domestic and global problems, it will be hard to realize the disappearance of progress and the chance to reach "the best of all possible worlds," and to realize that they are allowed only to long to replace a "hardly bearable world" with a "bit more bearable world." And the "bit more bearable world" is a higher point in the global configuration, not a lower one. It means integration into the European structure and not staying outside.

---

[52] Characteristically, Hungarian governments have hardly been able to influence the direction of foreign trade in which the historically traditional partners (Germany, Italy) have the greatest influence. Both the Antall and the Horn governments, however, did their best to keep up a certain mix in capital investments among the United States, and, within Europe, among Germany, the Netherlands, Austria, Italy, France and in Asia between Japan, South Korea.

[53] In 1989, the government of Miklós Németh cherished the hope that leaning on the support of the European Community it could escape the policy of restrictions proposed by IMF. Europe had proved to be unwilling and unable to counterbalance IMF on that issue, hence the government had no alternative but to implement the policy of restrictions. Late 1994 and early 1995 the Horn government cherished the hope that leaning on German support it could counterbalance the American influence and the restrictions could be escaped. It was disappointed in its expectations: the German policy took a stand in favor of the restrictions and the speeding up of the privatization.

Course of Constraint or Scope of Mobility

The Versailles system of 1919 is often blamed for enabling the great powers to create small states without deciding upon their economic integration and system of security. The system of great powers of the post-1989 period faces a similar dilemma. It created dozens of countries or allowed them be created without having projects about, interests in, and capability for integrating them. While "Pax Americana" and its helpless younger brother "Pax Europae" have approved boundaries and national movements, causing much harm as well, they have pushed those countries into a vacuum that is so familiar from the twenties. The recognition of the autonomy of countries is undoubtedly a step forward and we can appreciate the fact that the Euro-Atlantic settlement is not intended to threaten the existence of any small state, but the countries left in a void are unable to stabilize themselves and to produce economic growth without additional help.

The release of the small states "from the bottle" was not the result of a deliberate policy. The United States and Europe have not even made up their minds whether they will use the small states squeezed between the European Union and Russia as buffer states, or rather consider the region a sphere of influence to be divided between them and Russia. As a global peace maker, the United States has been obliged to intervene in the area without having serious long term interests.[54]

As for security, Hungary has fallen into a paradoxical situation. Her negative experiences of a security vacuum and the proximity of Russia, an authoritarian great power, makes her strive for integration into an international security and economic system even if that sys-

---

[54] Finally, the United States has been forced to participate in the conflicts of former Yugoslavia. We should not forget, however, that the peace making in Bosnia is of secondary importance compared to the conflicts in Latin America, the Middle East or South East Asia. Tony Judt draws attention to the possibility that the new American role may result in conflicts between the peacemakers of Europe on the one hand, and the United States on the other, conflicts that are familiar from the interwar period. Tony Judt, "What are American Interests?" *The New York Review of Books*, October 5, 1995, pp. 37–38.

tem shows little willingness to admit her. Paradoxically (from the point of view of security) she has reason for jubilation if the results of the peacemaking process in Yugoslavia prove permanent because in that case the East-Central European logistic center of the United States and the NATO will stay in Hungary. And that will mean her defense by a great power, cooperation with a great power and constantly living under the eyes of global opinion.[55]

The results of the American and the Russian elections in 1996 may prove decisive for the period until the end of the millennium. The resurrection of American isolationism and a Russian great power neo-nationalism of any kind may cast a shadow not only on the world but particularly on the intermediate European area. The impact of these two elections on Europe is even more complicated because they do not take place at the same time and, consequently, will give no possibility of choice to the small East European states and to the European Union that is unable to make decisions for the time being.[56]

The year 1996 may turn out to be a milestone in the European unification process too. The internal debates of the European Union have grown rather harsh by the time of the Intergovernmental Conference (IGC). That may probably be the last chance to reform the European institutional system but, precisely because of the differing national interests, the transformation will be put off again. In all probability, passive drifting will continue and, along with it, the tacit or overt acceptance of the two-stroke development of the European Union.

On the one hand we find the antifederalist British who, insisting

---

[55] We can count among the bitter historical memories the several similar French peacemaking interventions in Central Europe in 1919–1921, including peacemaking in Hungary in 1919. For the countries of the Little Entente, the French presence was of course a guarantee of their independence and autonomy and of possible intervention against Soviet Russia. By this historical parallel, I only wanted to hint at the fact that the security systems established by great powers are durable only if the temporary peacemakings are followed by institutional integration. Yet, much as France was not strong and interested enough to maintain the security system, NATO, in its present-day form, is institutionally unfit to integrate the small states.

[56] See, "Why 1996 matters the year the questions start being answered," *Economist*, January 27, 1996, pp. 19–21.

mostly on intergovernmental connections, reject the "hard core" plan, and are essentially for the establishment of a free trade zone. Hungary could also find a place in that looser non-centralized Europe, and Great Britain supports the admission of Hungary. On the other side, one can find the Germans and the Benelux states. The German policy prefers European competitiveness and mercilessly dictates the implementation of the Maastricht criteria on all countries. Germany proposes a federative model and a system of decision-making that is based on the majority principle and, since she knows that most of the Union members are unable to follow the "German pace," she supports the "core Europe" concept ventilated in the Schäuble-Lamers study. Germany is also for the admission of Hungary, fully aware that Hungary could not join the inner circle.

The French events in the second half of 1995 drove the political forces of France from the middle of the road between the British and the German points towards British skepticism. France persisted in the policy of the "hard franc" and tried to implement institutional reforms but had to face a huge opposition. It has become uncertain whether she will be able and willing to bear the burdens of the European Monetary Union (EMU). By 1995 it became clear that the French-German axis functioning between 1949 and 1991 had weakened, consequently the political basis of the European Union had also become unstable.[57]

Jacques Delors, who may be the one most interested in the preservation of the Robert Schuman-Jean Monnet legacy, recently published an appeal. He proposes a French "pact of confidence" in addition to the "pact of stability" of Theo Waigel, the German minister of finances. The "pact of confidence" (*pacte de confiance*) means that

---

[57] The "Europeanization" of the western part of Germany by France and the preservation of the French economic balance by an economically stronger Germany made up the axis of European politics. Skeptics say those days are gone because of the East European transformations and German unification. According to Tony Judt, the same thing happened to the Austrian-Prussian alliance on which the balance of the continental Europe was built; it collapsed due to the transformations in 1848–1849. See, Judt, op. cit., p. 27.

the signatories take upon themselves that they will really harmonize their macroeconomic policies. That is to say, that pact would provide the European Union with financial means,...so that it could realize common projects in the field of infrastructure and it could develop its key sectors. The signatories should also take upon themselves to openly regard employment as a priority as important as financial equilibrium. I would like to remind everybody that as early as the birth of the Maastricht agreement I proposed that the problem of employment should be among the criteria. The national delegations did not accept it.[58]

Competitiveness or democracy that is the European dilemma according to Dahrendorf. "The monetary system is a big mistake, an adventurous, venturesome and mistaken goal, it does not unite but rather divides Europe. The plan of the monetary system imposes the German code of behavior on other countries, who don't want to behave the German way, Ralf Dahrendorf says. He thinks that the monetary union will not be realized but the possibility of its establishment is going to threaten continuously all that has been achieved through the unification of Europe. The greatest danger ahead for Europe is that more and more people are apt to sacrifice a part of their freedom in exchange for economic improvement and for a safer public life, thus,

---

[58] "Europe: L'appel de Jacques Delors," *Le Nouvel Observateur,* February, 1–7, 1996, p. 28. When asked what would happen if Germans disagreed, Delors answered as follows: "Perhaps I am not conceited saying I am very popular in Germany. First of all, because there no one doubts that I am a European. Second, because I supported German unification from the very beginning. That very friendship urges me to speak openly, nay, with brutal openness. That is why I am saying to my German friends aloud: 'If you want to make experiments alone and if you refuse to cooperate with your partners in European macroeconomic policy, that means that you do not respect the spirit of this not only financial but also economic union.'" Incidentally, Delors thinks that the "pact of confidence" presupposes a conference in France, in the framework of which the economic and social partners should talk with one another, at last. They should talk on not only the wages but also on the invest-ments as well as the active employment policy and the research goals.

they would even accept the path of Malaysia or Singapore. According to Dahrendorf, the real challenge is "the intelligent reform of the social state."[59]

The closer we are to the Intergovernmental Conference, the more views collide. Anyway, the growth in the number of Euroskeptic countries does not improve the possibilities of a large-scale and mature reform.[60]

As far as enlargement towards East Europe is concerned, both clear-cut stands are for this policy. The British and the German views contain entirely different things, however. If she is asked at all, Hungary has to avoid very cautiously any kind of binding position, any position that may cause difficulties for her. Its range of movement is narrow. The debate is going on above it but not about it.

Because of the European Union's inertia, things are probably going to move along the same course, and Hungary will rather be able to join in via her micro connections. With the main financial institutions, companies able to export, and public utility services of Hungary having passed into the hands of transnational enterprises and financial institutions due to the partly turnkey, partly privatization investments between 1989 and 1996, we are more closely linked to Europe and to the global economic space than we would be in the case of a Brussels declaration of admission. It does not mean that Hungary should not do her best in order to be admitted by the European Union; we have to see, however, that it is more and more difficult or impossible for the investors to move out of Hungary and they are forced not only to maintain their investments but to develop them.[61]

---

[59] "'Alle Eier in einen Korb' Lord Ralf Dahrendorf über die Gefahren der Währungsunion und die Krise Europas," *Der Spiegel* 50, nos. 11–12 (1995).

[60] A good summary on the preparations of the conference and on the national views is Tamás Szűcs, "1996=1984? Bevezetés az 1996-os Kormányközi Konferencia előkészületeibe," *Európai Szemmel*, nos. 3–4 (1995). An article from the French point of view: Jean-Claude Casanova, "Pour la constitution de l'Europe," *Commentaire* (Summer 1995). Another one from the British point of view: Kristy Hughes, "The 1996 Intergovernmental Conference and European Union Enlargement," *International Affairs*, no. 1 (1996).

[61] In contrast with the Czech situation, where the capital that flowed into the country is contained in bonds and short term securities, in Hungary, the over-

We are going to be bound to Europe neither by the Hungarian government nor by the European Union. The European Union is unable to accept Hungary in the short run. The Hungarian government is only hardly more able to lead Hungary into the Union. The links are being established and shaped by the myriad of ties among the multinational enterprises, services, small enterprises, the regional and municipal cooperations, the private consumers, the civic organizations. In this sense European integration has already arrived. A region of Hungary, perhaps Pannonia, perhaps Budapest-Hungary has already linked herself to Europe. That is within the range of a small state's mobility.

---

whelming part of the capital is invested in manufacturing enterprises and public utility services, from where it is impossible to withdraw quickly and even a slow retreat or divestment is very costly. Thus, the investors are forced to "civilize," or "lift" the territory of investment (either Hungary or some of her regions and cities) because they have started to finance and run their own factories, insurance companies, banks rather than Hungary as a whole.

György Csepeli

NOT KNOWN, ONLY FELT
*Representation of National Sovereignty
in Hungarian Society Today*

The collapse of the post-war status quo in Central and Eastern Europe signalled the spectacular emergence of nationalism. The question is whether this nationalism was a specter from the past, the era preceding World War II, or something new?

Before answering this question, I would like to explain what I mean by nationalism. Nationalism is a collective buttress for the modern individual, with both cultural and political impact. Cultural and political nationalism are routinely differentiated (and frequently contrasted) in the pertinent literature.

The boundaries of the nation envisioned by cultural nationalism are spiritual, and the themes, values and relationships involved by national reality construed within these boundaries gain expression in public discourse woven of personally meaningful and emotionally powerful narratives. Tacit agreements govern the rules of such discourses, the norms of participation, and the role of speakers.

The boundaries of the nation envisioned by political nationalism are described and defined in relation to geographical coordinates, and the subjects, values and relationships of the national reality construed within these boundaries appear in the form of legal and political narratives, which concern publicly determined and sanctioned references, the sovereign national state first and foremost among them.

In my view, the question has to do with a historical time-lag which, at least in the development of European nations, means the appearance of cultural nationalism followed by political nationalism. However, any differentiation between the two phases can only be relative. Neither phase is devoid of some elements of the other, and the terms we use refer only to the preponderance of these elements. Cultural nationalism is also political nationalism insofar as it implies, willy-nilly, the project of the national state, while political nationalism is cultural nationalism insofar as it cannot dispense with the enormous socio-psychological force of culturally construed meanings in the naturalization and legitimation of the status quo. Characteristically, already in 1580, the Elizabethan poet Edmund Spenser aimed to give the political form of monarchy a content peculiar to the English language.[1]

In my opinion, the emergence of nationalism in Central and Eastern Europe after 1989 cannot be unequivocally interpreted as a manifestation of the specter of cultural nationalism, but must be considered as the resurgence of political nationalism instead. It is a paradoxical product insofar as this region was organized under the auspices of socialist internationalism by the will of the victorious Soviet Union, while its former allies looked the other way. The authors of socialist doctrines could never really come to terms with the persistence of nationalism in society, hence they strove to create ideological defense mechanisms by means of which they could eliminate any evidence which contradicted their tenets.[2]

The adherents of the founding fathers, who succeeded in realizing some of the dreams of their forerunners in Russia, were intent on working out efficient techniques of exerting direct and indirect influence in the spirit of internationalism. But they based these techniques on administrative organizational units which subsequently became the foundations for nation formation in the political sense. The process of nation formation got under way even within the Soviet Union, but gained an especially powerful momentum in the subjugated societies of Central and Eastern Europe, where cultural nationalism permeated the memory of each.

In the beginning, the fight against nationalism in the European socialist countries seemed successful. The main reason being the oppressive power of the socialist state over its subjects, who were virtually incapable of resisting the all-inclusive economic, political, and ideological centralization. But it would be misleading to think that

---

[1] Richard Helgerson, *Forms of Nationhood: the Elizabethan Writing of England* (Chicago, 1992).

[2] Roman Szporluk, *Communism and Nationalism* (Oxford, 1988).

repression by itself is enough to crush bourgeois society, distort the ideals of enlightenment, and destroy human dignity. The idea of state socialism invaded backward and underdeveloped societies, it was attractive to the new intellectual elite, as an ideology of modernization; in fact, as a modernizing force, it actually liquidated feudal remnants and created modern needs. As long as the program was credible, nationalism was, perforce, in a state of inertia.

Furthermore, the fight against nationalism succeeded because nationalism in Central and Eastern Europe could never assume a broadly comprehensive political form, whereby certain groups in the region would be able to define their boundaries not only with the help of historical and cultural narratives but also create internationally recognized states for themselves, allowing them control over economic resources within a clearly specified geographical range; finally, allowing them legitimacy via democratic institutional systems and roles established in conformity with the political values of the Enlightenment. The historian Joseph Rothschild saw it as a positive development that the various treaties signed at Versailles after World War I led to the creation of nation-states forming a zone between Germany and the Soviet Union. However, he could hardly refute the argument that these nation-states were too short-lived to acquire solid experience in nation-building and, hence, they fell one after the other when the Red Army overran the region in 1944–1945.[3] As a matter of fact, the ephemeral autonomy of these small East and Central European states, which emerged from the ruins of the Habsburg, Romanov, and Ottoman empires, proved that they were too weak to resist the temptation of conceiving the nation as a variant of *Gemeinschaft*, which is defenseless against the racist interpretation of the concept, instead of conceiving it as a political community of citizens determined by the *Gesellschaft* model. The Central and East European nation-states had no chance whatsoever to ward off the military consequences of Soviet occupation; neither did they have much of a chance to ward off its political consequences, because the Yalta

---

[3] Joseph Rothschild, *Return to Diversity. A Political History of East Central Europe since World War II* (Oxford, 1989).

Conference virtually precluded it. On the other hand, Soviet occupation received strong support from the antifascist ideological discourse on liberation, the moral conclusions of which compromised the earlier nationalist discourse. Cultural nationalism suffered a historical defeat because it could not prove that it is irreconcilable with fascism.

Considering all this, it is truly surprising that nationalism revived once the Soviet sphere of influence ceased to exist. All the same, the question remains: Should we consider this as a resurgent manifestation, as a specter from the pre-socialist past, or are there other interpretations capable of also taking into account the unintentional consequences of the "building of socialism?" I definitely wish to argue for the latter, notwithstanding the fact that we are witnesses to national animosity throughout the region, as well as to frenzied efforts to realize the obsessive idea of ethnic purity. It is also easy to show that the founders and manipulators of some of the political parties and programs hardly differ from their predecessors who entered the scene sixty years ago and ended on the gallows as war criminals. My proposition is that we are witness to the advance of political nationalism aimed at the creation of constitutional statehood, at the development of *Gesellschaft* type political nations based on civil society, the market economy, and civic status. The disputes tormenting the post-socialist nation-states are rooted in the ideological and psychological dilemmas of political nationalism; they have nothing to do with tribalism[4] with the obsession with ethnic purity, and are only indirectly related to the model of cultural nationalism.

State socialism had a paradoxical effect on nationalism. While successfully crushing cultural nationalism, its impact on political nationalism was quite the opposite. Generally, analysis of the relationship between state socialism and nationalism does not reveal this duality. The political elite of some countries was more tolerant of cultural nationalism, while elsewhere the elite did not abandon internationalism. Romania is an example of the first category, East Germany of the second. A scale, from official denunciation to open support, may be used to measure the attitudes towards nationalism than can be

---

4 D. Horowitz, *Ethnic Groups in Conflict* (Los Angeles, 1985).

observed among the political elite of former socialist countries. Nationalism never represented a force of any considerable influence on the fate of the "peace camp," and it was more a result than a cause in the chain of internal and external events which led to the disintegration of the camp.[5] But, then, why did nationalism emerge so openly following the collapse of state socialism?

The end of the Cold War also brought the visible order of the world to its end. Everything in the "peace camp" became questioned except the boundary lines between the individual "barracks," which turned out to be state borders. Previously, these borders partitioned the units constituting the Soviet sphere of influence. It was Stalin who said that these units were national in form, but socialist in content. In spite of the internationalist homogenization of the countries within the Soviet sphere of influence, the realization of this principle had serious consequences, particularly momentous in Central and East European countries where the "national form" demanded greater attention than in the heart of the empire. The accusation that the Yalta Conference had Sovietized Central and Eastern Europe is a commonplace, but it is a fact that it was this Conference which enabled the small Central and East European states to achieve all of the requisites of their nationhood in the political sense. There was never any doubt that the Baltic countries could not achieve this status; the Western powers however, never recognized their annexation to the Soviet Union, and so their "national form" persisted therein.

The Central and East European countries had forty years to gain an experience of what it is to possess the requisites of nationhood in the political sense. Poets, teachers, linguists, or ethnographers may create a nation in the cultural sense, but it is not their job to operate the government, army, police, customs guard, border guard, postal service, justice, railways, etc. A nation that wants to be more than an act of will and imagination must have its own currency, a capital, public buildings, embassies abroad. Any group may be defined as a nation in the cultural sense if it has a national stock of songs, folk cus-

---

[5] Jadwiga Staniszkis, *The Dynamics of Breakthrough in Eastern Europe* (Los Angeles, 1991).

toms, faith in the existence of its own national character as well as literary and historical narratives which help keep the nation "awake." It would be an exaggeration to say that it was the men of letters who kept national consciousness awake in each of the "socialist community of nations," or that certain political requisites were completely forgotten. In fact, the single way of filling the vacuum that state-socialistic ideology had created by leveling and inverting positive social identity, was by national identification, which was tolerated under the label of "socialist patriotism" and which was very much alive in some countries.

Nevertheless, the unhappy coexistence under Soviet repression had one novel result, perhaps the most important novelty of that age. For the first time in their history, these countries learned the meaning of permanent state boundaries, which are guaranteed by the international community and are, at the same time, sacred and inviolable in the psychological sense.

While the founding fathers of socialism predicted the withering away of the state, their pragmatic followers recognized that the building of socialism must be started and escalated only in states where conditions are ripe. Accordingly, they emphasized the importance of state boundaries, especially that of the "peace camp" as whole. Experience and paranoia both explain why the leaders of socialist states paid so much attention to this boundary line. The Berlin Wall is a particularly dramatic example. The borders between the "fraternal" socialist countries were also highly revered, and even Big Brother became obsessed with the idea of the impassability of its own borders, which official documents called "sacred"—an unusual word in an atheistic system.

The leaders of the Soviet bloc attributed such great importance to the question of borders that after lengthy negotiations with the West they signed the Helsinki Accords in 1975. The Accords restated the obligation of the international community to defend the unalterability of existing borders (except in cases where borders are changed peacefully and by common consent). From the point of view of the West, appeasement of the Russians was a symbolic act only, since Western countries had more important things to worry about than to toy with the idea of changing borders. Soviet politicians failed to notice the decline of Western interest in the border question. In return for the recognition of the status quo, the "peace camp" recognized human rights. Soviet-bloc countries thought that they had made a good deal when, in fact, they only got what they already had. On the other hand, recognition of human rights made the insecure structure of socialist law and order ideologically defenseless and indefensible. The Helsinki Accords had a large share in helping liberal democratic ideals and values de-legitimize state socialism forever.

The Russians were trapped by their own border fetishism.[6] They failed to see that the borders between West European states had gradually lost their significance. The resources of a national vision focusing on territory ran out. European economic, cultural, and political integrational institutions were established, which transcended the competencies based on the sovereignty of the nation-state.

Border fetishism outlived the disintegration of the "peace camp." After the "socialist content" disappeared, the "national form" became the determining feature of countries passing from state socialism toward pluralistic democracy and market economy. We might even say that these countries, like the West European nation-states of a hundred years ago, assumed a state-nationalistic character. The long desired national sovereignty of Central and East European nation-states, when finally achieved, already reeked of "second-hand freshness" at birth (to use Mikhail Bulgakov's expression, originally applied to fish). This sovereignty was the product of Soviet imperial administration. That is to say, the local bureaucratic and cultural elites that came into being and the appropriate institutions that were established in some of the imperial provinces during the decades of state socialism, saw a justification for their existence in the discovery of national sovereignty. By the end of the twentieth century, Central and Eastern Europe caught up with nineteenth century Western Europe.

Nation-state fetishism, by locating the state within strictly defined geographical boundaries, uses the human body as a metaphor to describe the nation. Fetishism in the psychopathological sense is

---

[6] R. Oschlies, "A nacionalizmus veszélyei Kelet-Európában," *Európai Szemle* 3, no. 2 (1992) pp. 77–88.

rooted in castration complex. Nation-state fetishism as a pathological kind of political nationalism is manifest in the fear of loss of territory. For instance, in the age of the Third Republic in France, the extremely popular children's book, *Le tour de France par deux enfants*, kept alive the pain over the loss of Alsace-Lorraine in generations of children.[7] In Hungary, Zsigmond Sebők's *Mackó úr utazásai* [Travels of Mr. Teddy Bear] did the same. In the story, Mr. Teddy Bear, travels across Central Europe, from the Carpathians to the Adriatic Sea, in the company of two bear cubs, Zebulon and Dorka. The political and travel narrative represents the Carpathian Basin as the body of the Hungarian state, its unity given once and for all. The book remained popular Hungarians growing up after the severely damaging Trianon peace treaty of 1920 and, in all likelihood, played a considerable part in the acceptance of the image of Hungary as a bleeding, mutilated country, nourished by the irrational complex of nation-state fetishism.

From the first moment of their establishment after World War I, the Central and East European small states were doomed to misery by their endless border disputes. Lithuania and Poland both announced a claim to Vilnius. Poland and Czechoslovakia both claimed the right of control over Teschen. Hungary wanted to regain from its neighbors the territories (or a part of them) it held earlier in Austria-Hungary. Bulgaria had territorial claims against Greece, Yugoslavia, and Romania. Romania feared that it would lose Transylvania, and subsequently had to accept the loss of Bessarabia. Yugoslavia, Austria, and Italy had mutual territorial claims. So many countries wanted a part of Albania that its very existence as a state was in jeopardy. Poland, Austria, Czechoslovakia, and Yugoslavia had only a brief existence before and during World War II.[8]

As mentioned above, Soviet influence in the region meant that the issue of border disputes became a fetishistic taboo, which some of the countries seem unable to shake off even in the present post-Soviet

---

[7] Emily Apter and William Pietz, *Fetishism as Cultural Discourse* (Ithaca, 1993.)

[8] Rothschild, op. cit., p. 89.

era. The non-aligned Socialist Federal Republic of Yugoslavia, situated just outside the boundary of the Cold War zone, was the sole exception. Its outside borders may have become a fetish, but not one of the leading participants in the Cold War aligned itself with the unalterability of the borders of the federation's member republics. When the Cold War ended, these borders instantly became fluid and the cause of bloody conflicts. Perhaps right at this moment they are being declared sacred and inviolable as a result of considerable international military and political pressure to this effect. Nation-state fetishism, the unintended product of the long reign of state socialism in Central and East European countries, may create fertile foundations for liberal democratic institutions and for a thriving, market economy based political nationalism.

Modernization has become the governing principle beyond the eastern borders of what was the Holy Roman Empire, and provides the standards for organizing Central and East European societies. There is no return, it seems, to the aggressive cultural nationalism of the past, and for several reasons. First, due to the fetish of state borders, no one dares assume the responsibility for a post-Yalta rearrangement. Second, market economy and pragmatic rationalism legitimized by the institutions of political democracy increasingly delegitimize such alternative zero-sum outcomes desirable for political manipulators of different nations in their international games. Third, in spite of the reluctance and wrangling of West European countries, the integration process has begun, opening the way to the European Union for the new nation-states, which already have defined themselves mainly in terms of political nationalism. Fourth, the global network as determined by new information technologies renders the earlier territorial distinctions between central and peripheral invalid.

Essentially, the problem is this: How soon will the Central and East European countries realize that immediately upon the successful creation of their national identity in accordance with the idiom of political nationalism, their task is to undo it as soon and as completely as possible?

It is a paradoxical situation that while in Central and Eastern Europe we are witnessing the evolution of the nation-state, in Western Europe the nation-state and its institutions have arrived at the reverse phase of devolution,[9] whereby organizations below and above the state level are strengthened. But we can see in the West, too, that the nation-state holding onto its memory of sovereignty does not accept automatically the consequences of defetishizing, which is part of the devolution process.

After World War II the problem of Alsace-Lorraine was solved as European integration improved, but it would be a serious mistake to assume that nation-state fetishism in Western European disappeared altogether. It is enough to refer to Great Britain's war in the Falklands, the conflict in Northern Ireland, the Basque question, or the conflict between France and Corsica, alleged to be of recent origins. All these however, do not alter the fact that the post-modern international scene indicates that the territory-oriented, fetishized nation image is disappearing.[10] The state nationalist narrative, assigning the metaphor of the biological self-evidence of the human body to nation-state borders, has become discredited.

A further paradox can be perceived in the fact that the post-modern intergroup discourse, which relegates nation-state sovereignty to the class of repressive myths, rediscovers the topos of cultural nationalism so familiar to Central and East European intellectuals who were socialized on the rhetoric of the "awakening nation." It may be the subject of another study to determine how essential is the similarity between the elements of post-colonial discourse, which argues for the rights of alternative cultural-historical narratives representing otherness, and the Central and East European "popular-national" idiom archetypically related to the Slavophile model. (To my knowledge, it was István Király who noted this analogy in the eighties.) In my view, if we consider the goal, differences are more important. Cultural nationalist policy conceives national identity in terms of a merciless "pedagogical narrative" that justifies the existence of the sovereign nation-state. According to Bhabha, post-modern national discourse prefers a narrative strategy stressing repetition, to the continuative and accumulative temporality of the pedagogical narrative. This nar-

---

⁹ G. Molnár, "Az új leviatán jogara alatt," *Magyar Hírlap*, October 13, 1995.

¹⁰ Michael J. Shapiro, "Moral Geographies and the Ethics of Post-Sovereignty," *Public Culture,* no. 6 (1994), pp. 479–502.

rative circulation makes the need for national cultural superiority, which is separable from the political program of cultural nationalism, an untenable proposition. Once the fear caused by cultural dissimilarity moves outside the sphere of the nation, the problem of "another people" will diminish. The possibility of realizing otherness by every individual constituting the nation will become the issue.[11]

The real challenge for European nations which have gone through the devolution phase will not come from Central and Eastern Europe. The envoys of marginality will come from all directions and they will claim the right of the representation of their own dissimilarity without it being the grounds for questioning their national identity.

In exploring the way today's Hungarian society perceives national identification, nation, and national sovereignty, we must begin with the problem which is connected to those mentioned above, namely, that the key terms of the vocabulary of national ideology (e.g., national self-determination, independence, sovereignty, state borders) derive their legitimate meaning from ideology and politics instead of logic, leading to a semantic diffusion we must deal with. As Boldizsár Nagy points out in his study in the present volume, "the word "sovereignty" does not have a meaning of its own, it cannot itself reveal what it signifies." This is only enhanced by what he states further, namely, that the speakers and the listeners are unable even to substitute conceptual apprehension with the understanding of a long linguistic description, given sufficient time and the availability of source materials. Nagy conducted a playful "test" with the participation of twelve social scientists (among them some contributors of the present volume) and sixteen fourth-year students of Budapest University's Faculty of Law. The analysis of their responses showed that they reached a nearly complete consensus (26:1) only on the statement that the Warsaw Pact, in force between 1955–1991, restricted Hungary's sovereignty. Yet, the text of the Warsaw Pact (or the much earlier Anti-Comintern Pact) cannot be accused of containing restrictions on

---

[11] Homi K. Bhabha, "Dissemination: Time, Narrative, and the Margins of the Modern Nation," in *Nation and Narration*, ed. Bhabha (London, 1990), pp. 291–322.

national sovereignty. It seems the experts do not know, but only feel that Hungary's sovereignty suffered mutilation on March 19, 1944, or on November 4, 1956.

In 1983, forty-eight percent of a sample of six hundred intellectuals agreed with the statement that national independence is "the freedom of action of the government within the limits defined by international power relations." In addition to the adherents of this pragmatic definition, two important groups of dissenters voiced their opinion. According to one, there is more to national independence; it means that the government has considerable freedom of action in international affairs. According to the other, which sticks to a more narrow application, national independence means "harmonozing national interests and the requirements of loyalty to allies."[12] As we can see, there is complete confusion in denotation not only among experts but also among intellectuals in general.

In the light of this incongruity among experts and university graduates (who can be considered the most competent on this issue), we are justified in assuming that the emotional connotations of the concept of sovereignty are even more characteristic if we examine, through a representative sample of the Hungarian adult population, what meanings the words—sovereignty, autonomy, independence, or supreme authority, state supremacy—carry for them when linked to the attribute national.

The situation is more favorable in the case of the attribute national, since its meaning concerns one of the categories that constitute social identification with a positive emotional force (gender, generation, religion, political orientation, social status, nation, etc.). Thus, the positive emotional connotation of the category Hungarian is extended to the category of national.

Empirical sociological data show that the word "Hungarian" has an elementally positive connotation in society, as it always had ever since empirical investigation was introduced in Hungary in the late sixties. (The situation is the same in other countries organized on a nation-state pattern.) The change of regime did not alter this fact.

---

[12] György Csepeli, *National Identity in Contemporary Hungary* (New York, 1997), p. 166.

Table 1 shows the data of a poll carried out in the fall of 1995 by TÁRKI (Social Science Research Institute) as part of the International Social Science Survey Project. The table contains only data pertaining to Hungary, since data on other countries participating in the survey have not yet been made available to us. The survey presented a few statements suitable for the measurement of positive emotional identification with Hungary and the Hungarians. The respondents were asked to indicate whether they agreed with each of the statements, or disagreed with them because of their own different views.

Table 1

Positive Connotation of the Word Hungarian

Statements	Agree (%)
I prefer being a Hungarian citizen over being citizen of any other country	87
There are certain things in today's Hungary which make me ashamed of my country	31
People must support their country right or wrong	58

Source: *TÁRKI*

The limits of the positive connotation of the attribute Hungarian are indicated in that only 24% of the respondents expressed the belief that "in general, Hungary is a better country than most other countries," and only 21 % agreed with the statement that "the world would be a better place if people in other countries were like Hungarians." Ethnocentric exaggeration is alien to the thinking of the majority of Hungarians today.

The TÁRKI data indicate that national identification in present Hungarian society is manifest not only on an emotional level, but is also expressed as a strong attachment on the behavioral level. Eighty-five percent of the respondents would not even consider emigration, and an even higher percentage (91%) expressed their attachment to Europe.

Although we could not expect an accurate definition of the concept of national sovereignty, the positive emotional power of Hungarian national identification is projected onto words that belong to the sphere of the concept of sovereignty, such as state, constitution, freedom. Therefore, we may question the effectiveness of a rhetoric founded on the concept of sovereignty.

In a survey at the end of 1995 (by Szonda-Ipsos) the respondents were each given a card with a list of various words, nine in all, preceded by the attribute Hungarian. We asked the respondents to select those expressions they find intelligible, with contents they can interpret in some way. Table 2 shows the results.

Table 2

Readiness to Interpret Words in a National Context

Expressions	Readiness of Interpretation (%)
Hungarian language	95
Hungarian state	94
Hungarian constitution	88
Hungarian freedom	67
Hungarian taste	64
Hungarian humor	60
Hungarian justice	51
Hungarian blood	47
Hungarian malediction	33

Source: *Szonda-Ipsos*

Table 2 shows that in terms of readiness of interpretation, only *Hungarian language* is more accepted than expressions pertaining to the political rhetoric of independence. This finding indicates that, in Hungarian society today, national identity is widely based not only on political but on cultural notions as well.

In the above-mentioned 1983 survey we asked the respondents to mark on a scale from one to five, the seven standard periods of Hungarian history with regard to independence. The overwhelming majority gave the lowest mark to the period of Turkish occupation in the sixteenth-seventeenth centuries (1.49). The age of King Matthias Corvinus in the fifteenth century was rated the highest for independence (4.83), with the Anjou period in the fourteenth century the next highest (4.26). The low score for Turkish occupation was followed by a gradual rise in average independence marks: the age of Maria Theresa in the eighteenth century with 2.54; the Age of Reform in the first half of the nineteenth century with 3.15; the era of the Austro-Hungarian Monarchy in the second half of the nineteenth and the early twentieth century with 3.23; the period between the two world wars with 3.31. At the time of the survey, any question concerning Hungary's contemporary independence would have been regarded as political provocation.[13]

The Szonda-Ipsos survey in December, 1995, focussing on the emotional basis of identification with Hungary and Europe, showed the preponderance of positive emotional elements. In both cases, those whose identification contained negative emotional elements constituted the minority. In neither case did positive identification assume extreme dimensions. Identification with Hungary was somewhat more positive than with Europe. According to the relative majority of the respondents (39%), Europeans have "only little" cause to feel proud, and "much" according to 29%. In the case of Hungary, the picture is balanced; respondents considered stronger and weaker identification justified in equal proportions (34:34). Denial of shame is quite characteristic—half of the respondents rule out the sense of shame with respect to both Hungarian and European identification. In addition, responses indicating a feeling of shame also tend to show restraint—respondents who acknowledge it say they have only moderate reason to feel shame whether they think of themselves as Hungarians or as Europeans.

Respondents in the TÁRKI survey rated various factors along a four-point scale, depending on the role each factor was assumed to play in the development of the sense of pride by reason of nationality.

---

[13] Ibid., p. 243.

Table 3

Sources of National Pride

Sources	Ratio of those who feel proud (%)
Sports achievements	81
Literature and arts	77
Science and technology	68
History	65
Military	22
Democracy	19
International political influence	14
Economic success	8
Social security	1

Source: *TÁRKI*

Hungarian public opinion shows considerable unity in the explanations given for the sense of national pride. The overwhelming majority assigns positive significance to cultural spheres. The primacy of such "romantic" subjects as history, arts, science, and sports indicates a continuity in the culturally determined nature of the development of Hungary as a nation, at least as regards underlying emotions. In comparison, the low frequency of reference to foreign policy, the economy, the military, democratic institutions, or social security indicates that the "prosaic" subjects constituting the ideological discourse of the modern nation-state play no part in the argumentation on national pride. It is a sign of the changing times that in the seventies people justified their national pride mainly in terms of economic achievements, mentioning culture and history only in the second place.[14]

Several data point to the dual nature of the ideological demarcation of national identity. The Szonda-Ipsos survey in the fall of 1995, using a five-point scale, revealed that the respondents rated mother-tongue as the most important factor in defining people as Hungarian. Table 4 shows the results in detail.

---

[14] Guy Lázár, *A magyar lakosság politikai-történelmi tudata a közvélemény-kutatások tükrében* (Budapest, 1983), p. 83.

Table 4

*Classification of the Criteria of Identification
as a Hungarian*

Statements	Mark (1–5)
He/she whose mother-tongue is Hungarian	4.0
He/she who proclaims him/herself Hungarian	3.9
He/she whose parents are Hungarian	3.7
He/she who is a Hungarian citizen	3.5
He/she who was born in Hungary	3.0

Source: *Szonda-Ipsos*

Another survey, carried out almost simultaneously, revealed similar findings. In this case, the respondents were asked to evaluate each criterion on the basis of its importance in making someone a "true" Hungarian. While the above survey presented the question of Hungarian national allegiance merely as a problem of classification, the following survey investigated the normative criteria of national identity and thereby made the ideological dimension inherent in the question explicit.

Table 5

The Criteria for Being a "True" Hungarian

Criteria	Judged important (%)
Considers him/herself Hungarian	98
Speaks Hungarian	96
Lives in Hungary most of his/her life	74
Is a Hungarian citizen	73
Was born in Hungary	66
Accepts the political-legal system	60
Is a Christian	36

Source: *TÁRKI*

Multivariable analyses support the expectation that basically two identification types of being Hungarian may be distinguished in Hungarian society today. One is based on citizenship rooted in the political concept of the nation, the other on mother-tongue originating from the cultural concept of the nation. The sociological conflict between the two frames of reference is minimalized by the fact that, whichever type the respondent belongs to, self-classification is the decisive factor.

The tendency of duality within the unit of self-classification has been present in Hungarian society since the seventies.[15] Mária Vásárhelyi's research in 1994 has shown that the change in the political system has not brought any change in this respect.[16] According to the majority of the respondents (59%), self-classification is more important in national identification than mother-tongue or citizenship. Only 17% said that birth should be considered important in identifying someone as Hungarian.

Submitting the results of the TÁRKI survey to cluster analysis, four groups were distinguished on the basis of their choice of criteria considered important in identifying someone as Hungarian.[17] The largest group (32%) consisted of respondents who were unable to choose from the criteria and judged all of them important. We called this the conformist group.

The second group (22%) consisted of those who did not consider Christianity and the political-legal system important criteria of identification, but approved the rest. Since members of this group deemed the psychological and citizenship criteria important, we labeled them liberal-national. Members of the third group (11%), labeled conventional, valued mother-tongue, Christianity, and self-classification highly. It may seem paradoxical that while both conformists and liberal-nationalists ascribed great importance to citizen-

---

[15] György Csepeli, *Nemzeti tudat és érzésvilág Magyarországon a 70-es években* (Budapest, 1985).

[16] Mária Vásárhelyi, "A nemzet és a területi kérdés a közgondolkodásban," *Jel-Kép*, no. 1 (1994).

[17] György Csepeli. and Antal Örkény, "Changing facets of Hungarian nationalism," *Social Research* (Summer, 1996).

ship, it was not emphasized as an important criterion of national identification by the liberals (35%) compared to the importance they
ascribed to mother tongue, self-classification, and democracy.

Resolution of this paradox is to be sought in the peculiar change
in the meaning of citizenship, the beginnings of which date back to
state socialism. In summarizing the research on national consciousness in the seventies, Guy Lázár wrote that

> in 1973, 73% of a nationwide representative sample said that
> they regard persons living in Hungary as part of the Hungari-
> an nation, while 24% said the same about Hungarians living
> in neighboring countries. This shows that, from the point of
> view of national allegiance, state borders are considered
> more important than language.[18]

The disintegration of the alliance structure of Central and East
European countries which had been imposed by force by the Soviet
Union led to the opening of the borders, and an acceleration of migration away from the privations of the East toward the Western welfare
societies. Its geographical location put Hungary in the "front line" of
migration, so previously unheard-types of immigrants were received:
war refugees, including Hungarian-speaking foreigners who claimed
to be part of the Hungarian nation.

Hungarian xenophobia, which had been ethnocentrically-based,
acquired a political coloration in the post-socialist period. While ethnocentric xenophobia draws the "outgroup margins" along the lines
of a common-origins consciousness and common cultural heritage
derived from the criteria defining ethnic group,[19] for political xenophobia, "outgroup margins" lie along the lines of the political community of citizens; it derives the passionate rejection of aliens not so
much from anxiety over democratic political rights, as from social
welfare rights belonging to citizenship and forming the constituent
elements of identity.

In this approach, citizenship is the vehicle for social welfare and

---

¹⁸ Lázár, op. cit., p. 52
¹⁹ Fredrik Barth, ed., *Ethnic Groups and Boundaries* (Boston, 1969).

economic rights guaranteed by the state, therefore, regardless of whether they fit other national criteria or not, non-citizen immigrants appear as undesirable competitors on the welfare and economic markets. Jürgen Habermas calls this variant of xenophobia "welfare chauvinism," which is taking on epidemic proportions in the European Union. Hungary is well on the way to catching up with the advanced part of Europe in the area of political xenophobia, if nothing else.

Hungarian public opinion is fairly united in its opposition to immigration on the whole (but divided on the issue of the immigration of non-citizen Hungarian nationals). The following table demonstrates this.

Table 6

Attitudes Toward Immigrants

Statements	Agree (%)
Hungary should take stronger measures against illegal aliens	91
Aliens are responsible for the increase in crime	74
Aliens take jobs away from native Hungarians	63
Acquisition of Hungarian citizenship should be made easier for ethnic Hungarian immigrants	53
Immigrants make Hungary more receptive to new ideas and cultures	20
Immigrants have a beneficial effect on Hungarian economy	8

Source: *TÁRKI*

Public opinion is more permissive on the question of admitting political refugees. Thirty-three percent are definitely for admission, while 23% would exclude even these refugees. The relative majority is undecided.

The importance assigned to the territorial integrity of the state constitutes an important aspect of state sovereignty. In the ideological discourse determining the political nation-state, the metaphor of "body" is often applied to denote "country," which explains the use of surgical terms (such as mutilation, amputation) in the terminology expressing concern for integrity. The concern for the "political body" is manifest in the fetishizing of state borders.[20] The formation of the Hungarian border fetish was encumbered by the fact that the consequences of the Trianon peace treaty were represented as a mutilation, creating the grounds for the political and psychological impact of the term "Truncated Hungary." This impact is a thing of the past, yet Hungarian public opinion is not united on the possibility of peaceful border revisions.

In the fall of 1995, 45% of the respondents agreed with the statement that "state borders in Central and Eastern Europe are unalterable whatever the inhabitants of the areas concerned think," and 9% agreed with the statement that "the borders in Central and Eastern Europe can be changed if the inhabitants of the areas concerned want it."

According to the results of the December 1995 survey, the overwhelming majority of the respondents (80%) considered the territorial partitioning of historical Hungary to have been an unfair decision; 13% deemed it a fair but incorrectly executed decision; and only 3% agreed completely with this 75-year-old event. In 1984, 64% of a sample of intellectuals disapproved of the decision, whereas by 1989 disapproval increased to 84% in a similar sample.[21]

In December 1995, 49% of the respondents believed that Hungary's borders are permanent and unalterable. (The frequency of this attitude increases with educational level and reaches 60% among those with higher education, which corresponds more or less with the result of the survey in the eighties.) One-third of the respondents hope that the borders may change to Hungary's advantage in the future. But almost one-third can imagine that the borders may also be changed to Hungary's disadvantage.

The frequency of concurrence with the opinion that the borders may change to Hungary's advantage decreases to a minimum (5%) if the precondition for change is an armed conflict. [22]

---

[20] Csepeli, György "A nemzeti identitás a posztszocializmus kontextusában," *Európai Szemle*, no. 4 (1995), pp. 15–25.

[21] Csepeli, *National Identity,* p. 194.

[22] *Medián Közvéleménykutatás az SZDSZ számára* [Medián Public Opinion Poll Prepared for the Alliance of Free Democrats], manuscript, 1992.

With regard to the near-disappearance of European borders, the relative majority seems to be a prisoner of border fetishism: according to 46%, the borders will not disappear anywhere in Europe. According to 24%, the western part of Europe will unite, leaving out Central and Eastern Europe. Nearly the same number of respondents (17%) expect Central Europe but not the areas east of Hungary to join united Europe. A similarly large group (15%) believes that the whole of Europe will unite and borders will disappear.[23]

In Mór Jókai's political science fiction, written in 1872 1874, Austria-Hungary is described as existing unchanged in the twentieth century, with the slight difference that Hungary is the leading country of the Monarchy and Budapest the seat of the Hungarianized monarch (called Árpád of Habsburg). Jókai would be satisfied to learn that in the fall of 1995, 89% of the respondents answered in the affirmative to the question: "Do you know anything about Austria-Hungary?" He would be less satisfied with the result that 77 years after the disintegration of the Monarchy only 18%of those who considered themselves knowledgeable, were sorry that the Monarchy disintegrated and history did not follow the path to the utopia Jókai had hoped for.

Nineteen percent of the respondents agreed with the statement that the Monarchy had been a "prison of peoples," while 30% rejected it. The ratio of respondents with a nostalgic opinion did not exceed 20% on other questions, which indicates that present Hungarian self-perception no longer contains the sovereignty-restricting, integrational tradition represented by Austria-Hungary.

As for the question of the new Utopia, 90% have heard that the European Union exists. It is the firm belief of 58% of the respondents that "membership in the European Union would be advantageous to Hungary." Nine percent believe the opposite, and one-third are uncertain.[24]

The survey by Szonda-Ipsos (in April 1996) showed that the majority of the population believes that joining the European Union

---

[23] Szonda-Ipsos, "Csatlakozzunk Európához?" *Magyar Nemzet*, May 6, 1996.

[24] TÁRKI Ominibusz-ISSSP, *A kutatás dokumentációja és alapsorai* (Budapest, 1995).

is "very important" or "important" to Hungary. Sociologically, the degree of importance assigned to membership depended mostly on the respondents, educational level and age. The higher qualified and the younger the respondent, the greater was the importance assigned to the integration process from Hungary's point of view, and the older and less educated they were, the less importance was assigned to it. At the same time, even in the least supportive groups (with at most eight years of schooling; the elderly) the importance of joining is rated higher than moderate (3). Fifty-nine percent of the population set the expected date of joining sometime before the year 2000.[25]

Respondents held NATO membership less important than joining the European Union. The attitude to NATO membership is positive in the case of 38% of the national representative adult sample, and negative in the case of 27% (25% were indifferent and 10% did not answer). While educational level was not a differentiating factor in the attitude to NATO membership, age was all the more so. The young and the elderly consider NATO membership more important than the average, the middle-aged do not. The majority (53%) expects the decision on membership before the millennium.

The majority (54%) support both integrations: the advocates of European Union membership also support NATO membership.

In order for a country to join the European Union or NATO, it must forego a number of requisites deemed important by the rhetoric of political nationalism. At the end of 1995, Szonda-Ipsos polled public opinion as to which requisites of sovereignty Hungarian citizens would insist on the most or would give up willingly. There were nine requisites which the respondents were asked to rank on a preserve-relinquish scale. Table 7 shows the results.

---

[25] Szonda-Ipsos (1996), op. cit.

Table 7

Insistence on Requisites of Sovereignty

Requisites	Mean rank (1–9 from high to low)
Own currency	3.0
Independent military	3.2
Independent ministry of foreign affairs	3.7
National border guard	3.9
Separate customs system	5.1
Hungarian passport	5.3
State railways (MÁV)	5.6
Hungarian standards	6.9
National postage stamp	7.8

Source: *Szonda-Ipsos*

Sizeable groups of the population feel that the state should insist on basically two requisites: its own currency and military. According to 2%, the former, according to 2%, the latter should be kept in any case. These are essential issues as shown by the fact that another one-third of the respondents ranked the two requisites in second or third position. Having an independent ministry of foreign affairs followed in third place. According to 13% of the respondents, the Hungarian state should insist on it unconditionally. Another one-third ranked foreign affairs second or third on the list.

These results demonstrate that Austria-Hungary as a model, in which the military, currency, and foreign relations were common affairs, would not be very popular even today. Few insisted on the remaining six requisites.

Maintenance of an independent military and a sovereign foreign policy were a matter of concern mostly for those with higher education. High school graduates, on the other hand, believe a Hungarian currency to be the chief requisite of sovereignty.

It seems that in public opinion Hungarian sovereignty is represented most meaningfully in the context of property acquisition. It shows the appeal of economic nationality that the majority of the respondents definitely reject the idea of permitting foreigners to purchase land. The overwhelming majority of Hungarians considers the learning of foreign languages necessary, and a part of them would, at the same time, protect Hungarian cultural products against foreign rivals. The aggressive assertion of Hungarian interests on the international scene is not backed by Hungarian society. It is worth noting that where global problems are concerned, not only restrictions on Hungarian sovereignty but also on national sovereignty in general in favor of international organizations undertaking the solution of specific problems (table 8) is seen as conceivable and desirable.

Table 8

Themes of Nationalism

Statements	Agree (%)
Greater attention should be paid to the teaching of foreign languages in schools	87
In the case of a few problems, such as environment pollution, international organizations should be able to enforce solution in individual countries	87
Foreigners should not be allowed to buy land in Hungary	73
Hungarian television should give preference to Hungarian movies and shows	42
Hungary should act in its own interests even this were to lead to conflicts with other nations	37

Source: *TÁRKI*

By now, the typical Hungarian national self-image is one of a "small people." Due partly to the suggestion of "lost grandeur" cultivated by Hungarian historiographic tradition as transmitted in history classes, and partly to the connotation of inferiority conveyed by the word "small," the geometric image of the country is a source of considerable psychological tensions. These are counterbalanced by compensation mechanisms very precisely described by the political philosopher, István Bibó.

Table 9 shows that, among those questioned, the most popular was a self-pitying statement according to which, "As a small people, we suffered and were worn down through the centuries, because of failures caused by forces greater than ourselves"; at the same time, there was strong agreement with the boast that "As a small people we were abandoned, yet did well for ourselves in Europe." The third most accepted statement was: "Throughout the centuries we lagged behind the economically and socially more advanced regions of Europe." A statement showing cultural bias and another complaining about the lack of kins of the Magyars were less popular, though the values were still higher than neutral, showing a tendency to agree. The exaggerated positive statement that "In crucial times we always stood in the forefront of human-social progress," was the least accepted.

Table 9

Small-People Consciousness

Statement	Mean agreement (1–5)
As a small people we suffered and were worn down through the centuries because of failures caused by forces greater than ourselves	4.4
As a small people we were abandoned, yet did well for ourselves in Europe	4.2
Socially more advanced regions of Europe	4.1
Our culture and intellectual achievements place us in the vanguard	3.9
Due to our isolation and lack of kins, the world never had a chance to learn our real merits	3.6
In crucial times we always stood in the forefront of human-social progress	3.4

Source: *Szonda-Ipsos*

Analyzing six patterns of national image schemes together, we found two characteristically distinct cognitive structures. The substance of the difference lies in the recognition or repression of backwardness.[26] These two cognitive types are good indicators of the apologetic and critical types of national identification, a discussion of which would take us in the direction of a cognitive-sociological analysis of national identity.

Such an analysis is not the purpose of the present study. Here we wish to call attention to the consensual effective and cognitive structures uniting Hungarian public opinion, instead of the differences explained by sociological and demographic variables.

Benedict Anderson defines the nation as an "imagined political community."[27] Empirical data make this definition more exact with regard to the Hungarian nation. Our interpretation of the above results confirms that the Hungarian nation may be defined as a political community which conceives itself in terms of cultural criteria. This conclusion suggests that the concept of Hungarian nation lies, somewhere, between the historically evolved "political nation" type seen in Western Europe and the considerably delayed appearance of the "cultural nation" type in Central and Eastern Europe. The power of the concept covers the already dead and the not yet born, giving the concept projecting the nation into eternity its psychological force. However, since the criteria for nationhood are a compound of cultural and political aspects, the origins of the sovereign condition of a nation are also dual insofar as they comprise both the soul, construed

---

[26] Two surveys, carried out at the end of 1995, are most frequently mentioned in the study. Data collection for the first took place in November 1995. The questions were compiled by the *International Social Science Survey Project* group with Antal Örkény, Mariann Sághy, and the author on the Hungarian side. The investigation was supported by OTKA (National Scientific Research Fund) in Hungary and data were collected by TÁRKI. We used the TÁRKI acronym to refer to this survey.

Data collection for the second survey took place in December 1995. Szonda-Ipsos was commissioned by the Millecentennial Memorial Committee to compile the questions. Tibor Závetz and the author participated in this work. We refer to this survey by the name Szonda-Ipsos. Both surveys were based on a representative national sample of one thousand people. Respondents were contacted in their homes with questionnaires.

[27] Benedict Anderson, *Imagined Communities. Reflections on the Origin and Spread of Nationalism* (London, 1983).

by national culture, and the political body. This forms the basis for the development of actual community-consciousness inasmuch as the majority identifies itself with the nation and shares the contents of the simple and communicable mobilizing faith derived from national identification.

Ákos Szilágyi

SOVEREIGNTY À LA RUSSE
The Parade of East European Sovereignties

Sovereignty has many meanings. Sovereignty is a category in international law, history or politics. It serves as an intermediary notion, a complementary term to "power," "authority," "independence," "autonomy." Sovereignty is the political legitimation of absolute power exerted on his or her domain by the medieval "suzerain" escaping from the supremacy of the pope and the emperor. It is the temporal alternative to God's "sovereign authority" in the sense of "independence without restrictions." Sovereignty justifies the state's monopoly on the use of physical force and decision on legislation, economy, politics and self-determination. It is claimed to be inalienable right of a monarch, of a people, of a nation, and of an autonomous individual. One speaks of external and internal sovereignties, sovereignty in the relationship with other states and sovereignty in the relationship with the subjects, or citizens of the state. There is the sovereignty of the undivided supreme power, of the branches of power divided by the contract of federation in federal states, the latter questioning the original absolutist as well as the modern nation-state concepts of sovereignty. Sovereignty is the right and ability to decide "on the exceptions" (*Ausnahmezustand*). Sovereignty can be seen as sovereignty of the law and order identified with the state and traced back logically and legally to the state and nothing but the state. Furthermore sovereignty can be *de facto* and *de jure*, restricted and unrestricted, partial or total, smaller or greater, matter of life and death or a burden to carry, achievement or handicap, "sacrosanct" or an object of trade.

Sovereignty took on various meanings from the pens of its theorists from Jean Bodin all the way to, heaven forbid, Andrei Yanuarevich Vishinsky, through Johannes Althusius, Thomas Hobbes, Hugo Grotius, Jean-Jacques Rousseau, Hans Kelsen, Carl

Schmitt. Thus it stretched from the doctrine of "absolute and permanent authority of a state" to the doctrine of "limited sovereignty." It was sanctified by international agreements from the Treaty of Westphalia to the Holy Alliance, from the Peace Treaty of Versailles of 1919 to the Paris Peace Treaty of 1947, and up to the most recent, post-Cold War Euro-Atlantic deal, the house of cards which was built in Dayton in 1995.[1]

The Cold War of Super-Sovereignties

Nothing demonstrates more sharply the vulnerability of traditional sovereignty than the dramatic melting away of Soviet sovereignty. This was the strongest one in the history of the twentieth century, a sovereignty that almost realized the ideal image of Bodin's concept. In several respects, we could describe the Soviet system as the exaggeration of the features of Western modernity, as a caricature of Western institutions and its categories of thought, in spite of the fact that it referred to itself as a critique and negation of all those. The "total state" and the "total party" themselves are nothing but the enormous caricatures and the execution, in the full sense of the word, of the "totalitarian" tendencies inherent in modern bureaucratic systems. In the same way the Soviet Union carried to the extremes the sovereignty of the modern state, a sovereignty deriving from the existence of a huge political and military power, and in this respect, we may well refer to the USSR as the "world champion of sovereignty." The unlimited independence and nature of the authority of this really sov-

---

[1] Cf. St. I. Benn, "The Uses of Sovereignty," *Political Studies* 3 (1955). In this seminal article the author presents six mutually exclusive meanings of sovereignty. See also W. J. Stankiewicz et al., eds. *In Defense of Sovereignty* (New York, 1969); F. H. Hinsley, *Sovereignty* (New York, 1966); A. P. d'Antreves, *The Notion of the State: An Introduction to Political Theory* (Oxford, 1967); J. A. Camilleri and J. Falk, *The End of Sovereignty? The Politics of a Shrinking and Fragmenting World* (Aldershot, 1992). On the interrelationship of sovereignty, federalism, and autonomy, see S. Lakoff, "Between Either Or and More or Less: Sovereignty versus Autonomy under Federalism," *Publius* 24 (Winter 1994).

ereign giant may be best expressed in a joke: "Question: What does the Soviet Union border upon? Answer: Upon whatever she wants to." In this respect, the Soviet Union's sovereignty was more than that of a huge nation-state: it was an imperial fact, an expansionist fact, a global fact, it embraced almost the whole world. That proved also to be its ruination in the end.

The Great Soviet Encyclopedia defined sovereignty: "the dominant characteristic of state power" which ensures that "by its authority or, in case, by force, it could exert influence in every area of society's life."[2] "That all-embracing, sovereign characteristic" of state power concerning society is what "makes the state independent internationally."[3] In short, sovereignty derives from state power. The more complete, more comprehensive, more irrevocable sovereignty is, the more solid is that power. This definition elevates the absolute monarchies' sovereignty concept to a totalitarian level. V. Tsimbursky, a Russian political scientist, notes that if the international independence of a state really depends on its authority and its power of influence and coercion, then there has never existed in history a state more independent than the Soviet Union.[4] But what was the use of that totalitarian interpretation of sovereignty? Did it have a function, did it make sense? Was there a "method" in that ideological speech of "madness?" We could rephrase the question this way: in what and why does the Soviet interpretation of sovereignty differ from the classical one? It differs in the same things and for the same reason its whole concept of political power generally does.

All political power, every institution and means of political power from the party to the state, from the legislative to the adminis-

---

[2] See the entry "Sovereignty" in *Bolshaya Sovetskaya Entsiklopediya* (Moscow, 1976), vol. 25, p. 26–65.

[3] Ibid.

[4] V. L. Tsimbursky, "Ponyatie suvereniteta i raspad Sovetskovo Soyuza," in *Strana i mir,* no. 1 (Munich, 1992), p. 4. From here on, I shall rely on Tsimbursky's differentiation between the two meanings of sovereignty: the actual fact of power on the one hand, and the recognition of the right to use power on the other. See also V. L. Tsimbursky, *Ideya suvereniteta v posttotalitarnom kontekste* (Moscow, 1993), vol. 1.

trative and the judicial powers, from the power of propaganda to the power of intimidation, is supposed to help smash the capitalist market of a given national economy together with the bourgeois society built on it, as well as help break up the world order of the globalizing capitalist economy, the "world system." Seen from that angle, that is in which the two interpretations, the Soviet and the classical ones, differ so radically because the former believed that the economy's power, whether national or global, can be smashed to pieces so that, the "realm of freedom" could take its place at once. Previous sovereignties, be these absolute monarchies, democratically elected parliaments, or dictatorships, had never intended to defeat the system of economic rationality, to smash the real world, to tear a nation-state from the world and to turn it against the world. The Soviet revolutionary socialist state concept had those aims in order to: to globalize and totalize a political power "confronting global and total economic power." It was due to that intention that sovereignty became a value (whereas the international attacks against this "real sovereignty" became "the treading on sovereignty"). The intrigue and criminal action of the global "class enemy" against the Soviet bloc of rock-solid super-sovereignty, aimed to break off a small piece and absorb real sovereignty into the global economy. This way and in this respect the Soviet Union became the "great protector" of sovereignties.

Economic globalization of the Western world wore away traditional national sovereignties, but some national sovereignties (especially in the Third World) hindered this globalization. These sovereignties got attached to the East European bloc of sovereign states and strengthened Soviet super-sovereignty. And vice versa: the fragments of sovereignty falling from the Soviet sovereignty bloc, particularly in East Europe and on the Balkans, but even in the case of China, strengthened the Western sovereignty bloc as a consequence of the logic of global confrontation. Most Central European countries, however, as well as the Baltic states wanted to wrest their sovereignty from the Soviet Union not for sovereignty's sake but, because that was the political precondition for integration into the Western economic organization and because only genuine sovereignty could be offered in exchange for economic advantages.

That is the reason why, while from the fifties and the sixties on, sovereignty was consecrated ideologically in the Soviet Union, the West started to analyze and criticize the traditional concept of sovereignty. In this respect, the leading role was played by the United States in whose constitution and federal system one can hardly find a trace of the notion of sovereignty, and which has frequent problems with the West Europeans; particularly with France's stubborn insistence on its sovereignty. That insistence was always received with understanding, warmth, and "don't give up" encouragement by the Soviet Union.

Recently in the literature on international law (in the writings of the Americans Jessup and Eagleton, the French Scelle, the Austrian Kelsen, etc.), as well as in the claims of prominent figures of international politics, there are more and more arguments that point to the obsolescence of the principle of sovereignty and demonstrate that the persistence sovereignty is detrimental to peaceful relations among states. By their reasoning, the partisans of the rejection of sovereignty want to be the pioneers of the world state, and also the destroyers of the obstacles hampering the global supremacy of the United States, the economically and financially strongest capitalist state. But for the very reason that the sovereignty of nation-states is a powerful obstacle to the realization of such will to supremacy, the Soviet Union and the so-called socialist countries firmly insisted on the principle of sovereignty and struggled for its intangibility. That struggle was supported by international law too: the United Nations Charter declared that, "The Organization is built on the principle of the sovereign equality of all its members" (Article 2, paragraph 1), and bans interference in the internal affairs of another state,[5] that is to say, the violation of the sovereignty of other states, notes the *Diplomáciai és Nemzetközi Lexikon* [Encyclopedia of diplomacy and international relations], compiled mostly from Soviet sources and published three years after the suppression of the Hungarian national uprising of 1956. The encyclopedia also gives a definition of sovereignty using the words of Vishinsky: "the condition of the internal as well as

---

[5] Gyula Hajdu, ed., *Diplomáciai és Nemzetközi Lexikon* (Budapest, 1959), p. 505.

external independence of a state authority from any other power."[6] It may be quite clear from this quotation why the slogan of "sovereignty for everyone!" became almost a Soviet doctrine after World War II. (Not in the meaning of the "Brezhnev Doctrine," of course, which was never issued by the Soviets, rather it was a Western demand that the Soviet Union, the greatest guardian of real sovereignties, account for its actions against real sovereignties.) Sovereignty obviously meant "our" sovereignty (a state could be "sovereign for us" and "sovereign against us") and, consequently, in reality, it meant opposition to the West and support for independence from the West, at least. Beyond that, the notion of sovereignty was also useful for rejecting out of hand the obligation for accountability for international norms and the general values not denied by the Soviet system at the theoretical level as "interference in domestic affairs." (Because the new, originally Western concept of sovereignty, that fits in the global economic order, selects several items from the exclusive sphere of authority of the nation-state and refers to them as European or global "common problems," and the nation-state is, in turn, entitled to handle those items only according to the norms of the international community, and only as a representative of that community. We shall see further below the way the new concept of sovereignty will grind down the old one, the way the recognition-based-sovereignty of the global economy will grind down Soviet sovereignty based on global political power.)

Until the end of the Cold War, the Soviet interpretation of sovereignty had an "anti-imperialist," anti-Western accent. It included the right of the sovereign states to oppose "economic and information imperialism," that is to say, the globalization of Western financial

---

6 Quoted in Hajdu, ed., op. cit. The history of the concept of sovereignty did not begin with Vishinsky, of course. The best summary of the revolutionary-class approach, characteristic of the twenties, can be found in Yevgeny Korovin, *Mezhdunarodnoye pravo perehodnovo vremeni* (1924), while in his *Ocherki po mezhdunarodnomu pravu* (1935), Yevgeny Pashukanis gives an outline of the etatist concept prevailing in the thirties. The debates of the age are reviewed in the short but excellent book: Iván Polzovics, *A bolsevizmus és a nemzetközi jog* (Budapest, 1938), p. 28.

world, and the extension of the Western humanitarian, legal, and political norms all over the world. In short, a state could be sovereign, in
the Soviet view, only against the West (in the Western view, just the
opposite: against the Soviet Union), and in that case, the given state
could count on the guardianship of the sovereign superpower, the state
in question, be it anywhere in the world (from Cuba to Angola, from
Afghanistan to Ethiopia, let alone the Arab countries). Its sovereignty
was worthless and weightless if not measured by Soviet standards,
that is, unless it was "added" to one of the super-sovereignties. From
that point of view, a sovereignty was already of value if it was *not*
added to the bloc of sovereignty of the global enemy (for example,
the neutrality of Austria or the special status of Finland in the Soviet
era, the latter being summed up in the malicious or bitter Western figure of speech "Finlandization," which saw a lost or robbed piece of
its own sovereignty in the sovereignty of Finland condemned to neutrality for geopolitical reasons). During the decades of the Cold War,
the same logic dominated in the West: sovereignty was of value only
if it contained separation or the independence from the Soviet bloc,
opposition to the Soviet expansion, including the so-called "extra-
bloc status," the status of the "non-aligned" (be they even "red" as
Yugoslavia or post-Mao China, quitting the Soviet bloc). Each crack
on the Soviet bloc's wall (1956, 1968, 1980) was referred to as movement towards sovereignty (strengthening "us," weakening "them")
from the Western super-sovereignty's point of view, just like all
attempts to let out or redesign the "Soviet straitjacket" (carried out in
internal affairs as in the case of Hungary or in external ones as in the
case of Romania)[7] were regarded as "sovereignizations."[8] Thus, dur-

---

[7]   Here and below, I use the concept of "sovereignization" in the Russian sense,
as interpreted by Polzovics. In this sense, "sovereignization" is to real and recognized sovereignty what "democratization" is to democracy, "liberalization"
to liberalism, "autonomization" to autonomy. "Sovereignization" is a watch-
word of the political struggle, used to back up the extension of the regional
power's sphere of decision and to recreate the legitimacy of the regional
elites' authority during the deconstruction period of the imperial structure.

[8]   See also Hélène Carrère d'Encausse, *Le Grand Frère* (Paris, 1983); and
Charles Gáti, *Füstbe ment tömb* (Budapest, 1991).

ing the Cold War, sovereignty was considered to have local value only. Real sovereignty began to be reevaluated in the framework of global opposition, and to depend on recognition; it was possible only if and so far as one of the super-sovereigns recognized it as its own, and that could take place only if the given sovereignty had said no to the other one (or to the other too). Central and Eastern Europe began to study the subject of sovereignty not in the post-1989 period but during the Cold War. That was the time when the region learned the lesson of Yalta: sovereignties "squeeze, embrace, hold tight" one another, so each practices self-determination.

In the end, however, it was not the military-ideological confrontation of the two world systems that decided the outcome of the super-sovereigns' Cold War; the strategic change carried out by the West, headed by the United States, made possible the changeover to the new concept of sovereignty corresponding to the globalization of the financial and information economy. Previously, independently of its compliance with Western norms (whether there was democracy or dictatorship, whether a given state respected human rights or not, etc.), any state could achieve recognition on the ground of the fact of sovereignty if that strengthened the Western super-sovereignty. Now recognition is linked not to the fact of sovereignty but rather to the democratic performance of the sovereign state; its human rights performance, its economic success. These amount to much more than the legal act of international recognition. That way, however, the "recognizers," that is, the Western powers as well as the international legal and political agencies have been entitled (by themselves, to a certain extent) to penetrate behind the ramparts of the sovereign states and to poke around in their dirty laundry. That strategic changeover had twofold sense: on the one hand, to undermine and "loosen" the Soviet super-sovereignty and, on the other, still by "rolling back" Soviet sovereignty, to carry out the globalization of Western norms, the material conditions of which had been established since the second half of the seventies, and the road to which was blocked by the monstrous political reality of the "Second World." The difference between the two concepts of sovereignty was most clearly demonstrated in the Soviet versus American interpretation of the role the United Nations was supposed to play. For the Americans, the United Nations was the "agent" of economic globalization, it was supposed to bring the world together with international norms, while the Soviet regarded it as the "agent" for the sovereign nation-state, the "mother-hen" of the newly hatched sovereignties, their breeder and protector. From the point of view of political globalization, the multitude of sovereign nation-states in the decades after World War II seemed to be hindering the process of economic globalization, smashing the economic fact of the world or, at least, tearing apart the economic net woven by the West; while from the point of view of economic globalization, the very expansion of unified norms through international organizations, the assistance of supranational political and legal processes of integration, consequently, the weakening of sovereign nation-states, the crushing of the sovereignties of "I-do-whatever-I-want-to-whatever-anyone-says," were and are still referred to as the guarantees for success.

The Withering Away of Soviet Sovereignty

Before the Soviet system emerged from the framework of "socialism in one country" and before it began to grow into a world system by incorporating the Central European sovereignties, the Soviet Union had not attached much importance to recognition by the West, and the West itself had been content to recognize the fact of sovereignty. (In the twenties as well as in the thirties, the Western critique of the "Bolshevik system" and the "Stalinist regime" had nothing to do with the recognition of the Soviet Union's sovereignty. And the other way around: the isolationist and internationalist Soviet Union of Stalin did not pay much attention to criticism by the West which, by the way, was a divided West fragmented into antagonistic nation-states, drifting towards war.)

Becoming a world system after 1945 meant that recognition by international organizations and the United Nations was becoming more and more emphatically an element of Soviet sovereignty. As a result, however, the fact of sovereignty was now in a dependent position. Doubtless, Stalin noticed the risks of dependence on recognition fairly soon. The antifascist coalition was based on that recognition from the very beginning: when the West, out of necessity, but not without principles, entered into an antifascist alliance with the Soviet Union, it also recognized that the latter was not one of the two (or more) totalitarian states but rather a great power qualified to liberate the world, a great power which, in sharp contrast to the Nazi regime, did not deny, in principle at least, the originally Western general values of freedom, independence, humanism, and democracy.[9] The recognition that was so useful to the Soviet regime of Stalin during the war became dangerous at the same rate after the war, when she had to comply with the norm not within the negative and extreme action of smashing the "evil of the world" but rather in with the proper positive everyday practice of the Soviet state. This recognition as a positive attribution of certain values (democracy, humanism, love of liberty) by the Soviet system involved the risk of the materialization of those values, which could have undermined the actual Soviet system.

After 1945, Stalin immediately began the maneuver of "separation" in order to restore Soviet sovereignty in practice, independently of any recognition. That is why the Stalinists began to take a Russian imperialistic turn, together with an ideological offensive against "kowtowing to the West," against "cosmopolitanism," and somewhat later with a wild political campaign ("we don't give a damn, whatever the West says, propagates, promises, loves or hates, we have our own, a separate and better, superior system of values, our own system of norms")! And that is also why the new form of self-isolation of the Soviet regime (in contrast to pre-World War II) took on an openly "Russian" character (in the most extreme form of the radical Russian chauvinism of the "Black Hundreds"). The refusal of Western or international recognition, as the self-defense of a regime

---

[9]   As Alan Bloom writes regarding the relationship of communism and liberalism: "Communism was a mad enlargement of liberal rationalism, and since then everybody realized that it was unsuitable and undesirable. Although fascism was defeated in the battlefields, its dark possibilities have not been exhausted entirely yet. If one is seeking for an alternative, there is no other possibility left, wherever one looks. I think fascism has a future, and it may be future itself." "The Need for Philosophy," *The National Interest* (Summer 1989).

founded on the real-sovereignty, could have been successful within the framework of "socialism in one country" (the case of China is a good example: the Chinese regime does quite well without Western recognition partly because of its non-European civilization, of course; and it is in no hurry to use the Western appreciation of its economic success to strengthen the sovereignty of the regime). It could not be successful, however, as a world system.

We have no space here to discuss the question whether the Soviet regime had any other choice after 1945 from an ideological, a geopolitical, a regional-imperial or a global-nuclear point of view if it wanted to survive, in other words, to become a world system (a choice that led to its collapse). We can claim that the challenge of becoming a world system was met by the Stalinist Soviet Union with a reflex-like reaction, and that reaction was inappropriate from the very beginning. Russian supremacy, the Russian imperial tradition, the enforcement of the Russian language and culture expropriated by the state and reorchestrated in a Soviet style, just when the Soviet regime went beyond its historical-regional boundaries, when it became a world system, inevitably provoked national resistances.

The expansion of Russian "national communism" brought into life the "national communisms" and "national anticommunisms" of Central Europe and the Balkans. Anticommunism and Russophobia meant the same thing in Central Europe at least until 1956 precisely because of the Soviet change of direction after 1945. Thus, Stalin's Soviet regime got into double trouble after 1945: as a world system it could not dispense with the factor of recognition, the precondition of which was the acceptance of Western norms (that was undermining the power base of real-sovereignty internally), while as a Russian regime, having chosen unrecognized isolation, it had to face the opposition and the endeavors to sovereignization of the Central European nation-states. The double answer to this doubly-problematic situation was corrected only after Stalin's death and particularly after the crisis of the Soviet regime in 1956: the universalist humanist rhetoric of "building of communism" in the Khrushchev era ("universal system" instead of a "Russian system," the "scientific-technological revolution," instead of "Russian science," as the language of the state ideology; the heroism of the "Soviet man," and of the "communist man" instead of the heroism of the "Russian man," who "conquers nature and even space") served much more suitably the purpose of political globalization than "Russification," which had left unpleasant memories behind; and the doctrine of "peaceful coexistence" involved a new formula of acceptance and sovereign for the adoption of international norms.

With super-sovereignties being mutually unsurmountable by military means and with the global strategy of the Soviet regime having changed, the system of relations between the West and the Soviet Union began to undergo a transformation too. While the fact of "sovereign Stalinist terror" had been acknowledged by the West, from the Brezhnev era on, through the peep hole opened by Khrushchev, the development of Soviet domestic policies (the violation of human rights, the persecution of the political opposition, of the dissident intelligentsia, of the independent artists, but also, retrospectively, the whole Soviet past overshadowed by the Gulag) became visible on the international political scene, and the Soviet Union was continuously called to account for the universal norms accepted *de jure* by the Soviets too. For economic considerations, but also in order to maintain and enlarge its world system, the Soviet Union needed Western recognition badly, although the dependence on recognition was undermining sovereignty based on coercive power. For this reason, however, Western values could not be realized within the framework of the Soviet regime, as was clearly demonstrated by the failure of Gorbachev's perestroika. The continuous Soviet defensive led to American victory in international politics. From the point of view of sovereignty, that process of retreat and deconstruction, from "peaceful coexistence" to the "Helsinki Conference," from "détente" to the withdrawal from Afghanistan and to the "new thinking," was the genesis of the recognition-founded-sovereignty, bringing about the birth of post-Soviet Russia.

The reinterpretation of sovereignty was forced partly by the West during the "détente" decades of the Cold War, but partly also, by the retreat of the Soviet regime, which had exhausted all the possibilities for further extensive industrialization and used up its military expansion, its resources for legitimization. It also lost confidence in its ideology, and proved to be helpless in face of the global economic and technological challenges of post-modernity. In its final perplexity, being concerned with a possible collapse, to gain time and for the sake of temporary stability, the Soviet leadership made a virtue out of necessity: the gradual withdrawal of the state from society into the deep recesses of totalitarian power, relinquishing the right to sovereign terror and bloodlust, the liquidation of privacy, and the total state management of the economy. These acts were perceived as the "thaws" and "spurts," lasting until repudiation of "reforms" and "renewals," of "concessions" and "waves of liberalization." The greater the danger the regime had to face and the closer it came to its end the more power it returned to society without being able to provide a form fitting the new situation. These concessions were given for the sake of survival. And it survived as long as it had anything to concede. It "conceded" then as long as it could, as long as it had anything left from the total system of power. Thus, by December 1991, after the decades-long process of "give back," the Soviet world system collapsed not with a bang but a whimper. The dissolution of the Soviet Union did not shake the world at all. It was the end of an era.

One of the most significant aspects of that "give back," which was not always easily distinguishable from "take back" and was never devoid of some wrangling, was the "give back" of real sovereignty, that is to say, the acceptance of international norms, and the attempt to change over to sovereignty based on recognition. It is not by chance that this attempt linked to the name and efforts of Gorbachev, the emblematic figure of the "give back" process, to the political campaign of "the ultimate dismantling" of the Soviet Union, which is to be filed in the history of politics under the entries "perestroika" and "glasnost." Gorbachev was the first and last Soviet politician who tried to found the sovereignty of the Soviet state on recognition, as his policies and political stature were dependent on Western recognition. What the West, personifying the international norm, did recognize in Gorbachev and in his new course was, however, not the fact of the Soviet state which was recognized *de jure* long before, but the efforts to approach the international norm. These yearnings were often repeated in the Soviet press of the period as "we want to be a normal country," which meant in the case of the Soviet Union, the dismantling, the "curtailment" of the Soviet type political system, of the total state's supreme power and, consequently, its political end. The world has never had a more recognized politician than the last leader of the Soviet state, as it hardly ever had a more recognized state than the Soviet Union of "perestroika." The narrower the meaning of the Soviet Union's sovereignty became, the greater was recognition. As a result, the recognition of the Soviet Union was the greatest at the very moment when it ceased to exist. Because of the nature of the regime, international recognition could be converted into neither the fact of sovereignty nor the strengthening of its legitimacy. Recognition-based sovereignty failed to save Gorbachev or the Soviet state. The greater the international recognition of Gorbachev became, the less domestic recognition he had, the latter being established on either the naked and/or ideologically decorated fact of power, or on nothing at all. But recognition was given for the very renunciation of power, the continuous renunciation of power for the sake of the Soviet ruling elite, Soviet society and the world in general.

Thus it is not surprising that, from the end of 1991, the very "idea of sovereignty became the specific means to be used in the 'self-destruction' of the Soviet Union" as Vladimir Tsimbursky puts it.[10] He rightly uses the word "self-destruction" for the process, although taking into account its peaceful, contractual form we should rather speak of "self-deconstruction" or "self-reduction." Beyond doubt, the edifice of the empire was not blown up by nations and ethnic communities,[11] rather, it was dismantled, willy-nilly, by the old and new central and local "clans" and "clan leaders" of the Soviet *nomenklatura* in the last moment, just before it could have been blown up by radical national movements. These "clans," "clan leaders" and "clan interests" backed both the CIS, the confederation of the former Soviet republics turned sovereign, and the furor of sovereignization

---

[10] Tsimbursky, op. cit. pp. 15–17.

[11] In his excellent analysis of the bargaining process between Moscow and the members of federation, Steven L. Solnick confirms this: "it seems very probable that the ethno-regional differences in Russia supported union rather than separation and fragmentation." Steven L. Solnick, "'Torg' mezhdu Moskvoy i subyektami federatsii o strukture novovo rossiyskovo gosudarstva: 1990–1995," *Polis,* no. 6 (1995), p. 96.

that erupted in the Russian Federation at the end of 1991, recorded as "the swarming of sovereignties" or "the parade of sovereignties." When, in accordance with the federation treaty, the former Soviet republics exercised their right to secede, they abandoned the Soviet Union together with Russia. The federation treaty was superseded by the confederation treaty of the CIS. The more or less radical separatist national movements were not in power in most of the republics, not even in the vicinity of power, as the subsequent presidential elections would demonstrate. All that happened was simply that those in the top republican positions of the Soviet *nomenklatura*, the former first secretaries, "did a somersault" and became presidents, while the first secretaries of the former autonomous territories and ethnic areas did the same inside their respective republics. For example, the declared sovereignty of Karabakh or Abkhazia gained no more recognition than the claimed sovereignty of the Gagauz, the Dniester Republic or of Tatarstan. The Soviet Union became, with the exception of the Baltic states, the Commonwealth of Independent States and the Russian Federation. That move was done under the pressure of necessity, of course: first, the old federal sovereignty had to be exchanged for the new nation-state sovereignty against local nationalist opposition, and the interests of the *nomenklaturas* of the republics coincided with the interest of Russia as well as of the whole community of nations, since neither of them wanted a nuclear great power to plunge into chaos; second, after relinquishing the Baltic states (which regained their sovereignty), the *nomenklaturas* of the republics had the choice between political somersault and self-destruction.

Against local nationalist opposition and the *nomenklatura* elite's drive to escape from central dependence, Mikhail Gorbachev, obsessed with the idea of recognition-based-sovereignty, had recourse to a referendum as the ultimate means of renewing the legitimacy of the Soviet state. The referendum was held in March 1991 without the participation of the Baltic states, Moldova, Georgia, and Armenia. Eighty percent of the voters of the remainder cast their ballots. 76.4% voted for a renewed Soviet federation. Significantly, in the Ukraine, eighty percent voted in favor of sovereignty inside the Soviet Union. In spite of that, on December 8, 1991, without any plebiscite, democratic authorization and Western recognition, the delegates of the three Slavic republics, representing the local *nomenklatura,* declared their sovereignty as an accomplished fact and stated that the Soviet Union "as an international legal entity and a geopolitical reality ceased to exist," and the Commonwealth of Independent States would take her place.

The West was and still is interested in the transformation and the renewal of the integrational framework of the former Soviet Union, in creating a democratic and economic basis for it, rather than in its dissolution into nation-states, and by the recognition of the transformation the West did its best to support integration such as the Russian Federation. Thus, when the West had to face the multitude of sovereign states scrambling for recognition instead of just the three sovereign Baltic states and a democratic federation, the pleasure it may have felt in the dissolution of the Soviet Union was tempered. The United States, the victorious superpower, was not a friend of nation-state sovereignty (in contrast to the Soviet Union of the Cold War), and had always preferred federation and autonomy. Moreover, with the end of the Cold War the sovereignty card had no significance. From the aspect of Western globalization, as long as it weakened Soviet super-sovereignty, sovereignty was considered to be a valuable political "good." It diminished the power of the Soviet bloc, which "blocked" the economic globalization of the West. The West, however, had no problem with the federative framework and global integration. It would have preferred a Euro-Asian economic model of integration in place of the Soviet Union or in an entirely new Soviet framework that would have participated in the global financial economy, rather than a legion of nation-states wrangling with one another and ignoring in a sovereign manner international norms, opposing globalization.

The three Baltic states, annexed in 1940, had always been a "foreign body" within the Soviet state structure, hence, their secession resulted in the fragmentation of the whole body. The leading politicians of the West undoubtedly wished the Baltic states would regain their independence, but for geopolitical and economic reasons, they did not want the collapse of the Soviet framework of integration and the swarming of never-had-been nation-states. The more so, since from the very beginning sovereignty, for the Baltic states (as for the

Central European states), meant the obtention of the sovereign right to join the European organization of integration (they were destined for that by their political traditions, economic self-interest and geopolitical circumstances). Most of the newly established *nomenklatura* nation-states, however, prefer to use their sovereignty to sustain the old Soviet regime and to reestablish its legitimacy under a nationalist aegis, and rather than to erect a political and economic system that would respect international norms. Paradoxically, the Soviet political and economic system was dismantled at the imperial center much more than in the now independent states of the imperial periphery: one could become "Russian" and demand the autonomy of Russia from the imperial center only on democratic grounds since Moscow, the heart of modern Russian statehood, is that center; whereas one could become "Uzbek," "Georgian" or "Turkman" in an antidemocratic way, turning sovereignty against international norms, using and interpreting it in the Soviet way: "the world," now reduced to Moscow, "is not entitled to interfere in our internal affairs." Thus, Russia proved to be the legal heir of the Soviet Union and she inherited also its sovereignty based on recognition.

Since the beginning, Russia's sovereignty has rested not only on the fact of a power possessing a nuclear force of deterrence but upon recognition. Russia accepts the Western norms, and she is aware of its dependence on recognition, of the fact that she cannot claim even her great power status without the approval and recognition of the Western powers. She continually feels obliged to give proof of her adherence to the principles of democracy, of human rights and of the market economy, in spite of all appearances to the contrary. Russia is continuously being tested by the West and is continuously begging for recognition. The well-known "shock therapy" of 1992, that is, the sudden introduction of market economy, as well as the sudden establishment of a constitutional state and of democracy after the bloody siege of the "White House" in Moscow suggested that in the future Russia was going to base its sovereignty primarily on recognition. (As regards the traditional interpretation of sovereignty, that amounts to the loss or renunciation of sovereignty. That is why the nationalist opposition continually refers to the system that developed during Yeltsin's presidency, which otherwise can hardly be seen as a parliamentary democracy of the Western type, as the "Provisional Occupation Regime" [the Russian acronym VOR also means "thief"]. It is called the reign of anti-national traitors who renounce Russia's sovereignty in favor of multinational enterprises, of international banking capital, of the "dark, mondialist forces," and whose fall and liquidation will be followed by the restoration of Russia's sovereignty.)

While frequently Russian respect for Western norms becomes questionable because of her actual political measures, still recognition is declared by both Russia and the West. We do not have to strain our imagination to find out how, in the Soviet era, the Western press would have presented the case of the "people of tiny Chechen" fighting for "freedom" and "sovereignty," or how, every October since 1993, the Western media would have recalled the terrifying vision of the "Soviet president" who had the "democratic parliament" stormed and shot at, how they would have exposed the burning "White House" in Moscow as the emblem of the "communist regime," as they do each year recalling the Tiananmen Square bloodshed and the figure of the Chinese student as he stood there in front of the column of tanks. It is more important that Russia's huge state and world system could no longer block the path of economic globalization, and itself is moving along the same course—Eastward. It is more important that Russia's sovereignty is dependent on recognition. And that this Russia has preserved its unity and has become remarkably more stable than expected two years earlier. For, from the viewpoint of the globalizing world, a contemporary Russia that is sovereign by recognition is preferred either to a hundred small nation-states sovereign by recognition or a single Iraq, with the size of Russia and independent of any recognition. The January 24, 1996, decision of the thirty-eight member Parliamentary Assembly of the Council of Europe was probably based on that consideration: by that decision Russia was granted membership in the Council of Europe, in spite of the brutal end to the hostage drama in Chechnia, and in spite of grave shortcomings in the area of human rights.[12]

---

[12] The admission of "real Russia" into the Council of Europe was not merely a symbolic ("Russia is part of Europe"), a political (supporting the "mediocre"

"The Flea Market of Sovereignties"

The more time passes since August 1991, since the miracle of the transubstantiation (and to a certain extent, but only to a very small extent, the metamorphosis of the Soviet Union into Russia), the more obvious it becomes that the driving force of this amazing, almost embarrassingly organic legal, political, economic transformation can be found among the specific economic, political and legal creations of the Soviet regime, and not among the external conditions and factors (the global strategic interests of the West, the American technological challenge under the impact of which the Soviet state bent, the rebirths of nations), nor in the activity of domes-

---

Russian democracy of Yeltsin before the presidential elections) and a pedagogic act (to teach the "barbarous Russians" to respect human rights, humanitarian principles, etc.), but also the beginning of the actual expansion of the European integration process towards East Europe under the aegis of the unified European system of norms. Russia has already joined a number of European conventions (particularly in cultural areas,) but if she is going to ratify the European convention on human rights and the attached protocols (that is, if Russia also recognizes as her citizens' personal right to turn directly to the European Commission of Human Rights, and if she recognizes the jurisdiction of the European Court of Human Rights and the law on communities), and if she, furthermore, is going to ratify the convention for the prevention of torture and inhumane treatment, the European charter of local self-government as well as the general agreement on the protection of national minorities, then, for the first time in her history, Russia will concede a small piece of her state sovereignty. On the other hand, as subject to European legal norms, she will be able to act within her own Euro-Asian organization of integration (CIS, Russian Federation) as the representative of Europe and as a force that is about to accomplish the European integration process, as the framework of integration by which the Russian regions and the Asian CIS members can link themselves to Europe in the fastest and the most direct way. That role is not the same as the Russian empire's former roles, however obvious the analogy with the Holy Alliance may be. No doubt Russia as a member will also be granted certain rights by the European Community, which embodies Europe, while she is to delegate a part of her sovereignty (in the traditional sense). See "Glavnoe ne rezultat, a protsess," *Kommersant,* February 27, 1996, p. 4.

tic social or political interests and forces (social classes, political parties, economic pressure groups). The autochthonous Soviet creations, the actual creations of the Soviet regime were the regions,[13] the legal-political-economic units of the Soviet administrative-territorial system. The Soviet regime did not produce social classes in the modern sense, neither did it tolerate the existence of political parties, or autonomous civic organizations. It regarded the formal distinction between state and society itself as an attack against state order (in Soviet terminology: "the Party and the people are one and the same").

The East European model[14] of development was different from the Western one in the sense that the state, which responded to external challenges, was always the prime mover of social change. In East Europe, the state has always been in charge of promoting enlightenment as well as capitalism, afterwards anti-capitalism, that is, communism or socialism, just like these days it promotes privatization that is, market economy and political democracy. The state has partly substituted the missing political, economic, social, and cultural institutions, partly eliminated the existing ones, and created institutions of her own from those components of the state organism that sprung to independent life, institutions that cannot be compared to anything else. Having stuck to their creator as parasites for a while, by the end these state components consumed its power entirely. A great number of small state monsters had been hatched from the egg of the monster state, and they united into a new monster state.

---

[13] According to Kagansky, the dissolution of the Soviet space into its "regional atoms," that is, the actual regionalization was nothing but the self-transformation of the Soviet space: (1.) the sovereignization of the regions, that is, of the structural components, then (2.) the decomposition of the Soviet state, that is, of the upper level, then (3.) the "collection" of the local components by the sovereignized regions and the reintegration of their own areas, and finally (4.) total re-creation of the space structure, including, the connections between the center and the regions, under the aegis of decentralization, autonomization, and decolonization.

[14] I use the concept the way Szűcs did. See Jenő Szűcs, "The Three Historical Regions of Europe: An Outline," *Acta Historica Academiae Scientiarum Hungaricae* 29, nos. 2–4 (1983), pp. 131–184.

So far, this formula, that is the decomposition of the state body, then the revival of the state pieces and, finally, their recomposition into a different state pattern, has been the solution to the enigma of East European transformations. The main question is whether the post-Soviet regional revolution differs from that formula or, on the contrary, business is as usual, the developments move along the regular course from pattern to pattern.

The formlessness of today's post-Soviet society also demonstrates this: we may speak about social classes or political parties only metaphorically. Between 1989 and 1991, Western "transitologists" were looking with their eyes popping out for the social forces, economic and political groups that, urged by interests and values, would establish both market economy and political democracy, but wherever they looked, as far as the eye of a political scientist could see, they found state and the *nomenklatura* of the party-state. It does not mean, however, that the Soviet state, the Soviet political system and planned economy as well as the imperial frameworks had been attacked and smashed by the "bandocracy"[15] (that is, the bureaucracy of the party-state interwoven with the underworld and the shadow economy) as a "new class." The role of the moving force, of the "active element" in the transformation of Soviet clan state socialism[16] into post-Soviet clan state capitalism was played not by the new or old classes, nor by the peoples and nations, but by the Soviet regions.

Clans, class-like formations, political parties, nations, ethnic groups, etc. could shape themselves and appear on the political scene only on the basis of the changes produced by the regional units established in the Soviet era, or through helping or hampering those changes, ideologically justifying and politically controlling them. It would be absurd to give an account of this structural meta-

---

[15] Cf. Ákos Szilágyi, "New Class Wanted (An Outline of Bandocracy)," *Társadalmi Szemle* 8 (1991).

[16] On the myth of the "new class," see I. Bunin, "Novye rossiyskie predprinimately i mifi postkommunisticheskovo soznaniya," *Liberalizm v Rossii*, (Moscow, 1994), pp. 46–48. For a comprehensive analysis of the political and economic clan system in Russia, see Zoltán Sz. Bíró, "Szomorú stabilitás: Oroszország 96 elején," *2000* (June 1996).

morphosis in the old modern narrative of the Soviet regime ("people's revolution," "political revolution," "social revolution," "great criminal revolution,"[17] *nomenklatura* revolution," etc.), whereas it is very easy to do that in the post-modern narrative of the "Soviet regions' revolution." All the rest, the civil wars, ethnic conflicts, the clashes between the branches of power, the power and fights of the clans, the social conflicts, the very division of the Soviet society into "up" and "down," into "pariahs" and "maharajahs" just followed (and not preceded, as in the traditional revolutions, like in the Russian one of 1917) the regions' revolution that pulled down the Soviet framework of integration. To this extent we are justified in describing the regions' revolution as a post-Soviet (and not anti-Soviet!) revolution.[18] It is not by chance that, until the end of 1993, the Soviet political system was formally preserved, and the ejection or the extirpation of the Communist Party from the state system meant only that the structural level of the Soviet super-state ceased to exist and the Communists had to become a party among other parties (in this regard, we cannot even talk about an anti-communist revolution, since the direction and the course of the structural transformation was determined not at the political levels but by the regional roles, situations, and interests). Because of all this, the post-Soviet revolution was also a post-modern revolution: it conspicuously lacked any future-oriented ideology or ideological voice of "anti"-ism in general; it lacked the people, the revolutionary masses, the "social charge," and it also lacked the revolutionary agency of political ideals and political passions (and, hence, it lacked terror, revenge, civil war and intervention, the usual stages of modern revolutions.)

A much more significant role was played by the electronic media,[19] however, which simulated the political revolution, the polit-

---

17 Among others, see the brochure "Velikaya kriminalnaya revolutsiya" by Stanislav Govoruhin, film director, journalist, politician and party leader (Moscow, 1993), and also the articles in the "national radical," or "ultranationalist" journals *Nash sovremennik*, and *Moskva* in the period 1991 to 1996.

18 See Kagansky, op. cit.

19 See Ákos Szilágyi, "Se csodák, se katasztrófák (Virtuális Oroszország)," *Mozgó Világ*, no. 1 (1996); and "Simulacrum Simulacrorum," in *A tények és a lények* (Budapest, 1995), pp. 76–161.

ical institutions, and even the economic institutions, and by the centralized monetary economy, which simulated the market. There was only one aspect in which the "anti-" had real content: it meant the negation of the "center," that is, the highest regional level of the Soviet imperial statehood, though that content was formulated by the Soviet regional units at different levels and ranks, giving purely economic, political, or national and/or ethnic characteristics to the negation, depending on the given stage of the regional struggle for independence, and on the hierarchical rank and character of the region.[20] The negation was formulated in one way in 1988–1989, and in another in 1991–1992, in different ways at the level of the Soviet member republics, at the level of autonomous Soviet republics, of the provinces and of the territories, at the level of the ethnically-based

---

[20] Russia was never a proper federal state. That would have presupposed that its territorial components of more or less equal size had uniform political status. As a matter of fact, however, in both demographic and economic aspects, there was a yawning gap between the "Russian" regions and the regions of the "autonomous nations," let alone their differences in political status. The foundation of this system had been laid down by the Stalinist constitution of 1936 when it connected two contradictory principles of state construction, namely, the ethnic and the territorial principles, dividing the peoples living on the territory of the state into nations "with coats of arms" and nations "without coats of arms." The former have territories, nation-states of their own, while the latter have neither territories of their own nor the attributes of statehood. Furthermore, the constitution provided the regions of different types and, as a result, their populations with different licenses respectively. A federal republic had a constitution, a parliament of its own, moreover, it was entitled to secede from the Federation, while an autonomous republic or area as well as a region on the province or district level (the Russian "oblast" and "rayon") had neither. Emil Pain writes "That complicated regional hierarchy could have hardly survived if it had not been consciously declarative....The collapse of the communist regime, however, brought back to the autonomous republics their rights guaranteed in the Constitution and they tried to fill the declarative norms of the Stalin-Brezhnev constitution with real content." Emil Pain, "Separatizm i federalizm v sovremennoy Rossii," in *Kuda idyët Rossiya* (Moscow, 1994), pp. 161–162. That, however, meant entirely different things for the Russian regions and for the ethnic autonomies, that is, the legal unequal status became the basis of real inequality. From then on, the Russian regions could not be satisfied with fewer licenses than the ethnic regions had.

regional units and, finally, at the level of the purely administrative territorial units. It is true that during the same period, depending on the state of political struggles, the regional endeavor for independence was formulated by every administrative-territorial unit Soviet republic, autonomous republic, autonomous area, province, territory, city in the same catchwords (like the changeover to "independent economic accounting" in the early years of perestroika, then the struggle for the status of "special economic zone," that is, the "zonification," and, from the beginning of 1991 until the end of 1993, sovereignty and sovereignization). The post-modern revolution of the Soviet regions promised and demanded not "peace" and "bread" and not even "jobs" or "freedom," rather sovereignty, sovereignty and again sovereignty.

In 1991, a competition for sovereignty began among the Soviet regions (that was called "the parade of sovereignties" by the Russian press) "and the politicians also had their own race in the field of promises of sovereignty, who promises and to whom more or even total sovereignty, in order to keep him in check or to have him pull his own regional level out from under his feet. For instance, Yeltsin promised sovereign status to the Soviet member republics, causing Gorbachev's all-Soviet regional level (the "super region" of the imperial or federative state) to lose its footing, while Gorbachev raised the legal status of the autonomous republics of the Russian Soviet Federated Socialist Republics's to the level of Soviet republics (also giving them the right of secession, an unprecedented move in Russian history) in order to weaken or hold in check at least Yeltsin's all-Russian regional level (the "super region" of the Russian Federation).[21] One may say that government politics played a sovereignty game in that period, and it was easy to foresee which regional level would be

---

[21] Sergey Shakhray, Yeltsin's ethnic advisor, who was for long the president of the State Committee for Ethnic Policies and coordinated the activities of the internal, security, and military forces stationed on the North Caucasian Russian territories, explained the explosion of the "Chechen region" by blaming Gorbachev for the war, which was a fatal mistake made by Yeltsin and the "democrats of August." *Kriminalniy rezhim, Chechnia, 1991–1995* gg. (Moscow, 1995), p. 5.

the loser and would collapse if the revolution of the regions won. As the creations of the Soviet political system were neither social classes, nor peoples, nor nations but administrative-territorial units, the regions and their independence and leveling prepared the demolition of the Soviet political configuration and "totalitarian" integration (and now reintegration within different frameworks and with different rights also depends on them). The non-regional political endeavors, economic interests, cultural value orientations also articulated themselves by the mediation of the regions and in the language of the regional politics, continually putting sovereignty into the center of their political outlook.

With the exception of the three Baltic states, sovereignty did not imply the establishment of nation-states or regaining the stolen or lost sovereignty, but rather the revolt of the Soviet regions, the local societies and/or the local elites against the Soviet center of power as well as the demolition of the highest regional level. Because of the Soviet Union's disappearance, every region could jump a level seen from that angle. Yeltsin was not found by accident in 1991 as the leader of Russian democracy, when he got himself elected as the president of the RSFSR (following the pattern of Gorbachev's Soviet presidential title and following the logic of the sovereignties' competition), or when, in December of the same year, after consulting the presidents of Belarus and the Ukraine, he "dissolved" the Soviet Union; he was rather the leader of the region of Russia, the leader of the regional revolution.[22]

---

[22] Yeltsin, Gorbachev, Nazarbaev, Kravchuk, Shushkevich and all the other former party secretaries, party secretary-generals who are now presidents of republics, used to be the leaders or chieftains of Soviet regions at different levels, rather than of peoples, nations, social classes, political movements, ethnic groups, and it was in this role that they made themselves recognized in the multifarious but sometimes interwoven roles of "the great Soviet reformer," "the popular tribune of the anti-bureaucratic revolution" or "the father of the people." Rhetorics and the roles were changing according to the situation (which regional force to contend with, against whom the regional chieftain has to articulate himself, in what kind of language was it possible to approach the passive majority or the active minority of a given region's population in a given period), whereas the content and the goal remained the same, namely, the self-transformation of the Soviet configuration—total disintegration as the precondition of a new integration.

That is the very reason why it was so difficult for him to check and limit that revolution, that is why it took so long and the Russian presidential state tried out so many versions to keep Russia, and the Russian Federation together between 1992 and 1993.[23] That is why the opening of Yeltsin's revolutionary performance was marked by the famous, and rather enigmatic sentence he pronounced (to the delight of the leaders of the Tatar Republic) in 1992: "Take as much sovereignty as you are able to realize."[24] And that is why in his fight against legislative power, he mobilized the ethnic regions, promising them even more sovereignty. As late as June 1993, he accepted the proposal elaborated by the leaders of the republics within Russia concerning the text of article 5 of the new constitution: "The Republics are sovereign states within the framework of the Russian Federation."[25] Such a concept of sovereignty is entirely missing from the constitution approved by referendum in December 1993. The revolution of the regions has been over for a while, the consolidation of the results of the revolution, that is to say, a reintegration, the building of a new structure of integration has been going on more or less successfully. By 1994, the "parade of sovereignties" had been replaced by a "recycling center of used sovereignties" as a Russian journalist summarized the consequences of "the sovereign-

---

[23] The Russian Federation in the aftermath of the Soviet Union's demise was not the same as the one of today. Several drafts of its transformation and new foundations were elaborated between 1991 and 1993. The realization of many ideas were tried out before December 1993, when the federative state organization, approved by referendum and formulated in the Constitution, was ultimately worked out. According to this Constitution, every subject of the Russian Federation has equal legal status (each one is an equal component of the federation), none of them is sovereign, nor has the right of secession from the federation. The real differences are, however, stipulated in so-called bilateral agreements. Some of them grant remarkable rights and make quite significant concessions to the republics.

[24] Yeltsin's famous phrase is quoted in L. M. Drobizheva, "Etnitsizm i problema natsionalnoy politiki," in *Kuda idyët Rossiya?* (Moscow, 1994), p. 191.

[25] For the complete text of the constitution of the Russian Federation see, Vladimir V. Belyakov and Walter J. Raymond, eds., *Constitution of the Russian Federation: with Commentaries and Interpretation by American and Russian Scholars* (Lawrenceville, Va, 1994).

ty revolution."[26]

In the first phase of the sovereignty revolution, the regions headed by the Yeltsin-led region of Russia defeated and liquidated the "super-region" of the Soviet state center; in the second phase, however, the regions attacking the new state centers, questioning the sovereignty of the new state centers, demanding sovereignty from them, suffered a devastating defeat at the hands of the new state centers not only in Russia, which obtained the largest part of the Soviet inheritance, but in Azerbaijan, Georgia, Tajikistan, and even in the Ukraine. Moreover, this took place at all those levels of the former Soviet hierarchy which remained there after 1991 (that is to say, not only at the level of the Russian Federation but also at that of the autonomous republics, the provinces, and the territories). "The process of regionalization obviously involves decentralization, whereas centralization is an ever-stronger trend at the level of the regions"[27] that was how Vladimir Kagansky summarized the situation of 1994 in his analysis of the transformation processes in the post-Soviet configuration. In the first phase of the regional revolution, the historical Russian state

---

[26] Boris Zhukov, "Punkt priyoma ponoshennih suverenitetov" (literally: Recycling center for used sovereignties), *Stolitsa*, no. 40 (1994), p. 5. In Zhukov's opinion, the reason why the total dissolution of Russia, that is, "the scenario of 1917 has not been repeated" so far at least, the reason why CIS is resuscitating (by 1994, all the late Soviet republics except the Baltic states had joined the Commonwealth), and the reason why the Russian Federation has remained together, is that the Russian "state democrats" have concentrated on economic questions instead of political-ideological ones. They have been "state nihilists" and the adherents of "shock therapy." "The democrats' aim was never the disruption of the Soviet Union. They have seen clearly the benefits of the unified state organization, nevertheless, they have not tried to preserve it at any price. Let the republics play the game of sovereignty and independence sooner or later, the logic of the economy is going to drive them back, they will be forced to work out the economic mechanisms of integration without which they cannot be viable...." Between 1991 and 1994, Russia was preoccupied by the real transformation of her economy rather than questions of official language, citizenship, or "reform without a shock." That is the reason why she has become a strong economic center of gravitation and that is why she has managed to keep her unity.

[27] Kagansky, op. cit., p. 126.

(i.e. the Soviet state) came into conflict with itself and divided into two parts: the Soviet presidential state of Gorbachev and the Russian one of Yeltsin. Likewise, in the second phase, the state of the sovereign Russian Federation produced the Russian state of legislative power (the Congress of People's Deputies), and the Russian state of executive power (the state apparatus of the president).[28]

The cause and the breeding ground of these conflicts and splits were not any social or political antagonism dividing Soviet society but regional emancipation, the landslide of the regional sovereignties that divided, even "dismembered" the political elite. The course of events demonstrated clearly that, in Russia, the subjects of politics or of history are not parties, classes, nations, not society, but states, more exactly the levels and units of state administration behaving as quasi-states (for example, the "presidential states" in 1991, or the quasi-states of the "executive power" and of the "legislative power," that is to say, the regions in both cases).[29] Since the beginning of the transformation, because of the non-structured nature of society, the importance of parties is negligible or secondary.

The State Duma, the "parliament of the parties" has been playing second fiddle, sometimes it has made a show of itself in the bicameral legislature established by the Constitution passed late in 1993. The Federation Council, however, consisting of two representatives delegated, not elected, by the regions recognized as the subjects of the federation, has been performing the duties of a moderate and prestigious upper house. (One of the two delegates representing a region in the Federation Council is the head of the local government, the other one is the president of the local Duma, that is, of the local house of representatives. They are elected to these posts locally, of course.) This arrangement clearly demonstrates who is the master, who are the masters in the household of Russian politics, who defeated whom, and what the consolidation of the regions' victory at the end of 1993 involved.

---

[28] See also Ákos Szilágyi, "Kis orosz államháború," *Szovjet füzetek*, no. 11 (1993).

[29] See also Ákos Szilágyi, "Az ellopott puccs," *Szovjet füzetek*, no. 3 (1991).

It is worth noting here, that even the most significant political parties lack real regional organizations or political representation in the respective regions. Quite to the contrary, the regions have or may have their own representation in the parties, and it is they who behave as parties, even if not in the sense of the classical definition of political parties. Regions behave and realize their interests sometimes as quasi-states, sometimes as quasi-parties and almost always as real corporations in the new Russian clan state capitalism. It would be a total misunderstanding of the metamorphosis of the Soviet system to suppose that all this belongs to the transition, to an "intermediary" phase, to development from the Soviet past to the non-Soviet future, to be followed sooner or later by the development of the structures of the Western-style market economy and political democracy. After all, "post-Soviet," in other contexts "post-communist" or "post-socialist," is frequently misinterpreted as "for-the-time-being-Soviet," as "unfortunately-not-yet-entirely-bourgeois-capitalist-and-democratic," not only by Western analysts but frequently also by the "post-Soviet" society's participants themselves. In the structural sense, however, "post-Soviet" is not something from which something different is going to spring up, but that other thing which the "Soviet" has become, and that other thing will differ permanently rather than temporarily from the Western model of development, as the East European model was always different even after its great historical transformations. Even in its rhetoric, the sovereignty revolution of the regions was not an anti-Soviet revolution, rather it was the emancipation of Soviet political institutions that were Soviet in their historical genesis as well as social functions; it was their emancipation from the old structure, and came to an end with the demolition of the old structure and the establishment of the new.

As far as political and civil freedoms and the relationships of ownership and legal institutions are concerned, all that distinguish the post-Soviet structure from the Soviet one are the consequences or results of the revolution of the regions, that is, of the specifically Soviet institutions, and hence they will remain gifts, withdrawable, constrainable, or extendable if needed, coming from the post-Soviet Russian state dominated by the regions clans, corporations, quasi-states. The growth of freedom in every field is undoubtedly a dependent variable, dependent on the state of the regional revolution. Of course, this very state, the state evolved from the revolution of the regions, brought the virtually permanent revolution of the regions to an end when, in October 1993, it liquidated the Khazbulatov-led Soviet Parliament, the legislative power that had made the most of the "Russian regions," and created a new one in its own image.

As sooner or later every permanent political revolution comes to a point where it has to face its own state-creature when it turns out whether the state, having become "counterrevolutionary," is able to consolidate the results of the revolution, or rather collapses and lets the revolution become chaos and its original (revealed or concealed, perhaps ever-obscure) meaning vanish. If, at the end of 1993, the revolutionary state of Yeltsin had not been able to stop the permanent sovereignty revolution of the regions, to stop the further dismemberment of the "self-dismembering Soviet configuration"[30] (and we are not speaking of the "Red-Brown conspiracy," the "communo-fascist" putsch attempt), then all that had been predicted for Russia since the beginning of 1992 would have happened: the dissolution of Russia after the dissolution of the Soviet Union, involving the danger of a mostly inter-regional civil war or Soviet restoration combined with reintegration.

The revolutionary Russian state, which was given the ultimate push (or the pretext) to pronounce the counterrevolutionary "Halt!" by the "state war" among the branches of power, did not eliminate but consolidated the results of the regions' revolution, not in the December Constitution but rather in the bilateral agreements signed in rapid succession, after the adoption of the Constitution. That is the only possible explanation for the fact that the regions suddenly gave up continuing their revolution of sovereignization. Although during the bloody October of 1993, the Moscow "White House" was bombarded by Yeltsin's tanks, although seemingly only the ambitious political chieftains (Khazbulatov and Rutskoi) suffered defeat and not the regions themselves, and although on the eve of the "mutiny," the regions tried to conduct themselves as a "third force" (the Council of

---

[30] See Kagansky, op. cit., p. 119.

the Subjects of the Federation proposed the common annulment of both Yeltsin's ukaze on the dissolution of the Supreme Soviet, and its parent body, the Congress of People's Deputies, and their motion of non-confidence), after December 1993, the spectacular retreat of the regions took place.

With the "mutiny" stifled, the republics were in a hurry to annul their decrees that had left the presidential ukaze in abeyance. In April 1993, it was doubtful whether every republic would allow the referendum to be held on its territory In December 1993, however, that question was not even raised, though the Constitution up for vote, in contrast with the previous Federation Treaty, annulled the item on the sovereignty of the republics and declared that every subject of the Federation had equal rights (that is, the Russian regions were granted the same rights as the ethnic regions). The Tatar Republic that had defined itself as "a sovereign state, a subject of international law" in 1991, nevertheless accepted the new constitution in 1993, which claims that the single source of sovereignty in the Russian Federation is "the multinational people," and its only vehicle is the Russian Federation herself. Moreover, Shaymiev, the Tatar president hastened to declare that "he does not strive for seceding from the Federation, on the contrary, his aim is to preserve its unity."[31]

The declaration of sovereignty was not the goal but the means to the regions' sovereignty revolution. The realization of state sovereignty was and remained difficult not only because of the lack of Western recognition (even in the case of the Chechen Republic, see further below) but mainly because in a state where eighty-two percent of the population is Russian (except for Armenia, it is the most homogeneous state in the ethnic sense), seven percent of the total population can hardly declare that fifty percent of state territory is "the territory of the sovereign statehood" of that seven percent. The original (native) population does not make up half of the population of those territories (there are no more than six republics in Russia where the Russians are in a minority: Dagestan, Ingushetia, Kabardino-Balkaria, North Ossetia, Chuvashland and Tuva); and we

---

[31] The words of Mintimer Shaymiev, the president of the Tatar Republic, are quoted by Pain, op. cit., p. 169.

should not forget the economic weakness and financial dependence of the ethnic regions, and the wave of sovereignization of the Russian regions themselves between 1991 and 1993.[32] (The Chechen Republic was the only one that attempted to realize total and real sovereignty politically, with well-known "success" and less well-known real goals.) The regions did not and could not become sovereign states; nevertheless, they reached their goals, namely, they became independent in a political and an economic sense, they established horizontal relationships with one another as well as with the center, and retained their actual right of veto against the center (for instance, some years ago, Saratov and Volgograd provinces blocked the reestablishment of the Volga Germans' autonomy). Almost everywhere they seized the licenses of the former regional levels above themselves (the Russian Federation and the former Soviet member republics seized the status of the Soviet Union; the member republics of the Russian Federation the status of the erstwhile Soviet member republics; the autonomous territories the status of the Russian member republics; the provinces and the territories that of the autonomous territories and so on).

Due to the sovereignty revolution, the political configuration of the Russian Federation became multi-dimensional and, due to the counter-revolutionary stabilization of the federative state, it did not explode. In the meanwhile, however, ownership, state oppression, power and the law became regional. The future of the Southern Kurile Islands, much debated by the Russian Federation and Japan, depends not only on the federal government but on the regional coalition called Far East, on the province of Sakhalin (since the islands belong to that province administratively) and on the islands themselves. The federative "counterrevolution" brought separatism rather than regionalization to an end. That is why, aiming at the completion of the consolidation process, the central government made up its mind to liquidate Chechen sovereignty, which for three years had been recognized by no one. The Chechen Republic turned out to be the Federation's only subject that had gone beyond the regional goals of the post-Soviet sovereignty revolution. It was the only

---

[32] On the sovereignization revolt of the "Russian regions" see Ostrovidova, op. cit.; Pain, op. cit.; and Korkya, op. cit.

region in the post-Soviet configuration where the political agents of separatism, supported by tribal and religious background, gained total victory over the forces of Soviet regionalism, if not in democratic elections but by resorting to terror. In all other regions, this kind of breakthrough of nationalist-fundamentalist separatism, inspired generally by the intelligentsia, was not successful or succeeded only temporarily.[33] That was also the case everywhere in the rest of the Northern Caucasian regions: the regional elites of the Soviet *nomenklatura*, the late party secretaries and presidents, the Moscow emissaries gained or regained power and gave sense to the sovereignization process.

Only Doku Zavgaev, the Chechen president, elected from party secretary by a large majority at the end of the Gorbachev era, did not succeed in this kind of political acrobatics, mainly because the "August palace revolutionaries" of 1991 assigned his place to Dzhokar Dudaev from Moscow. The Russian democratic politicians around

---

[33] From this point of view, Dudaev seemed to be the "third force"; he opposed not only the political forces of Soviet regionalism (Doku Zavgaev, the Soviet president of the republic and his teyp) but the "Daymokh," the traditionalist political movement of the Chechen intelligentsia as well. When, in June 1991, under pressure by the chauvinists (the Vajnakh Democratic Party of Zelimkhan Jandarbiev, the party of B. Gratemirov, called Islamic Road and the "Gulam" movement), Dudaev was elected president of the Executive Committee of the Chechen People's All-National Congress, the movement of the traditionalist intelligentsia, headed by Lecho Umkhaev and Salambek Hajiev, abandoned the Congress. Later, when he got himself elected president by 15% of the Chechen voters (the fraction of the Chechen people which participated in the presidential elections called in late 1991), with the political struggle between the president and Parliament, between the teyps of the president and those of the opposition was becoming rather acute, Dudaev carried out a slaughter among the intellectuals. Having removed or executed his rivals one by one, in a decree he banned the Grozny congress called for December 25–26, 1993, by the 129 *teyps* and the Chechen diaspora, at which the delegates would have called parliamentary elections for April 1994 and discussed the possible ways of settling the Chechen situation. For details, see Vadim Korotkov, "Chechenskaya model etnopoliticheskih protsessov," *Obshchestvenniye Nauki i Sovremennost*, no. 3, (1994); Aleksandr Yanov, "Chechenskiy ekzamen," in A. Yanov, *Posle Yeltsina* (Moscow, 1995), pp. 88–111; as well as two official propaganda publications and collections of documents, *Chechenskiy krizis: ispitaniye na gosudarstvennost* (Moscow, 1995); and *Kriminalniy rezhim.*

Yeltsin, who had been Russian intellectuals the day before, these politicians of the victorious Russian Region, that is, the Russia of Yeltsin, were hardly aware what kind of revolution they were helping triumph, how deeply Soviet this anti-Soviet revolution was and that their "state nihilism" (market economy is everything "state is nothing!") would become senseless as soon as the sovereignty revolution of the Soviet regions reached its goal, that is, as soon as the regional level of the Soviet super state collapsed. (They were no longer needed after that. They can choose whether to leave voluntarily or be fired, or they themselves may turn from "state nihilists" to etatists, "*gosudarstvenniki*" and "*derzhavniki*.")[34]

Thus, the "August democrats" of Yeltsin knew neither that they met their match in the person of Dudaev, the former brigadier general of the Soviet army and former member of the Soviet Communist Party, nor did they known the difference between sovereignty as a regional political claim and sovereignty as a tribal-religious political claim. They did not know that Dudaev was not the "national-democratic" chieftain of the regional revolution, like Ruslan Aushev, his former fellow-soldier, who became the president of the Ingush Republic also after August, and not a nationalist intellectual of deranged mind, like Gamsahurdia, the ill-fated Georgian president. Nor did they realize that raising him to power they would start the avalanche of a tribal-religious civil war[35]

---

[34] For example Andranik Migranyan, who switched from Gorbachev's presidential advisory board to Yeltsin's and, in addition to fabricating an ideology backing for the Russian intervention in Chechnia on the grounds of the necessity to reestablish and maintain the Russian great state ("derzhavnost'") at any price, also became one of the authors of the new Russian foreign policy doctrine. From the end of 1993 on he pressed continuously for the replacement of Kozyrev who adopted a "shuttlecock policy." See Andranik Migranyan, "1995: a nagy fordulat avagy a teljes összeomlás éve az orosz államiság történetében," *2000* (March, 1995), pp. 8–11; and Ákos Szilágyi, "Hungary Through East European Eyes," in *Kormányunk a mérlegen, 1990–1994* (Budapest, 1994).

[35] "...for three years, an average of thirty people per day were executed in Chechnia, and essentially there was a civil war. Peace-loving citizens perished, people who didn't want to die for Dudaev"—wrote Zhukhovitsky, the correspondent of *Literaturnaya Gazeta* at the beginning of 1995. (Quoted in Yanov, op. cit. p. 89.)

and a federal Russian-Chechen internal war as well. Let us take a closer look at what they did not know or did not want to know, in what else (except the person of its leader) the Chechen region differed from other Soviet regions, and why the avalanche did not bury the whole of Russia, as had been predicted, hoped, or feared by many people.

Why did the regions' sovereignty revolution not come to an end in Chechnia in late 1993? Why had the federal government felt obliged to use military force to curb the sovereignty revolution, and why did it not succeed quickly? Chechnia is perhaps the only unit of the Soviet administrative-territorial system that has not become a Soviet region, that has preserved its archaic tribal-national social system and a religious structure based on it, in spite of Soviet-type bureaucratization, modernization, and urbanization. The two stage deportation of the Chechen population demonstrated how intractable a problem the Chechens proved to be for the Soviet state (as they had been for tsarist Russia, as shown by the first Caucasian war which lasted for fifty-five years).[36] The closed nature and the cementing force of Chechen society were, however, not weakened, but rather strengthened by state terror, particularly those of the ever-revolting, mountain Chechen tribes, suffered from the relocation which have always been opposing (in these days as well) the ethnically and tribally fairly mixed, more peace-loving, in Soviet style urbanized, lowlands Chechens. For instance, during the deportation of his family to Kazakhstan, Dudaev himself, who belonged to the Yalhoroy *teyp* (national-territorial community), through the mediation of his brother, Bekmuraz Dudaev, came close to the *vird* (secret Sufi fraternity, religious community) that was considered to be the youngest, the most aggressive and socially the most radical within Kadiriyah Islam that united one of the branches of the *virds*.

Kadiriyah opposed not only the Russian state but the other great branch of the *virds*, called Naksbandiyah founded by the Caucasian

---

[36] See Mikhail Pokrovsky, "Zavayovanie Kavkaza," in M. Pokrovsky, *Diplomatiya i voyni tsarskoy Rossii* (London, 1991), pp. 179–229 and Abdurakhman Avtorkhanov, *Imperiya Kremlya* (Garmisch-Partenkirchen, 1988), pp. 143–192.

freedom fighter, Imam Shamil, and its conservative theocratic order was unacceptable to the followers of the "true road" (tariqat) propagated by the Kadiriyah. (Shamil persecuted the Kadiriyah like the Russian authorities did, because it threatened his theocracy too.)[37] Thus, in Chechnia, not the region, the new Soviet administrative-territorial formation but *teyp* and *vird*, the archaic tribal-religious units, that survived even the Soviet era, turned out to be the institutions of the post-Soviet political developments. The *teyps* and the *virds* (overlapping the *teyps*) established political parties and states (we should not forget that for a while beside Ichkeria, Dudaev's Chechen Republic, there existed a Tereki Chechen Republic headed by Umar Avturkhanov, and the two republics stood and fought against each other), and demanded sovereign status for the state organizations they occupied.

As a matter of fact, Soviet-type regionalism, represented by Doku Zavgaev, had to fall in 1991 because, in contrast with the rest of the Soviet regions, including Northern Caucasia, it involved the political and economic supremacy of his own *teyp*, the Nizhaloi national-territorial community rather than that of the regional Soviet elite. (When he was elected president, the members of that community swarmed the structures of power. In that context, being a Communist meant belonging to Doku Zavgaev's *teyp*, while being a "national-democrat" meant belonging to rival teyps.) Tribal-national as well as religious communities and clans of the same kind have existed in other Soviet regions too (for example, the Kuliabs, the Kharms, the Parims, the Hissars, the Khojens in Tajikistan, the Zhuzs in Kazakhstan), but they had either united with the regional elites or were so weak that their victory was out of question (or, for example, in the case of Tajikistan, their victory was prevented by the intervention of Russia).

As a consequence, the triumph of the sovereignization revolution, the end of the Soviet central state, resulted in the liberation and strengthening of the regions all over the post-Soviet sphere except the Chechen area where the regional unit fell, together with the Soviet central state, and was replaced by the *teyps* and the *virds*, the tribal-nation-

---

[37] See Pokrovsky, op. cit., and S. Kurginan, V. Solokhin, and M. Podkopaev, "Suverenitet i piratstvo," in *Chechenskiy krizis: ispitanie na gosudarstvennost* (Moscow, 1995), pp. 14–17.

al communities. While the "sovereignty parade" of the Soviet regions, depending on the respective regional level, gained either state sovereignty or actual autonomy, that is, could establish the minimal preconditions for a new, non-Soviet type economic integration (the new "sovereignties" did not curb, but rather accelerated the reintegration processes), the sovereignty of Dudaev's Chechen *teyp*-state, a sovereignty based on unconcealed tribal power, involved ultimate and total secession, the total impossibility of reintegration of any kind. And not just because of personal or tribal-religious group obsessions. The fact of the *teyp*-state's sovereignty served neither the realization of a newly engendered nation's self-determination, nor its integration into the community of the nations, it was rather supposed to justify the unlimited power of a tribal-religious community acting as a state. This is the deeper explanation why, in spite of Dudaev's attempts, the confrontation between the Chechen Republic and the Russian Federation has not become a new Caucasian war even after the rude and senseless military intervention of the federal authorities, that is why the "Chechen case" has been an isolated case in the Caucasus, in spite of quasi-national, freedom-fighter, sovereign, Moslem rhetorics[38] (isolated even in the Moslem world, except for the Chechen diasporas in Turkey and Jordan).[39]

---

[38] In the fall of 1994, Dudaev turned to the peoples of Dagestan with calls as follows: The Muscovite (*sic!*) has already overstepped every measure in his hatred for us. We have never needed the help of Dagestan so much, since the future of all of us depends on these days, and not only in Chechnia but especially in Dagestan. Stand up! Take your future in your hands or entrust it to those capable of heroic deeds in struggle and of peaceful labor, stand up and see that we will be stronger than ever. We have never been closer to freedom than in these days. Stand up and let all those and their offsprings be despised who are unable to give a helping hand on the battlefield when the great call sounds. Stand up, Dagestan, stand up in the name of Allah, the Compassionate, the Merciful! Amen!" (Quoted in *Kriminalniy rezhim,* p. 51.)

[39] Dudaev's appeal to the Islamic state also found no response: "The Chechen Republic is the first to declare its boundaries open and crossable, and it turns to Dagestan, Azerbaijan, Iran, Iraq, Turkey, the Central Asian countries—Kazakhstan, Uzbekistan, Tajikistan—the Arab states, Pakistan and every Muslim country and people to call upon them to follow its example" (June 1994). Quoted in *Kriminalniy rezhim,* p. 50.

Dagestan, North Ossetia and the Ingush Republic acted as normal post-Soviet regions during the sovereignization process between 1991 and 1993. They were fundamentally interested in keeping away from the storm-center of warfare, as otherwise they could not have consolidated the results of the sovereignization revolution, namely, political and economic autonomy (beyond the intricate historic network of sympathy and hate among the Caucasian ethnic groups, and beyond the differences between the cultural character of the religious-tribal communities). The meaning of the sovereignty declared by Dudaev's *teyp*-state went beyond not only post-Soviet regionalism but beyond all the possible aims of traditional and post-modern state nationalism as well. In reality, that sovereignty involved not the proclamation and gaining of national independence from Russia but the independence of a "pirate-state," which originated from the wedding of a tribal-religious community and a modern, international mafia community, independent from any kind of international law, norm, or rule, whether economic or political.

The post-modern fragmentation—from regionalism to ethnicizing nationalism and tribalizing nation states—serves the liberation from the organizations of integration which are not viable economically and obsolescent politically, and a faster and more profitable integration to real economic organizations. This kind of fragmentation helps globalization[40] (and I do not think post-Soviet regionalism would be an exception). The Chechen *teyp*-state's sovereignty is based on real tribal conditions and has served the total isolation from the world, in the interest of the free pillage of the world. Dudaev's *teyp*-state, which has liquidated the supra-*teyp* "national-democratic" Chechen intelligentsia, which has lacked even the external attributes of democratic legitimacy, which has steadily kept the population under oppression, has been able to survive only as a "pirate-state" in the post-Soviet configuration from the very beginning, that is, it has been sustained by the increasingly international Russian mafia, interwoven with the political-economic clans in Russia and not by the *teyps* and the Islamic world.

---

[40] See Ákos Szilágyi, "Virágozzék ezer nemzetállam!" *Politikatudományi Szemle*, no. 2 (1995), 102–110.

The "Chechen mafia" is no more than a part (though not insignificant) of the mafia world covering the whole post-Soviet configuration.[41] The sovereignty of Dudaev's Chechen state was different from the sovereignty of the Soviet regions not only in that it stretched the revolution of sovereignty as far as total separatism on a tribal-national basis, but also in the fact that the Chechen *teyp*-state, which refers to Islam, actually embodied the sovereignty of a "pirate-state" of the Russian mafia, of bandocracy, that is, a shadow economy, a black market economy, and an underworld interwoven with the state-government bureaucracy and with the organizations of force.

If the federal power was unable to break that sovereignty for nearly two years, it is not only because the federal authorities have been making mistakes after mistakes, not only because the brutal military intervention has turned almost the whole of the Chechen people against federal power and made the previously isolated and unpopular Dudaev a national freedom hero, and not only because the Chechens are famous as good soldiers,[42] because they are fanaticized

----

[41] During the three years of sovereignty, Chechnia became the center of banditry, of forgery, of drug-trafficking, gun-running, and smuggling. For example, 90% of the forged money in circulation in Russia was produced in Chechnia; 42% of the frauds and defaults in the Russian sphere of banking (900 billion rubles) in the first half of 1994 were committed by Chechen citizens; 1,700 freight cars were looted in the Grozny area every month, 120 unregistered airplanes took off with contraband merchandise. In 1992 the republic produced and sold 450, 000 tons of petroleum products without a single dollar of revenue for the Chechen National Bank. According to other data, in 1991 and 1992, the country exported petroleum products to the value of 25 billion dollars, while it is not known where that sum went, or who shared in it. See the details in *Chechenskiy krizis*, pp. 12–13, 33–36; and *Kriminalniy rezhim*, pp. 21–24.

[42] During the fifty-five-year long Caucasian war, Shamil's 20,000-strong insurgent army carried on the struggle against the Russian army of 200,000 soldiers (in the last years of the war, the number increased to 280,000, whereas the Russian army deployed against Napoleon numbered only 240,000). The situation today may be even worse than 150 years ago. By 1996 the federal military contingent stationed in Chechnia has reached 42,000. The strength of the Chechen army with the foreign mercenaries is 11,500. One may add the portion of the civil population that the Chechen fighters can mobilize as militia, or about ten persons per fighter. *Kommersant*, no. 9, March 19, 1996.

by Islam and harbor long-standing hatred for Russians, but mainly because the federal power must break the enormous Russian mafia interwoven with the post-Soviet political and economic elites, if it wants to drive back Chechen sovereignty to the level of the autonomy of the post-Soviet regions. In Chechnia, the federal army fights neither against Dudaev, nor against the Chechens, or the Islamic expansion but against the Russian mafia—that is, against itself, at least partly—which renders the sufferings the war has poured on the peaceful civil population even more outrageous. A worse terrain and means to fight against the only real danger threatening Russia could hardly have been found. (This has occasionally given rise to a suspicion that there are conflicts of interest between the Russian mafia clans.)

The federal government could have stepped in politically against the sovereignty of the Chechen "pirate-state" by questioning its democratic legitimacy, and by initiating, together with international organizations, a referendum and democratic elections;[43] the military or police intervention against this sovereignty of a very special nature would have been useful only if the federal government had previously managed to break the influence and power of the Russian mafia on the federal level. The power of the Russian mafia, which played an active role in the regional revolution and created a "pirate-state" of its own in the Chechen *teyp*-state, should have been eliminated in the new Russian state itself so that the Chechen "pirate-state" could be liquidated afterwards. In fact, it is not the "Chechen nut" but the "nut of the Mafia" that has proved to be too hard to crack for the Russian state. In spite of the state rhetoric, it was not the territorial unity and integrity of the Russian Federation that was at risk, but the political and economic unity and integrity of the state of Russia as a precondition of the post-Soviet configuration's economic reintegration. And this unity and integrity are not threatened by anything but the Russian

---

43 See Aleksandr Yanov, "Chechenskiy ekzamen," in *Posle Yeltsina* (Moscow, 1995), p. 90: "Free elections in Chechnia! That could have been and should have been the slogan of liberal Russia well before the start of the crisis of December 7, 1993, but that democratic way of escape, instead of the aggressive solution, did not even cross their mind."

mafia. Neither the expansion of NATO nor the separatism of the ethnic regions mean as great a danger to the sovereignty of the Russian Federation as the Russian Mafia that plays an increasingly important role in the political-economic system of clan capitalism and in the new class of bandocracy.[44]

---

[44] This conclusion, which may have seemed exaggerated some years ago, is already backed by the frightening diagnoses produced by the intelligence of the American and the Russian governments. In the first days of May 1996, the director of the CIA claimed during a congressional hearing: "the CIA believes that the mafias play a significant role in the shaping of Russian internal and foreign policies. It may distress the foreign governments supporting Yeltsin, but that is the truth, and national security interests compel the USA to take that factor into account." (*Népszabadság*, May 3, 1996, p. 20.) The Russian weekly *Kommersant* reported that: "Some analysts believe Chechnia herself has a subordinated position in the 'system,' the nerve centers being located in Moscow and Istanbul." In "Zveno v prestupnoy tsepi," *Kommersant*, no 19 (1996), p. 11.

János Mátyás Kovács

IMAGES OF SOVEREIGNTY
Austria's Changing Identity

> Austria-Hungary is no longer. I do not care to live else-
> where. Emigration is out of the question. I live
> with a torso and convince myself that it is perfection
> itself.
>
> *Sigmund Freud*

Lately, my letters from far-off United States are again addressed "Vienna, Australia." This was not always so. For a while, in the midst of the Kurt Waldheim scandal between 1986 and 1992, my overseas acquaintances were able to distinguish temporarily between the home of tame Alpine cattle and that of the wild kangaroos. This sudden geographical enlightenment was due exclusively to the forgetful president of the Austrian Republic who, when nominated for the post of United Nations Secretary General in the seventies, neglected to mention in his curriculum vitae the fact that he had been a Wehrmacht intelligence officer in the Balkans during World War II and a witness, if nothing else, to highly suspicious events. In 1986, however, Austria stubbornly went on to elect Waldheim president, who was then boycotted for years by the West.

But let us forget this sensational scandal and return to Austria's dull—"Australian"—everyday life. I would not go as far as to say that First Lieutenant Waldheim's reluctant withdrawal—without offering apologies or a formal resignation—evoked a cathartic change in Austrian mind[1] and started an "everyday era" of Austrian history.

---

[1] See W. Johnston, *The Austrian Mind* (Berkeley, 1972); P. Bettelheim and R. Harauer, eds., *Ostcharme mit Westkomfort: Beiträge zur politischen Kultur in Österreich* (Vienna, 1994); G. Botz and G. Sprengnagel, eds., *Kontroversen um Österreichs Zeitgeschichte* (Frankfurt, 1994); and E. Bruckmüller, *Öster-reichbewusstsein im Wandel: Identität und Identität und Selbstverständnis in*

What actually happened was that the president's affair coincided with the beginnings of the reinterpretation of Austrian collective identity (if there is such a thing). It accelerated the self-examination whioh had long been urged by the "other Austria"[2] which wished to break through the collective amnesia while attempting to bring a touch of reality to Austria's delusory history and adjust the remainder of the Austrian Miracle to Central European slouching. The evolving self-image of Austrians may be somewhat blurred today, still, it is far less deceptive than it was only a decade ago. We might even call this new-fangled, somewhat uncertain soberity a normalization of Austrian identity.

Why do I speak of self-identity if it was the Austrian variant of state sovereignty I was asked to discuss? The reason is simple: Austria's postwar history of forty years is a perfect example of showing how the individually weak, but collectively strong pillars of

---

den 90er Jahren, Schriftenreihe des Zentrums für angewandte Politikforschung (Vienna, 1994), vol. 4. On the Waldheim case, see the studies by Gerhard Botz, Robert Knight, Félix Kreissler, Siegfried Mattl, and Wolfgang Neugebauer in Botz and Sprengnage, eds., op. cit.; and also the chapters by Breuss, Liebhart, and Pribersky in S. Breuss, K. Liebhart, and A. Pribersky, *Inszenierungen* (Vienna, 1995); R. Menasse, *Das Land ohne Eigenschaften, Essay zur österreichischen Identität* (Vienna, 1992); A. Pelinka, *Zur österreichischen Identität: Zwischen deutscher Vereinigung und Mitteleuropa* (Vienna, 1990); R. Sieder, H. Steinert, and E. Tálos, eds., *Österreich: 1945–1995: Gesellschaft, Politik, Kultur* (Vienna, 1990); R. Wodak et al., *"Wir sind alle unschuldige Täter"*: *diskurshistorische Studien zum Nachkriegsantisemitismus* (Frankfurt, 1990); Kurt Waldheim, *Die Antwort* (Vienna, 1996).

2 "Other Austria" is a generic term used to describe the intellectual kinship of the one-time Austrian resistance movement, the anti-nuclear and ecological movements of the seventies, and the current groups of republican (leftist-liberal, alternative, critical) intellectuals, see Breuss, et al., op. cit. See also J. Haslinger, *Politik der Gefühle: Ein Essay über Österreich* (Darmstadt, 1987); R. Menasse, *Die sozialpartnerschaftliche fsthetik* (Vienna, 1991); Menasse, *Das Land ohne Eigenschaften*; R. Menasse, *Histerien und andere historische Irrtümer* (Vienna, 1996); W. Müller-Funk, "Das Land des Lächelns," in *Der Intellektuelle als Souverän* (Vienna, 1995); G. Nenning, "Neutralität und Realität: Eine unnötige Unterscheidung," in H. Krejci, E. Reiter, and H. Schneider, eds., *Neutralität—Mythos und Wirklichkeit* (Vienna, 1992).

national identity prop up the precarious sovereignty of a small country and how the erosion of some of these pillars would render it shaky again. I would like to discuss the imaginary, yet real pillars of state sovereignty, a kind of "virtual sovereignty" which successfully displaced (or complemented) the sovereignty created and protected by material authority—as long as it could. I shall speak mostly about neutrality since it carried the greatest weight among the pillars of national identity. I should like to show how the idea of neutrality conceived by Realpolitik rose to mythical heights, why it lost most of its meaning with dizzying swiftness, and how today's Austrian politics tries to part with it as quietly as possible.

* * *

I am going to tell a story, a personal rather than a disciplined one. I am not an international lawyer, or a political scientist, nor a historian working on Austria. I also admit that other than the personal socialist experience of "limited sovereignty," I did not have much to do with the legal mysteries of state independence. Sociology will often provide the keynote in the story and, though I am an economist, I shall rarely mention the economic aspects of sovereignty. I have only one reason for joining this circle of experts and a very prosaic one at that: for almost ten years now I have been commuting between Vienna and Budapest, I read the newspapers and attend conferences in both countries. The radical (yet quiet) revision of the Austrian concept of sovereignty conceived in the fifties has been taking place right before my eyes. Possibly, I am not so close to Vienna that I would not see the forest for the tree, nor so far from Budapest that I would not guess what in Austria's history of sovereignty may be of interest to the Hungarian reader. And since this history does not lack irony, at times even the grotesque, please excuse some occasional teasing remarks. Teasing—why deny it—frequently conceals jealous acknowledgment.

Being Innocent after Divorce

> Austro-fascism and national socialism were wed
> in an ideological marriage; we may concede Austria was not a
> virgin raped, yet forced she was (and how) and only
> then did she give herself.
> *Félix Kreissler*

Bella gerant alii, tu felix Austria nube...—the image of a lucky (happy?) empire which expands and prospers cunningly by way of marriages rather than war is not merely a memory of a bygone era. It continued to constitute an important element of Austrian national identity even after 1955, when the Austrian State Treaty restored, so to speak, the independence and territorial integrity of the Second Republic. Undoubtedly, in the fifties, Austria was in dire need of a little happiness in order to recover from the adversities of the twentieth century. Defeat in World War I and the collapse of the Habsburg empire, the Austro-fascist degeneration of the First Republic, the fatal polarization of political classes and the *Anschluss*, degradation of Austria into *Ostmark* then complete absorption into the Third Reich and, finally, another defeat in World War II all played parts in the near erasure of the country from the map as a sovereign state. For ten years after 1945, it awaited the decision on its fate (would the Allied occupation forces and the four military zones remain, would there be a German style division of the country, or would it be swallowed by the Soviet Union—as were its Eastern neighbors), until, allegedly, it regained sovereignty as well as its national self-respect. This time it did not have to marry but it took all the more effort to keep from entering a bad marriage or, more exactly, to survive a divorce case.[3]

---

[3] See Botz and Sprengnagel, eds., op. cit.; P. Dusek, A. Pelinka, and E. Weinzierl, *Zeitgeschichte im Aufriss: Österreich seit 1918* (Vienna, 1988); W. Mantl, ed., *Politik in Österreich: Die Zweite Republik: Bestand und Wandel* (Vienna, 1992); A. Pelinka and E. Weinzierl, eds., *Das grosse Tabu: Österreichs Umgang mit seiner Vergan-genheit* (Vienna, 1987); H. Portisch, *Österreich I*, vols. 1–2 (Munich, 1994); H. Portisch and R. Riff, *Österreich II*, vols. 1–4 (Munich, 1995); Austria. Bundeskanzleramt, *Rot-weiss-rot-Buch, Gerechtigkeit*

During the Cold War the Allied parents went their separate ways and sought long for a solution to the complicated issue, namely, that if one could not have custody of the child then neither should the other. Meanwhile, the child could feel like anything but grown-up. Since 1918 there was plenty of time to get used to being humiliated. Having shrivelled from a monarchy into a republic ("a state no one wanted") it was under the control of the League of Nations for a long time and matured under harsh conditions, surrounded by the Little Entente, Italy, and Germany, only to become one of the states of the Third Reich after the *Anschluss*.[4] Up to 1944 Winston Churchill wanted to wed Austria to Bavaria and establish a South German confederation (or a Central and Southeast European or Danubian confederation including also non-Germanic peoples). The Soviets, who previously spoke about the restoration of an independent Austria, occupied (liberated) most of the country in 1945 and established themselves in the eastern provinces. In fact, in 1950 they had the daring, though not the power, to impose a delayed "popular-democratic" turn. Earlier Austria already had to relinquish South Tirol to Italy; after World War I it successfully opposed Slovenian territorial claims, but after World War II Tito's army reached as far as Klagenfurt, and again there was talk of dividing the Burgenland between Yugoslavia and Czechoslovakia. Clemenceau's ghost haunted the Alps, who had said when the Monarchy disintegrated: *"Autriche—c'est le reste."*

---

für Österreich! (Vienna, 1946); G. Stourzh, *Geschichte des österreichischen Staatsvertrages: 1945–1955* (Vienna, 1985); G. Stourzh, *Vom Reich zur Republik: Studien zum Österreichbewusssein im 20. Jahrhundert* (Vienna, 1990); E. Weinzierl and K. Skalnik, eds., *Das neue Österreich: Geschichte der Zweiten Republik* (Graz, 1975); E. Weinzierl and K. Skalnik, eds., *Österreich: 1918–1938: Geschichte der Ersten Republik* (Graz, 1983).

[4] After occupation by or union with Germany the country became the *Ostmark*, a name reminiscent of the Middle Ages. Later it was renamed the Alpine and Danubian Reich Provinces. At this time, in order to resolve the contradictory situation of "Eastern Reich" within the Third Reich and to obliterate the last linguistic memorial to independent statehood, the denominations, Ober- and Niederösterreich (Upper and Lower Austria), were also erased. Thenceforth these provinces could only be called Ober- and Niederdonau Gau.

"Truncated Austria is not a country," the Austrian irredentists would have proclaimed between the wars had they been familiar with the Hungarian slogan; anyway they, too, sought Nazi Germany's patronage—and we know with what results.

But do we really know? I doubt it. Speaking for myself, it never occurred to me to try and find out why a "state treaty" instead of a peace treaty was signed with Austria after 1945. Lawyers, however, know that the country simply did not exist from the point of view of international law, it had to be defined as a state. By others—for the lack of anything better. Decency demanded a return to democracy. Again: led and supervised by others, for the lack of anything better. However noble the goal (the majority of Austrians were probably not convinced of it at the time), a paternalistic situation like this does not usually help a country's self-respect.

Not so in Austria. Paradoxically, at first it was mostly in the Austrians' interest to contest their own statehood in order to avoid being named a defeated and guilty country, thus, liable to pay reparations. They again made use of Hans Kelsen's idea that had worked so well in legal disputes after the collapse of the Monarchy. The first postwar Austrian governments declared: we did not start the war, how could we, when we were not yet a state—or no longer a state. Germany is responsible for everything that happened after March 1938, not Austria, only a few Austrians committed war crimes, whom we will punish, but until then give the country generous support. If Germany is the sole culprit, then all German and Germanized assets in Austria belong to the liberators, the Soviets said and the other Allies gave a nod of assent. This meant that the Soviet Union, which could not interpret the concept of German assets broadly enough, became seriously interested financially in postponing military withdrawal. For ten years German assets were the pretext for putting off withdrawal, and afterwards the Soviet Union exacted exorbitant reparations from enterprises it had stripped bare in the meantime. Perhaps Kelsen's idea was not so good after all.

In addition, whenever the opportunity arose, the Soviets raked up the old accusation of Austria being an accessory to crime. The Allied Powers failed to define clearly Austria's position in spite of the fact that in 1943 they had decided at their Moscow meeting that Austria was Hitler's first victim,[5] not his henchman, and as a subjugated country it did not enter the war of its own will. Under Soviet pressure a passage about the joint responsibility of Austrians was also included in the Moscow Declaration, which formed the basis of all subsequent negotiations. Under these conditions, Austria could hardly be a victor or, at least, an innocent victim, yet definitely worthy of independence. More exactly, it could be made independent. It was already known who would guarantee this independence, but not who it was to be independent from. Certainly from Germany, no matter how many Germanies there were. The victorious powers were united in not wanting to see Germany and Austria under the same roof. Everything else was determined by given geopolitical positions. Anything could postpone the final settlement: from the Sovietization of Eastern Europe, through the Trieste tug-of-war and the Korean war, to the German question. True, these "anythings" were weighty problems, but—trusting in the strategic importance of the Alps— Austria, too, could consider itself a weighty issue.

Austria's defenselessness was enhanced by the fact that, though innocently this time, its fate again became linked with Germany's. Every settlement proposal, whoever made it, was weighed from the point of view of the precedent it would create for German reunification or partitioning. This was especially true of the question of neutrality. I am talking about the neutrality that became the cornerstone of Austrian identity, the celebrated associate concept of sovereignty, virtually a state philosophy from 1955 onward. Too bad that the idea did not come from the heart. Too bad, because Austria had to pay for sovereignty partly with neutrality, however profitable the latter eventually proved to be.

---

[5] The Austro-fascist opposition to Nazism (the oppression of the nazi *Putsch* in 1934, the distance Dollfuss and Mussolini kept from Hitler, Schuschnigg's attempts to postpone the *Anschluss*, etc.) hardly explain the decision. The Allies did not wish to face a Greater Germany again after the war. In the meantime they would have liked to urge Austrians to turn against the "subjugators."

Neutralized But Free?

> We, Austrians want to be neutral primarily in terms
> of ourselves. Neutrality is a wonderful way to sneak
> out of our own history.
>
> *Armin Thurnher*

Legend has it that Austria had longed for neutrality for decades and could hardly wait after its occupation to give voice to this desire. It reasoned and wheedled to make the reluctant Allies see this as the most advantageous solution. The whole world conspired against it (accordingly, the main sin of the Cold War was probably that it prevented the settlement of the Austrian question), but the country took the matter into its own hands and proclaimed neutrality. I know I am exaggerating. Let me say by way of excuse that I have just finished struggling my way through a large part of the almost endless literature written on this myth.[6]

The idea of neutrality did appear once in a while in Austrian political discourse after both world wars, though much less articulately and more ambiguously than later. Actually, the original version (Kelsen's, of course), also known as quasi-neutrality, calls only for the mere fact (but not necessarily a declaration of the fact) that the country does not join non-neutral countries, does not start a war and, if there is a war, will elect to stay out.[7] The memory of the *Anschluss* induced the leaders of the Second Republic to note wisely that "it

---

[6] See the most frequently mentioned and most objective comprehensive legal works of Manfred Rotter, *Bewaffnete Neutralität. Das Beispiel Österreich* (Frankfurt, 1985); M. Schweitzer, *Dauernde Neutralität und europäische Integration* (Vienna, 1997); Verdross, *Die immerwährende Neutralität Österreichs* (Vienna, 1977); also Verosta's, Ermacora's, and Zemanek's. Schlesinger's book is a good example of a foreign critical analysis of the subject. T. Schlesinger, *Austrian Neutrality in Postwar Europe* (Vienna, 1972).

[7] On the concept of quasi-neutrality, see F. Ermacora, *20 Jahre österreichische Neutralität* (Frankfurt, 1975); Manfred Rotter, *Die dauernde Neutralität* (Berlin, 1981); Verosta, *Die dauernde Neutralität: Ein Grundriss* (Vienna, 1967). World War I peace treaties neutralized Austria to prevent its union with Germany. In the twenties and thirties Austria was accountable for its neutrality to the League of Nations in order to be eligible for vitally important loans.

would have been better to stay out of the whole thing" and "the West was in no rush to intervene." At first, a number of Social Democrats—brooding over the skirmishes between the *Schutzbund* and the *Heimwehr* in the thirties—were averse even to the idea of a new Austrian army. Young and old (the old most certainly) wanted to join the West, but the political elite were afraid that combative support of this desire would be tantamount to declaring the country divided, and quite likely part of the country would then be caught in the Soviet sphere of influence. They thought that it would be best to keep a friendly distance from the Soviet Union; this, however, would require the simultaneous withdrawal of the Western powers; but if the West leaves, who will be there to protect Austria should the Soviet Union change its mind? Consequently, Austrian statesmen thought twice before they mentioned the word neutrality. Little was said about the Swiss example, so frequently cited later. Actually, the occupying powers were also hesitant when they were not improvising.

Initially, the Soviet Union was afraid that if it gave up Austria, it would encourage the neighboring countries to follow suit. Concurrently, by way of explaining the presence of Soviet troops in Hungary and Romania, the Soviet Union argued that these ensured the supply lines for the army stationed beyond the Leitha River. At the same time, the United States and its allies worried that Austria's neutrality would break the strategic line which extended from Italy to Norway (greatly worrying the Soviet Union), and which was to become the NATO chain of countries. They did not relish the idea of supporting the establishment of a peaceful Danubian confederation either, nor did the Soviet Union, for different reasons, as it may have lead to handing over the country to the enemy. Although the neutralization and demilitarization of Austria seemed a logical solution to the stalemate, it might have tempted Germany, not to mention the Central and East European states, to request similar treatment. They might have rightly asked if they could also be granted neutral status. The strategic vacuum that demilitarization might have created also alarmed the generals on both sides. What if the enemy fills the vacuum first?

For this reason, prolonging the zone system seemed a tolerable compromise until a few important decisions were reached in the region (communist takeovers in Eastern and Central Europe, the establishement of the Federal Republic of Germany (FRG), the German Democratic Republic (GDR), and NATO, NATO membership of the FRG, etc.), in other words, until the new division of Europe was accomplished. Austria had to wait patiently for the first wave of a reduction in the international tension after Stalin's death. And also for the Soviets to be finally willing to relinquish the German enterprises they had confiscated. Meanwhile, Austria may have thought that the two blocs would celebrate the end to the ten-year-long wrangle with its help, but in honesty it had to admit that slowly but surely its sovereignty was rationed out. The Western states were faster, the Russians slower to portion out freedom.

The Allied Council interfered in high state affairs of the Second Republic with less and less frequency. Legislation of constitutional laws required the preliminary consent of the Council and it had the right of veto, as far as the lower level legislation was concerned, within a one month period. Austria proved a diligent pupil in restoring capitalism, which explains the increasing inactivity of the Western members of the Council. They frowned only when the other ally, the Soviet Union, attempted to discipline their pupil. In the evolving Cold War they were becoming increasingly involved with one another, and the cunning pupil began to fish in troubled waters. Let a brief list suffice here of the abundant "occupation school" regulations which Austria sought to abandon later on. In 1950 the Austrian government asked for the following modifications: to cease charging the expenses of the occupation to the country; to return a number of seized houses and apartments; to end military justice, not to arrest Austrians, and to allow Austrian police to arrest members of the occupying forces if they violate Austrian law; to restore to Austria the right to issue visas; to allow local forces to supervise the zones if occupation troops remain; to end censorship of the press and postal services (as well as school textbooks), confiscation of books, banning theatre productions, interference in radio programming; to cease free hunting and fishing by allied officers, to void the requirement of way-bills in domestic transportation, and permits for erecting pylons, for maintenance work on roads; to reinvest the president of the republic with the right to grant amnesty, to lift the obligation on Austrian authorities to answer every question raised by the occupation forces. All this took place in the fifth year of democracy. Another three years had to pass before these requests were examined. Not in the least because of the cooling of atmosphere among the "school staff" between 1949 and 1953.

Solving the Austrian question was not a pressing issue, especially not for the Soviets, although in the spring of 1949 it seemed the Austrian State Treaty was about to be signed. Tito had broken relations with Moscow, alleviating the fear that the territorial claims of Yugoslavia would torpedo the treaty. By the end of 1947, the Soviets agreed to the redemption of confiscated German assets by cash payments and in kind. Austrian leaders would have agreed to the establishment of a "Soviet economic enclave"[8] after the departure of the Red Army, but the Western allies warned that on the pretext of protecting its property the owner might return at any time—armed. At this time no one, except Austria, mentioned that the country might eventually have its own army. There was also complete silence on the question of neutrality.

Meanwhile, President Harry Truman proclaimed the policy of "containment" and Secretary of State George C. Marshall his recovery program; neither was independent of the Greek civil war and the communist grip on Eastern and Central Europe. Unafraid, Austria accepted assistance under the Marshall Plan and the Soviet Union paid almost no attention. The Christian and Social Democrats (ÖVP and SDÖ) joined forces and expelled communists from the government and the political police. Still the Soviets said nothing. Although in 1948 they did attempt to set up a blockade similar to the one in Berlin, they gave up after two days. The Austrian government acted in increasingly open complicity with the Western powers and became alarmed only when, with the establishment of NATO in 1949, United States policy stiffened; the Pentagon overshadowed the State

---

[8] This would have included primarily industrial and commercial enterprises, including the oil fields in Lower Austria, appropriated by the Administration of Soviet Property in Austria (USIA). These enterprises operated within a plan system serving mainly indemnification purposes and also the strengthening of the influence of the Austrian communists. Portisch and Riff, op. cit.

Department and American generals began to speak about extending the occupation at a time when the Austrian State Treaty seemed already in sight.

The German knot was impossible to untie, but the Austrian held promise in the view of the negotiations in the spring of 1949. The great powers were adding finishing touches to the 1947 agreements and then parted in the knowledge that they would be celebrating in the fall. Neutrality was still not mentioned. Yet again, a few things intervened: the Soviet atomic bomb, communist victory in China, the break between the GDR and the FRG and, of course, the Trieste crisis. Austria was not invited to join the NATO, but was expected to hold out for a few days if attacked from the East. Then came the Korean war and the sad lesson was learned: wherever the Western powers move out, the East moves in. Thus, Moscow's willingness to withdraw became immediately suspect. Military strategists began to show appreciation for Austria. In the words of an American general: it took half an hour to fly from Munich to Milan, now—if we leave Austria—it will take two hours because of the need to bypass Switzerland and fly over France. Soviet command knew that it had more things to lose if the Pentagon won and the Americans stayed in Austria. True, the Red Army could also stay in the Danube region, but the mountains, the fearsome Alpenfestung, as they learned in World War II would belong to the enemy.

The Soviet threat was very real at that time. In the fall of 1950 the Austrian Communist Party, in a last effort, attempted a takeover, taking advantage of the popular dissatisfaction with the economic stabilization program. An interference by any of the occupying powers would have—it is better not to even think about it. The government, however, remained firm and the Social Democratic unions proved stronger than the communist activists. Needless to say, this capacity for democracy did not enhance the Soviet's trust in Austria. The Soviet Union must have known that if the country were divided, it would not be able to pacify the Soviet zone. The Western powers were not so hopeful. They decided to stay until the country became economically stable and a sort of army (*B-Gendarmerie*) was established in their zones. In all seriousness, they were getting ready to evacuate the government and the male population of military age to

Italy.[9] They did not really seek consensus with the enemy, only probed its flexibility in a brief agreement in 1952 (timed provocatively to coincide with the anniversary of the *Anschluss*). With sham naivety they proposed to withdraw, to guarantee the 1937 boundaries, to return all German assets to Austria, and to prohibit only political flirtation with Germany.

The Soviet Union reacted angrily: citing Austria's quiet rearmament (not without reason), the conciliatory treatment of Nazis (also with some justification),[10] the Trieste question, etc., they became obdurate. This lasted until the Russian troika assumed power after Stalin's death and the Austrians gathered enough courage (and permission) to take the initiative. In the summer of 1953, following innumerable negotiations and signing of all sorts of partial agreements, events accelerated (with Nehru's mediation). Austria tentatively mentioned that it would not join NATO after the Soviet Union withdrew its forces but form a neutral zone with Switzerland. But what are the guarantees, politicians asked in Moscow and Washington. All the same, both sides felt that there was something to the idea. The great unknown was hidden in the precise meaning of neutrality. Diplomats demanded that their legal advisors help them define the concept so that it would satisfy everyone, but their side would profit from it. Or, at least, lose little by it. Solving this puzzle took another two years.

The Soviet Union stated that the necessary precondition for withdrawal was that Austria would not join either of the blocs and that final withdrawal would take place only after the peace treaty with Germany was signed. Initially, the West rejected both proposals (but Austria resented only the second) then, after long deliberation,

---

[9] The recent discovery of illegal arsenals in various parts of the country caused a scandal. When the Western Allies withdrew from Austria, they left these behind just in case.

[10] True enough, after long deliberation of the question, the Western powers, as well as the Soviet Union decided not to object to the participation of the VdU (Union of Independents) in the 1949 elections and their use of pan-German propaganda for winning over pro-Nazi Austrians who were given back their right to vote. The Social Democrats, prudently, also supported the new party hoping it would steal votes from the Christian Democrats. See Portisch and Riff, op. cit.

accepted the first if the Soviets gave up the second. Even so, the Americans found it hard to reconcile themselves to the idea of neutrality and dissuaded Austria from playing with this inflammatory word. They advised that Austria should not promise more than that it would not enter any military alliance and would not like to see alien troops on its territory because they, the Americans, would not want to keep arguing with the Soviets about what the United States or Austria did to violate that neutrality. Austria should also insist that the Austrian State Treaty did not extend to demilitarization. If it becomes absolutely necessary to declare neutrality, then Austria should do it as a state made sovereign by the Austrian State Treaty. The United States will not give guarantees, only secure Austria's borders which can be defined, at least.

The Soviet Union continued to demand various things (for instance, that Austria should not join the United Nations or any Western coalition), did a bit of blackmailing in calculating the price of the indemnification of German assets, but it was obvious that the most important issue for them was to link the German settlement with the Austrian (or, vice-versa), with the notion that they might be able to exact concessions from the Western powers. This created another deadlock, and the temporarily stationed troops stayed. The Americans augmented NATO with West Germany and the Soviets were toying with the idea of the Warsaw Pact. Khrushchev ousted Malenkov from power and suddenly said to Austria: forget yesterday, from now on the Soviet Union is ready to talk about the Austrian State Treaty independently of the German question. It was the time of the famous Moscow Meeting (Viennese politicians were strongly requested to appear in Moscow in the spring of 1955) which was to become the leitmotif of the foundation myth of the new Austrian state.

"We brought our liberty from Moscow." "Our dream of ten, seventeen, thirty-seven years has come true" (depending on where one begins to count). "We were hard as steel or bending like reed in sending 'negotiating' the Russians out of the Alps. What the West was unable to achieve, we accomplished (paid for)," said Austrian statesmen, like Julius Raab, Leopold Figl, Adolf Schärf, and state secretary of foreign affairs Bruno Kreisky, congratulating themselves. Among themselves they joked: "Finally, we have liberated ourselves from our liberators." The Americans were quick to note the Soviet Union's hasty concessions at the bilateral negotiations. Moscow even offered Austria the opportunity to buy back the oil fields and the Danube Shipping Line which the Soviet Union had always considered strategically important, in return for a declaration of Swiss-type neutrality.[11] It was not neutrality in the ideological sense of the word, that is, the Soviet Union did not question Austria's Western orientation, and even ceased obstructing its admission into the United Nations. Lastly, just before signing the Austrian State Treaty, it consented to striking the, as it were, humiliating passage on joint responsibility for Nazism, and did not even set a ceiling on Austrian military strength.[12]

Why the rush? the West asked suspiciously. They did not abandon their Austrian friends even in Moscow (they were present during the bilateral negotiations, and they, too, consented to the clause on neutrality), so there was no danger of a secret clause being added. The West relaxed only when it became apparent that whatever ulterior motives the Soviet Union had (Khrushchev's opening toward peaceful coexistence, attempts to lure West Germany before its rearmament, to make money quickly, etc.), they were not very dangerous. West Germany was securely within the NATO, Trieste in Italian hands, and the Eastern bloc was crumbling since the Berlin uprising. After all, another buffer state beside Switzerland and Yugoslavia, would serve our own protection, the western powers thought. Perhaps the Soviet Union would also relax once the Warsaw Pact legitimized its presence in Central and Eastern Europe.

And for the first time in history, the Soviet Union showed real trust. They agreed to leave out the declaration of neutrality from the Austrian State Treaty, withdrew their troops within a few months, and gave the Austrian government the opportunity to make the pledge of

---

[11] Although, at the end of the war Austria rapidly nationalized German and Germanized enterprises to avoid their legal acquisition by the Russians (and thus invented the concept of anti-Soviet nationalization), in the end it could, at best, pay compensation for its own possessions.

[12] Everyone was happy, except Adenauer, who fiercely protested nationalization and compensation for German assets. Dismissal of joint responsibility for Naziism did not improve Austria's image in German minds.

neutrality in full possession of liberty, after the euphoria of independence had subsided. These few sentences, which were refined in the months between May and October 1955 became part of the Constitution[13] and, more important, interpretative comments were also formulated by the government during this period. There was a need for the attributes of neutrality to be defined with utmost care, because "only" the following were settled during negotiations with the former Allied Powers: Austria shall not enter any military alliance in the future; shall not permit establishment of foreign bases on its territory; shall defend its neutrality by every means. Instead of the simple attributive "permanent" interpretation of the Constitution confirms the "perpetual" (*immerwährend*) nature of Austrian neutrality. It also confirms that this neutrality is (a) voluntary, not imposed, that is, Austria was not neutralized; (b) armed (*bewaffnet*) even if only for the purpose of self-defense, that is, the country was not demilitarized; (c) not ideological, but expressly military in meaning, that is, there is no economic, political, and cultural neutrality (or keeping equal distance from the blocs) and the state declaration of neutrality does not restrict the individual in exercising human and civil rights; (d) even in peacetime, neutrality presupposes active, constructive, war-avoiding behavior, that is, in colloquial terms, "we'll behave, just leave us alone."

This was when the legal dogmatic dispute and foreign policy maneuvering (or, somewhat maliciously, shuttlecock policy) began on the part of Austria. Pacifying gestures, omniscient explanations, let Austria decide what was and what was not covered by the concept of neutrality. Meanwhile, the apologetic Austrian position would become crystallized at the same time as practice softened to the

---

[13] In the words of the Constitution: "(1) For the purpose of the permanent maintenance of her external independence and for the purpose of the inviolability of her territory, Austria of her own free will declares herewith her permanent neutrality which she is resolved to maintain and defend with all means at her disposal. (2) In order to secure these purposes Austria never in the future accede to any military alliance nor permit the establishment of military bases of foreign states on her territory." (Federal Constitutional Law of 26 October 1955 on the Neutrality of Austria, *Symbol* 59/f, Article 1.)

Soviet Union's disadvantage. A survey of the events of the four decades after the Austrian State Treaty was ratified shows the following balance in "neutrality affairs": Austria gained admission to the United Nations, EFTA, the Council of Europe, it reached an agreement with the Common Market and, after many years, after the EEC became the European Union it became a member; in contrast, the Soviet Union has only one thing to be proud of (if we consider formal institutions), namely, that Austria joined the Danube Commission at the end of the fifties, and there were two lasting "refusals": Austria did not join the institutions of European integration until 1995; it is still kept out of/keeps away from NATO, and; at most, flirts with the idea of Partnership for Peace.[14] It is a fact that Austrian neutrality was very profitable for its Eastern "liberator" (from diplomatic mediations, through the tolerance of international espionage and evasion of technological transfer prohibitions, to the undisturbed arrangement of intervention in 1956 and 1968), yet it was unable to enlist Austria among the non-aligned states. Austria was an observer, since anti-imperialism held no attractions for her, nor did it want to be identified with the Third World.

Austria acted friendly with everyone, knowing that the Soviets and the West alike were watching Argus-eyed, and if it did not want to "die of neutrality"[15] it had to find loopholes and the means of self-justification that would satisfy both sides. Deep down, the Soviet Union was afraid of NATO expansion in Austria and accused the successive Austrian governments of a "cold *Anschluss*." The United States, on its part, suspected Austria of being too keen on its role as an "active neutral nation," overdoing it, almost sounding like a member of the "peace camp." But let us not rush ahead.

---

[14] The South Tirol question, Austria's most complicated neighbor squabble to-date, is hard to classify in this respect, since Austria's sovereignty (more exactly, the sovereignty of Austrians living across the border) is restricted by Italy, a NATO member state. It even blocked Austria's overtures to the Common Market in the sixties.

[15] The description was used by the Social Democratic Vice Chancellor Bruno Pittermann in the fifties. The exact term was "starve to death."

Precarious Sovereignty

> State form: democracy. Austria has a government nurtured
> by the people and a people tortured by the government. In
> addition, Austria is forever neutral and 'forever' in Austria
> means as long as it is allowed.
> *Peter Orthofer*

What was the price of new state sovereignty aside from pledging neutrality? The declaration of perpetual neutrality, when dictated, is not a glorifying act for a sovereign state even if—let us assume for the moment—it was the desired goal. What were the concrete obligations involved? The prohibition of *Anschluss* could hardly have bothered Austria, nor the—by now rather absurd—preclusion of any agreement with Germany (which one?), that would have prepared the way to an eventual union (theoretically, every Common Market agreement was of this type).[16] By 1955, Austria had carried out a sort of de-Nazification to comply with the stipulation of the Austrian State Treaty, and no one expected it to begin the purges again; the regulations banning neo-fascism had also been enacted long before. Upholding the dethronement of the Habsburgs, as demanded by the Allied Powers, has always been the principal constitutional requisite serving the interests of the Second Republic. As to the rule that German citizens could not thenceforth serve in the (at the time) non-existent Austrian military—well, so much the better; the Austrian State Treaty specified the rank above which ex-Nazis could not serve in the military (I liked the ban on fascist propaganda screenplay writers the best); the country was not allowed to buy German and Japanese (civilian!) aircraft; it had to tend the memorials and cemeteries of the Allies. Bagatelle.

---

[16] Union with East Germany, had it survived after 1989, would have been an interesting—though legally inconsistent—historical turn. Austria, which had traditionally close business relations with East Germany, was quick to recognize it when it was established and mourned a little when it ceased to exist (R. Münz, "Grüner Pfeil, blauer Helm, weisser Fleck: Nachrichten aus dem neuen Deutschland, Mit einem Seitenblick auf Österreich," *Transit* 10 (1995).

The issue of the redemption of German assets (which the West generously disregarded) was more unpleasant though it affected the spirit of the nation less than its pocket. Every country is free to run into debt without necessarily incurring a restriction on sovereignty. Yet it is not a pleasant thought that the collector may come with tanks. The proudly proclaimed "armed neutrality" seems more like the case of a little boy whistling in the dark. The fact is that the Austrian State Treaty prohibited the production and deployment of nuclear weapons, heavy artillery (with a range of over 18 miles, for instance), and bombers. I do not think that the prohibition on having submarines injured Austria's self-esteem, but the ban on missiles (even defensive missiles) might have. Interestingly enough, Great Britain, remembering its experience during the war, insisted on the inclusion of this clause. Austria was forced to destroy even the designs of the banned weapons. Moreover, the Allies reserved the right to prevent the deployment of any newly developed weapon in the region between the Neusiedler (Fertő) and Constance (Boden) lakes.

The Allied Powers kept their eyes on Austrian generals. The size of the army to be established was never officially limited but, miraculously, to-date it has never exceeded 50–60,000 men (the original concept specified an army of 53,000 men and an air force of 5,000). In the absence of surface-to-air missiles, Austrian airspace was wide open (and the cosignatories of the Austrian State Treaty flew in and out at will; for instance, a Soviet military air-freighter in 1968), which made the Austrian military command think about proclaiming some of the large settlements "open cities." The former allies also kept track of what weapons the other was offering for sale. Thus Austria was better off producing its own arms or acquiring them from neutral Switzerland or Sweden if it wanted to develop its military. And it had little choice, since at the outset the *Bundesheer* (federal army) had only second-hand (primarily Western-made) weapons left over from the war.[17]

It is a fact that in 1955 foreign troops left the country in haste (the four elephants got off the boat, the locals said), and ever since a doc-

---

[17] See Ermacora, op. cit; Portisch and Riff, op. cit; E. Reiter, "Die Neutralität ist kein sicherheitspolitisches Konzept der Zukunft," in Krejci, Reiter, and Schneider, eds., op. cit.; Rotter, op. cit.

ument signed by the victor powers guarantees Austria's boundaries. Moreover, it is perhaps not a negligible fact that thenceforth the government of this sovereign republic was responsible exclusively to the Parliament rather than the Allied Council. It feels different to know that instead of foreign troops, government members hunt in the Alps; that the state president once again has the right to grant amnesty. This was not an easy period for Austria, however. Unquestionably, its sovereignty was dictated, rationed out, a kind of gift which may be filled with content and reinforced from the inside, though obviously the means of doing so were also considerably restricted. There was no military offensive capability to strengthen this shield of sovereignty, and a victorious repossession of South Tirol was out of question, as was a possible campaign to take, for example, the city of Sopron on the Hungarian border. Instead, the Austrian State Treaty prescribed what ethnic groups (Slovenes, Croats) Austria must live in peaceful coexistence with inside its borders.

What cannot be accomplished by force, diplomats and businessmen will accomplish, given enough self-confidence. If two adversaries keep you in check, play one off against the other. If you must give in, hold up your head and do as if it were what you always wanted and prepare a new tactic. Make a virtue of necessity. Do not forget your hinterland and take care conflict does not arise there. Reading the memoirs of the great generation of Austrian political elite[18] shows these to have been the—somewhat old-fashioned—recipes they learned from the skirmishes preceding the Austrian State Treaty. They did not leave much to chance, though they could have, since luck was on their side.

Hinterland? It was more like "a hinter-nation". Under Hitler the National Socialists (Germans and Austrians) argued that the principle of *ein Volk in zwei Staaten* (one people in two states) violated the national sovereignty of the Germanic peoples. According to them, the *Anschluss* ended this violation forever, though Austria did lose its

---

[18] See K. Gruber, *Ein politisches Leben* (Vienna, 1976); Bruno Kreisky, *Zwischen den Zeiten* (Vienna, 1986); Bruno Kreisky, *Im Strom der Politik* (Vienna, 1988); J. Raab, *Ich glaube an Österreich* (Vienna, 1995); A. Schärf, *Österreichs Erneuerung: 1945–1955* (Vienna, 1955).

sovereignty in the process, but who was going to mourn for it? Well, there was plenty of tears between 1945 and 1955 until the State Treaty returned a large part of its independence, thereby giving Austria a historic opportunity to accomplish what the First Republic could not. Namely, to turn state sovereignty into national sovereignty, to establish a nation-state in the middle of the twentieth century with considerable delay, indeed to invest the *Staatsnation* with the attributes of *Kulturnation*, and thereby strengthen and internalize state sovereignty. Every single one of the thirty years after 1955 was in favor of this and so Austria remained a united whole. Germany, on the other hand, was divided; its eastern half attempted the same trick to create sovereignty under incomparably worse conditions and much more clumsily. The western half had a guilty conscience because of Hitlerism and/or was arrogant enough not to trust the success of the Austrian *Kulturnation*. So West Germany did not intervene.

The Austrian State Treaty ensured greater state sovereignty than national legitimacy. The country had to derive its legitimacy from its own (if possible, pure) sources. What is an Austrian if not a German? Until 1918, the answer to this question, inescapable since nineteenth-century German unification, was: a Habsburg subject; between 1918 and 1945 the answer was this: an Alpine ("better") German; by 1955, what could be said was void of dignity: an Austrian is a German whom the Allied Powers do not consider German (or do not label a Nazi out of kindness, but insincerely). This sorry opening could have served as grounds for self-pity in playing the part of a small-state victim licking its wounds until the end of eternity, but there was also a forward way out. After a few years of some thinking and much work it was possible to imagine an Austria inhabited by Austrians and defined by Austrians. The somewhat insecure Austrian sovereignty was buttressed with new pillars of national identity and after a while the Austrians believed that the independence they were once given was complete and theirs forever, in fact they had deserved it, they had actually fought for it. Maybe this was the real Austrian Miracle.

Identity in the Golden Age

> Today, if someone asks an Austrian in England:
> Are you German? most say: No, I am an Austrian.
> Fifty or sixty years ago the answer would have been
> a great deal more complicated, something like this:
> Yes but from Austria. Or: I am a German-Austrian.
>
> *Gerald Stourzh*

Let us forget the darker side of national identity for the moment, since Austrians, too, tried to talk about it as little as possible, putting their faith in the liberating effect of repression—and making Sigmund Freud turn in his grave. Let us take the Austrian novelties of evolving national identification (self-deception) in the fifties, sixties, and the seventies. Although some of these ideas were already present in post-war (also prewar) political discourse, the work of elaborating them and their official synthesis was done in the Kreisky era. Briefly, and ignoring the order of importance, they are the following:

1. Austria was Hitler's first victim. The Moscow declaration of 1943 in which the Allies acquitted Austria of joint responsibility, in addition to easing reparations, also greatly eased the country's feelings of guilt. In the spirit of the declaration, the raving crowds on the Heldenplatz in Vienna greeting Hitler's entry into Austria in 1938, the 99.73% result of the plebiscite in support of the *Anschluss* (even if we know how such data come about), the many concentration camps, the Austrians joining the SS, the Austrian origins of Kaltenbrunner, Eichmann and others, the entire history of Austro-fascism, and, of course, the German nationalism of Austrian Social Democrats, were all forgettable and to be forgotten.[19]

---

[19] In 1918, Karl Renner, the first interim chancellor of the First Republic, proclaimed German Austria and even wrote its national anthem; in the twenties and the thirties, as a moderate Social Democrat, he sought cooperation with the Christian Democrats; in 1938 he voted in favor of the *Anschluss*, as he put it, "happily"; in 1944, he wrote a letter to Stalin discussing the future of socialism in Austria (and also mentioned that he had met Stalin's comrades-in-arms, Lenin and Trotsky [!]), and finally, he became the first president of the Second Republic trying to free itself of its German past. This "master builder of two republics" is rightly considered the symbol of Austrian continuity in the twentieth century.

Anyone who did not wish to remember asked: let's have a look at the dictionary and see since when does *Anschluss* mean only joining (perhaps even volunteering) and not territorial annexation?[20] How about the great many anti-fascists of the Austrian resistance, should they be forgotten? If the Germans occupied Austria, how could Austria be held responsible for war crimes?[21]

These were the first building blocks of national solidarity after the war. The surviving Social and Christian Democratic leaders said: We bitterly blame ourselves only for forming rival political camps in the thirties, seeking to destroy each other, instead of fighting fascism. But these camps disappeared in the concentration camps. In Dachau we learned to respect social peace forever. We continue to fight old and neo-fascists: ours is perhaps the most stringent law in Europe prohibiting a recurrence of Nazi crimes (*Wiederbetätigung*),[22] and we have Simon Wiesenthal, the merciless hunter of Nazis. Soviet Jews emigrate via Vienna. Our banner, coat-of-arms, our national anthem are innocent.[23]

---

[20] It is no accident that in 1989 the official term for German reunification was *Zusammenschluss* expressing reciprocal will, which in 1938 was still used interchangeably with *Anschluss*.

[21] The fundamentally Communist and Catholic organized resistance did good service in showing Austria as a victim after the war. It was Waldheim who destroyed this myth before the world when he said that he was (only) doing his duty together with hundreds of thousands of his compatriots. See Walter Manoschek's article in Sieder, Steinert, and Tálos, eds., op. cit., and Gerhard Botz, Hans Safrian, and Walter Manoschek in Botz and Sprengnagel, eds., op. cit., as well as Anton Pelinka's study in Mantl, ed., op. cit.

[22] It was a strange example of law interpretation when at the end of the eighties a representative of the Green Party carried a Nazi flag into the Parliament to protest Waldheim and was warned that the use of Nazi symbols was prohibited by law.

[23] Already in 1919, against Social Democratic opposition the Babenberg banner of red, white, and red won over the German black, red, and gold tricolor which, after the war, hoped to symbolize the affinity to Germany, the traditions of 1848, and the break from the Habsburg age. The present coat-of-arms of the country was also created by the First Republic: one-headed eagle with the Mauerkrone on its head, holding a sickle and a hammer in its claws to express the unity of the three social orders: the bourgeoisie, the workers, and the peasants (note, this is not the communist symbol). In 1945, at Renner's proposal, a broken chain was added to indicate Austria's liberation from fascism. The eagle is not two-headed but discretely carries the German colors to date. The

What about the fact that justice was served with the execution of a few dozen war criminals and that already in the 1949 elections parties were competing for the votes of ex-Nazis who, until then, were denied civil rights? What about the fact that Austria forgot to compensate the few survivors of the Holocaust (a German problem, it was said, and they were left out of the State Treaty)? What about the fact that the word *Kzler* meaning camp resident was an expression of contempt for a long time after the war? What about the fact that the new Austrian army invited Wehrmacht officers into its ranks? What about the fact that in 1949 a pan-German party (the legal predecessor of Haider's FPÖ today), at times showing strong Nazi sympathies, was reestablished? What about the fact that the *Turnerbund* and various ultrarightist fraternities were permitted to organize again?[24] What about the fact that not until the mid-eighties—and under external pressure—was it discovered what Waldheim did during the war. Well, let's relegate these facts to the subconscious!

2. *Austria is a German-speaking but a non-German (non-Prussian) country*, deserving the same recognition in the community of nations as the two Germanies or Switzerland. It is not one of the German states but itself a republic of federative *Lands*. It is smaller but not inferior. Moreover, it had legal continuity: it has been called *Ostarrichi* thousand years ago, its historical predecessor is the Habsburg, and not the Holy Roman Empire; Francis Joseph I, and not Wilhelm II; the First Republic, and not the Weimar Republic. Let us forget the Austrian feelings of inferiority accumulating—and what is

---

story of the national anthem is even more circuitous. After a brief hiatus, Haydn's composition, the *"Gott erhalte,"* was the anthem of the First Republic with words expressing pro-German sentiments and which was later rephrased and became known as *"Deutschland, Deutschland über alles"* to the same melody. After the war the Christian Democrats tried to save the melody by softening its military, march-like structure, but were voted down in 1947. (After it became known that the Germans do not want to return the "annexed" music either.) The music of the finally accepted anthem based on a tune allegedly by Mozart and a competition decided on the text which describes the natural beauties of Austria. See Breuss, Liebhart, and Pribersky, op. cit.; Menasse, *Das Land ohne Eigenschaften*.

[24] See H. H. Scharsach, *Haiders Clan: Wie Gewalt entsteht* (Vienna: 1995).

worse, probably justified—since the German unification and the defeat at Königgrätz in 1866, the Austrian plans for constitutional modification concerning the establishment of German Austria (Deutsch-Österreich),[25] and the insatiable desire of certain provinces (primarily Salzburg and Tirol) between the wars, but before the *Anschluss*, to join Big Brother. Moreover, let Austria create its independent culture (and maybe language) by setting up Austrian Cultural Institutes beside the world-wide network of the (German) Goethe Institutes and by dubbing German movies (or at least commercials). Austria is not Europe's China as (the German) Karl Marx contemptuously called it, nor is it the place where the Balkans begin as liberal Germans had always jeered because of its feudal sympathies, bigoted religiousness, and gut-level *étatism* (*cf. Obrigkeitsstaat*). Beethoven was Austrian, Hitler was German—it has been said maliciously that this switch of nationality has been the basis of the Austrian *Kulturnation* ideal since the fifties.

3. *The authentic model of "social partnership" (Sozialpartnerschaft) guarantees the Austrian Miracle.* It is a kind of social market economy like its German counterpart, but more charitable, less market-oriented, more agreeable and nature-friendly. The welfare state, a carefully nurtured hybrid of Christian social teachings and the traditions of "Red Vienna," flourishes in the two- (more exactly, two and a half) party democracy. A coalition of "black" and "red," Christian and Social Democrats governs the country together with corporations they control (or which control them), and tames the class struggle to accomodate parity committee negotiations. The time lost in strikes is measured in minutes (on an annual basis), welfare benefits are increasingly more generous. The social peace dreamt about in concentration camps has been realized and although political camps still

---

[25] Negotiations on the question of unification were so far advanced that Vienna was almost named the second capital of Germany. However, the victorious Western powers intervened and the country was named *Republik Österreich* instead of the commonly considered South East Germany, Higher Germany, Danube Germany, etc. (Renner's favorite was *Republik der Deutschen Alpenlande*.) In consolation, Austria was allowed to retain German as the state language and the German tricolor in its coat-of-arms. See Stourzh, op. cit.

exist, they cooperate. When the Christian Democrats were squeezed out of the coalition (between 1970 and 1986), the Socialists continued where the coalition left off. They are called "red," but actually they are hardly even pink. They refuse to have anything to do with communists and keep only the "Austro" from their former Austro-Marxism. The clericalism of "blacks" is also slowly disappearing and their agrarian sympathies are diminishing. Both camps tend toward the social-liberal center. The ongoing chaos of the period between the two world wars has been replaced by political stability—the elite has learned the lessons of history.

What is to be forgotten amid all this positiveness? The parity game mocked by the names of *Proporzsystem* and *Parteibuchwirtschaft*, the state divided and used by the two parties (the SPÖVP Union Party, as Jörg Haider called them), on the basis of "I scratch your back, you scratch mine," corruption, waste, and impotence, the decline of parliamentarism into corporatism, indeed, a corporatism not regulated by law, excessive state intervention in the economy, cronyism, nepotism, authoritarianism, the weakness of civil society. *Kammerstaat* and *Beamterstaat* (chamber state and state of bureaucrats). A republic without republicans (real liberals). The western-eastern slope in the political culture of the country. The traditional opposition between the conservative "Alpine" Austrians and the more socialist-liberal "Danubian" Austrians.

4. *Austria is becoming increasingly rich*, leaving behind not only its eastern neighbors (including East Germany), but also catching up and, in many respects, overtaking the more advanced states in Europe (including West Germany) and the world. In spite of fears following 1918, Austria, a small country, is proving vigorous indeed. An undying merit of the Austrian Miracle is that rapid economic growth matched increasing social equality, the state matched the market, employer the employee. Domestic small and medium enterprises developed together with mammoth (including foreign) enterprises, Alpine agriculture with urban industry and tourism; meanwhile, territorial distribution of growth improved and environmental protection was exemplary. Austria did not turn inward, but followed and often overtook international trends, for instance, in the development of small enterprises, services, and pollution control, as well as in human capital investment. Forgotten was the first push given by the Marshall

Plan; the European (German) hinterland; the inflow of German capital, the undeclared currency union with West Germany; the informal "COMECON membership;" the wasteful big state industries and pumping of subsidies into agriculture; the overregulated domestic market; the backwardness of Burgenland, etc.

5. *Austria is a small Central European mediator* (bridge, turntable), which participates in international life in beyond its size. Here, again, Central Europe is the keyword to distinguish Austria from Germany and denote the country easternmost West, and not westernmost East, as some might think. The memory of the Monarchy shines through this notion: accordingly, Austria, though not the military power it once was, is economically and culturally a small-scale regional great power amid perhaps the most liberal iron curtain states which were forced to adopt communism yet preserved common traditions. For this reason and because its neighbors are "only" Warsaw Pact countries but not the Soviet Union, no one should dare compare it to Finland (Austria is not a subcase of Finlandization), though it, too, maintains very friendly relations with the Soviets. Like and in competition with Switzerland, Austria attracts international economic and political institutions (OPEC, UNIDO, Atomic Energy Commission, etc.), as well as informal networks. It mediates not only between East and West (Helsinki process), but also between the advanced and developing worlds, especially the Middle East. There is order within its close environment it manages to solve even the most sensitive issues (South Tirol, Carinthian Slovenes), and when political refugees from the East knock on its doors (1956, 1968, 1981), they are admitted, and relations with Hungary are an ideal example of neighborliness.

Central Europe means Europe but never Eastern Europe. Austria moves toward Western Europe with deliberate steps: for reasons of neutrality it chooses the less tightly woven EFTA instead of the Common Market, then builds a bridge between the two organizations, trades freely but does not integrate. As the home of the Pan-European movement and a neutral country, it favors a united Europe without blocs. Until that time, it remains Atlantist in spirit—though it is not part of the NATO military structure—and a member of the developed (free) world. At the same time, being a neutral small state which never possessed any colonies overseas and is not hampered by geostrategic considerations, it shows greater understanding for the problems of the developing countries than the great powers. Let there be no misunderstanding: Austria is not a part but a custodian of the Third World. In Hugo von Hofmannstahl's words: Austria is on the receiving end in relation to the North and the West, and on the giving end in relation to the South and the East.

Things to be forgotten: Germany and Italy are also Central European; the mythical elements of the concept of Central Europe; the resistance of the Common Market to Austria's admission; the small violations of neutrality; the developing states are a business ventureas well; Austria is a messenger, not an independent mediator, etc.

6. *Austria is a real (multi)cultural great power with jovial citizens, an island of peace and happiness* (Insel der Seligen).[26] It is a country with an imperial history, cultural world heritage, untouched nature, of Habsburgs, Wolfgang Amadeus Mozart, Franz Joseph Haydn, and Beethoven, and also—as the anthem says—a country of mountains, valleys, and rivers, inhabited by convivial (*gemütlich*), life-loving people who exude the air of *Ostcharme mit Westkomfort*. Low crime rate, intact families, though the rate of suicide may be a bit high. The Republic is proud of the historical mixing of peoples on its territory (this, among others, predestines it for independence amid the Germanic peoples), of being a nation that is inclusive rather than exclusive. The Republic is proud of its aristocrats, though—officially—it does not allow the use of titles. The Viennese cookbook is full of Hungarian and Czech/Slovak recipes, the operetta is full of fun-loving Hungarian hussar officers, the arts and sciences are (until the end of the thirties) full of Jews. If German kinship must be mentioned, then the vivacious Bavarians are the link, they are the French of Germany, the main Catholics, who—to say something about folk culture—also wear Lederhosen and like Schrammel music.

Everyone fits into the common history. Theodor Herzl, Franz Kafka, and Sigmund Freud, but also Karl Lueger and Engelbert Dollfuss, all the Social Democratic and Christian Democratic leaders

---

[26] Pope Paul VI's description of Austria.

and their lieutenants, every Habsburg, except those living, but even they are being slowly accepted. It is better not to mention Hitler's Austrian origins. Let us not pry into popular anti-Semitism, with or without the Jews, or the traditional and general contempt for the neighboring peoples, primarily the Yugoslavs (derisively called *Tschusch*) and, to a degree, the Italians, nor into the periodic hatred of Germans depicted as Prussians (*Piefkes*) and the aversion to the Swiss. Let us not ask whether Austrian literature is German, nor why German, Swiss, and Austrian television broadcast Musikantenstadl at the same time every month. Might there be an all-German folklore after all and, God forbid, an all-German people?

Let us stay with the joy of life. The Blue Danube Waltz is just as much part of the Austrian image of *savoir vivre* as Wienerschnitzel, the Wiener Sängerknaben just as much as the Sacher cake, Mozart just as much as the Mozart Kugeln. The spectacular Viennese Spanish Riding School, Schönbrunn, and the Opera Ball are blended with the charms of "the Styrian oak" Arnold Schwarzenegger, Sissi (the affectionate name for Elisabeth, the wife of Austria's Emperor Francis Joseph I) and Kaiserschmarren (a kind of dessert), Jugendstil and the Prater, Stephansdom and Heuriger stand together. So does Baroque and the yodel. Austrians are a little old-fashioned, but not museum pieces. They are not boring and rigidly upright; being decent (anständig) does not exclude being resourceful and a little slipshod.

The above constituents of Austrian identity—characterizing the golden age of the 1970s, early 1980s—obviously overlap, and frequent repetition only reinforces this mix. This is especially true if we consider that not only statesmen and political pamphleteers worked on it, not only "red" and "black" leading intellectuals strengthened the faith of Austrians who were eager—and who is to blame them?—to associate their self-image with something morally superior (and more successful) than the image of war criminals, but everyday experience and the outside world also seemed to justify this massive success propaganda (also shaped by the professional state advertising agency, the *Österreich-Werbung*).[27]

---

[27] The first postwar official Austria image was presented by E. Marboe, *Das Österreichbuch* (Vienna, 1948).

In American and Soviet war movies the Nazis were Germans, not Austrians; world television news showed Bruno Kreisky happily embracing Josip Broz Tito and Yasser Arafat; John F. Kennedy and Nikita Khrushchev shook hands in Vienna; Waldheim was two-term United Nations Secretary General. Wherever Austrians went in the world, they could do so with heads held high, they were liked and acknowledged, and could return home feeling "we count," "we are small but strong," and "there is no place like home."

An experienced Hungarian will soon discover in the above identity elements of the traditional Central European small-state some traces of the odd sense of pride in "we are different/better," "we are in between," "we are a little ambivalent." This is the special Austrian way (*Sonderfall Österreich*), as they liked to say. Nevertheless—for the first time since the disintegration of the Monarchy (except for the attempt at Austro-fascism)[28]—self-interpretations contain not a sense of defeat, guilty conscience, bitter self-pity, or resignation. There is no longing for old fame, no sense of ill-fate. The self-portrait of Austria is not one of a country caught between shores, eroded by permanent internal conflicts, not a frontier fortress of the West under siege, not a pawn pushed to and fro on the chessboard of nations. Instead—and please excuse the profane simile—Austria is the tail that wags the dog: it shows the door to the occupying powers, creates its own state philosophy and social organization, entrusts itself with international mediation. Meanwhile, harmony rages in the country. It seems as if the "god of the Austrians" were reading some American pop psychology book before starting creation, the key phrase being: think positive. The people react well: every survey shows that they feel great and increasingly Austrian in the new roles they play.

---

[28] Austro-fascism or clerical authoritarianism? Was Dollfuss the harbinger of Nazism or the champion of " state resistance"? Was it the original model experiment of corporatist organization or an Austrian variant of national socialism? Is it a new Austrian national consciousness or a conviction that "Austrians are better than Germans"? The dispute about Dollfuss, Schuschnigg, and their ideological associates still continues. See Gottfried-Karl Kindermann and Karl Dietrich Bracher in Botz and Sprengnagel, eds., op. cit.

Mock them as we might, by the end of the seventies Austrians convinced themselves that basically all was well. It was easy, especially since basically all was really well, and the resultant surprisingly homogeneous national consciousness made things even better. The difference between provincial, ethnic, and political camp identities lessened, and decision through consensus became dominant. The concept of nation made use of relatively few atavistic symbols, it was not very historicising, and incorporated a set of new myths, some of which were based on pragmatic motives, for instance, neutrality. Kreisky, or Emperor Bruno as he was fondly or mockingly called, represented the return of *gloire* (I mean, *Glanz*) to Cis-Leithania. Is it possible that finally the Austrian state truly became a nation? In any event, October 26, the day neutrality was proclaimed and which was called the Day of the Flag for ten years, was renamed the National Holiday (*Nationalfeiertag*) in 1965. Thenceforth neutrality deserved special mention (if not the first in order) in the enumeration of the fundamental elements of national identity.[29]

There were many things the shapers of national identity had to overcome. Almost everyone at the time considered the First Republic a temporary formation. The Central European curse also afflicting Austria was that, generally, patriots were not republicans and republicans were not patriots. Dollfuss' clerical-nationalist program was stillborn. The persistent Germanophile sentiments of the social democrats (socialism together with the more advanced brother) enabled the communists—also ordered by the Comintern—to discover the "thousand-year-old" Austrian nation together with the Christian Democrats and the legitimists, of course, and against the Germans. It was based on traditional opposition between Prussia and Austria complemented by some national characteristics, to expose German nasti-

---

[29]   See Bruckmüller in Mantl, ed., op. cit; Bruckmüller, Fellner, and Haas in Botz and Sprengnagel, eds., op. cit.; and also Breuss, Liebhart, and Pribersky, op. cit.; Bruckmüller, op. cit.; M. Gehler and R. Steininger, eds., *Österreich und die europäische Integration 1945–1993, Aspekte einer wechselvollen Entwicklung* (Vienna, 1993); F. Plasser and P. A. Ulram, *Österreichbewusstsein und nationale Identität. Ein empirischer Forschungsbericht* (Vienna, 1991).

ness. The result was a counter-identity: albeit the Christian Democrats laid greater emphasis on the Catholicism of Austrians than the communists, they agreed that as a race (!) their people differ from the Germans due to the great Danubian mix of ethnic groups. With some exaggeration, the anti-Semitic line was handy and only the word "German" had to substituted for "Jew." And, of course, another language called "hurdistanisch" had to be introduced in schools, which was German, of course, but was known as the "school language" for years after the war under the cultural ministership of the conservative Felix Hurdes. It became (and still is) fashionable to speak in various local dialects instead of *Hochdeutsch*. If Hitler had only known how well he united the Austrian nation![30]

Gradually, the Social Democrats also came on board, especially when they formed the government by themselves. Kreisky's rival, Josef Klaus, pictured on the 1970 ÖVP election posters as the "true Austrian," (against the Austrian Jew Kreisky) nevertheless suffered defeat, and the winner started stressing how Austrian he was. He linked the concept of nation with modernization and openness, on the one hand, and subtly rehabilitated the Habsburgs, taunted the Germans (while the economies of the two countries became meshed in an unprecedented way), the Israeli, and the Americans, and lectured the Russians, on the other. He did not believe too much in the traditions of Austrian federalism, and planned to raise strong national identity to replace provincial identities. The Austrian Economic Miracle helped accomplish this. Four Austrian competitors in the first three places, roared a television reporter.[31]

All noteworthy surveys up to the second half of the eighties show that Austrians increasingly looked on their state as a nation. In the

---

[30] See Fellner and Haas in Botz and Sprengnagel, eds., op. cit.; Gerhard Botz and Albert Müller in E. Gehmacher, "Europa nur für Gewinner? Die Meinungsbildung um EWR und EG in Österreich," in Krejci, Reiter, and Schneider, eds., op. cit.

[31] See Hans Eder in Sieder, Steinert, and Tálos, eds., op. cit.; Ernst Bruckmüller's article in Mantl, ed., op. cit., and P. Gerlich, ed., *Sozialpartnerschaft in der Krise: Leistungen und Grenzen des Neokorporatismus in Österreich* (Vienna, 1985).

mid-fifties nearly half of the respondents considered Austria to be part of the German *Kulturnation*. In three decades this declined to one-fifth. The less educated and the younger the respondents, the more they believed themselves to be Austrians. They did not derive the nation from the state or the constitution, they did not call it a home-land, they had no particularly romantic notions about it. *Heimat* was the immediate locality, the province, especially in Carinthia, Tirol, and Vorarlberg. Based on these observations, the majority of Austrian historians in the eighties rejected the German theory of "three German states, two nations, and one people" in their own *Historikerstreit*. Austria is not only an independent state, but also a *Kulturnation*, therefore, how could it belong to a one and only German people?—they asked.[32]

Sitting on the Fence

> Assuming that Austria's neutrality is as perfectly voluntary
> as some say, the question remains: is it possible to ask a
> nation to pay taxes, serve in the army, obey the law, respect
> the national banner, all of which give evidence of and
> symbolize what the nation should not do. Restrictions
> imposed on a community can hardly constitute its essence
> unless we are talking about a penitentiary.
>
> *Thomas O. Schlesinger*

How much of the sheen of the above success attributes of national self-identification is reflected in sovereignty? Let us take the example of the interpretation of neutrality again. For decades, Austria has been demonstrating how the dogmatically consistent (originally Swiss) concept of neutrality can be tempered—almost imperceptibly—so that it does not impede the development of the Austrian Model and curtail the flight of political imagination. This is how its

---

[32] Botz and Sprengnagel offer a good review on the main stages of the debate. With the exception of Fritz Fellner, the better-known historians of modern Austria—Ardelt, Botz, Csáky, Hanish, Rumpler Stourzh, and Weinzierl—launched a joint attack against the introductory study by Karl Dietrich Erdmann. Botz and Sprengnagel, eds., op. cit.

leaders wanted to avoid a tragicomic ending wherein the celebrated neutrality which was to serve sovereignty would preclude strengthening the other pillars of sovereignty.

Meanwhile, Switzerland was mentioned with diminishing frequency. Unlike its alleged example, Austria joined the United Nations immediately upon signing the Austrian State Treaty in 1955 risking that, though a neutral country, it would have to obey binding resolutions (e.g., war sanctions) adopted without its consent. Since the beginning of its membership it has been busy issuing statements on the conditions under which it would have to refrain from carrying out United Nations resolutions. In 1956, Austria stood by watching as the Soviet Union overran a neighboring state which had just declared itself neutral. From the early sixties it aspired to join the Common Market, which would have also entailed consequences that violate, indeed rule out neutrality, for instance, in case a member state, with which Austria maintains close economic ties, enters war. Not to mention the expected political solidarity. Austria wanted the benefits of membership without its disadvantages, to be inside as well as outside. In the words of the British ambassador in Vienna, Austria wanted to sit on top of the fence while others did the dirty work. The West was becoming suspicious, so it was time to formulate a flexible interpretation of neutrality in order to dispel the misgiving that the country might be trying to take a free ride. How can a policy be morally vindicated which allows the Communist-organized World Youth Rally and the rightist Sudeten Germans' meeting to take place in Vienna; which asks to share in the fruits of the Common Market while saying that, being a neutral country, it wants to be left out of certain economic warfare measures; which, when denied admission into the EEC, hints at being invited to join the COMECON; which makes moves to arm itself, yet expects to be protected.

What was there to say to all this? Be offended and ask: weren't you the ones who wanted it to be like this? Or retort by listing the advantages the West enjoyed as a result of the Austrian *Ostpolitik*? Or perhaps sing the words of the hymn of *Realpolitik*: "You try surviving in the shadow of the Iron Curtain." Or, could the people of a small tormented country rely on anything else but their resourcefulness? Others would do the same, western states do not always act in solidarity either. I would not say that the Austrian political elite missed these opportunities to score political points, but they considered it far more important to avoid portraying the concept of neutrality as a "necessary evil." Looking ahead and carefully nurturing the identity of its citizens, Austria began to explain how great it was to be neutral. This moral deficit had to be made to disappear especially since no plebiscite was held to authenticate the parliament's declaration of neutrality.

The cosmetic revision began when neutrality was declared. With the propagation of neutrality, Austria contributes to world peace and to eventual disarmament. Austria helps to smooth over international conflicts, admits refugees (would it have helped the Hungarians or Czechs had Austria provoked the Soviet Union, they reason), and is always ready for goodwill and humanitarian missions. It joined the United Nations, among others, because it felt it may be needed there. It hurries to Cyprus (to mediate between two NATO member states), to Egypt etc. to keep the peace. Austria liked to call itself parliamentarian (*ehrlicher Makler*) and medical orderly. This part of the neutrality doctrine was devised for public consumption.

In the field of international law, Austrian neutrality sought the broadest interpretation and the ensuing gray area allowed it to select convenient interpretations. The pledge of perpetual neutrality means neutrality in both peace and war. Proclamation of an active neutral policy means responsibility for the future consequences of decisions. Even though Austria is militarily neutral, it must know that a hermetic isolation of military affairs from the economy and politics is not possible. Bearing this in mind, Austrian politicians reasoned: let's talk as much about neutrality and about as many of its elements as possible but keep the options of interpretation under our control. After all, Austria is a sovereign state. The imposition of the Swiss model left it no other option; the concept could not be narrowed down to the maxims of "we shall not join any military alliance" and "we shall not allow foreign troops into the country." If Austria is to be neutral, let it be very neutral. What is there to risk? That the Soviets would object to Austrian officers watching American movies on television? There is more to win. The country can always reject their overtures saying, "sorry, our religion (i.e., neutrality does not allow it." As for the West, it has made so many concessions already that Austria will manage somehow. In this respect, however, they miscalculated somewhat. It took over thirty years after the first attempts in the early sixties, after a long wait and humiliating rejections, not entirely due to the stubborn objections of the Soviet Union, to gain admission into the realm of the European Union. Furthermore, just like before the ratification of the State Treaty, geopolitical rearrangement was again necessary for Austria to become "interesting" again.

Yet Austria was also lucky. Discounting Soviet interventions, there was no serious military activity (war) in its vicinity. In the Security Council the two sides kept one another in check, and thus there were no United Nations resolutions adopted that would impose obligations violating Austria's neutrality until the Gulf War. Civil war did not erupt in South Tirol, and Austria also took care to make sure it would not. Furthermore, the fact that the traditional guidelines laid down in the 1907 Hague Convention on what a neutral country can and cannot do largely lost force, also worked in Austria's favor (can a missile fly over neutral airspace; what constitutes economic, psychological, information warfare; what happens if a war is waged without having been declared; does satellite intelligence gathering violate neutrality; etc.). It was easy to fish in troubled waters.

It was possible to vote now this way, now that in the United Nations, even in the Security Council (on Rhodesia, South Africa, Cyprus, Middle East), being flexible in interpreting the rule of impartiality, claiming that Austria was only representing "collectively neutral" United Nations resolutions. It was possible to say that there was no war in South Tirol and, therefore, the training of terrorists in Austria was irrelevant. Austria could ask who was to decide which of technologies it sold to the Eastern bloc were strategically important. Or, to declare that arms exports, if not sent to warring countries, is honest business. If I understand correctly, the distinction between the law of neutrality and the policy of neutrality provided the doctrinal justification for this reasoning.[33] Reputedly, the latter offers greater scope for free calculation of actions. Prudence was required only in

---

[33] See Ermacora, op. cit.

taking care that during these diplomatic sleights of hand neither the opposition nor the critical intellectuals become too bold, and that they do not strike a discourteous note in dealings with either military bloc. Although, when neutrality was proclaimed, it was also said that it imposes no obligations on the citizens, yet self-restraint was the main unwritten rule of conduct.[34] Let us do things our own way, Austrian politicians argued. We will escape the traps of neutrality gradually and quietly and thus extend the boundaries of sovereignty. The time was the late seventies, early eighties.

Virtual Sovereignty

> Where there is a national soccer team and a National
> Bank, there must also be a nation.
> *Bruno Kreisky*

What does all of the above say about sovereignty? Why do I consider this sovereignty to have been virtual? Let me say in advance that I use virtual in the original dual sense of the word and by no means pejoratively, that is, in the sense of "seeming." In Vienna this is called "real-fiction." This is how less sovereignty becomes more. It is not simply a case of a footman dressed like a king or an animal puffing itself up to appear larger. Austria did not just imagine its own importance. Although, in the fifties, it had very little to start out with on the road to self-construction but it was able to win the respect of its immediate and broader environment in excess to its strength. It would be unfair to call this contemptuously a pretence. If anyone, it deceived only itself insofar as it became perhaps too absorbed with self-construction as the years went by. According to the writer Robert Musil, the Austrians' sense of opportunity is more highly developed than their sense of reality.

---

[34] In 1968, during the Prague intervention, the head commissary of the ORF instructed his colleagues as follows: "In view of the unrestricted freedom of the press we enjoy, we must exercise utmost self-control. As the voice of free and neutral Austria we cannot be party to speculative journalism....We must take utmost care especially in live programs....Rather risk a discrediting technical breakdown than make irreparable political blunders." Ibid., p. 253.

The (insecure) sovereignty, restored by the grace of the Allied Powers, and the neutrality Austria was talked into were in fact something very little to start with. But the Austrian State Treaty concealed a much greater scope of activity than expected. It soon became obvious that the East did not object to Austria's Western orientation, while the West tolerated flirtations with the East. Its busy activity between the two blocs, the performance of minor services in the role of mediator, as well as the acquisition of special expertise from Eastern Europe and building a complex network of contacts therein, helped Austria rise to the heights of world politics. When the East came too close for comfort (1956, 1968), the West protected Austria's sovereignty. When the West tried to exert its influence (EEC), the Austrians could always argue that the Soviets would not like it. When Austria talked about its role in building a bridge between East and West, it was actually to praise its enclave position. The country followed a similar strategy later in the dialogue between North and South, thus collecting credits from all points of the compass.

While politically guarding, economically it consolidated its sovereignty. Good-neighbor Austria supplemented its irrefutable domestic economic achievements with advantages obtained by playing the *Mitfahrer*, a guide and sometimes a free-rider, in East-West (then North-South) business relations. Technological transfers and trade in raw materials, re-exportation of commissioned work and transit traffic, financial services, capital exportation and tourism—a mediator or immediate beneficiary in all these spheres, Austria made profit at minimal political expense and without being under duress to compensate for economic losses. (For instance, it did not have to invite Communists into the government or subsidize outdated industries in exchange for Soviet oil shipments.) Neither the Common Market nor COMECON imposed any real restrictions on it, instead they both helped to extend its decision-making power in the world of economy.[35]

---

[35] See S. W. Arnott, *The Political Economy of Austria* (Washington, 1982); F. Breuss, *Österreichs Aussenwirtschaft: 1945–1982* (Vienna, 1982); S. Richter and Klára Székffy, *Ausztria gazdasága* (Budapest, 1987); E. Streissler, "Das Ende des Keynesianismus," *Wirtschaftspolitische Blätter,* no. 3 (1982), and Gunther Tichy in Mantl, ed., op. cit.

Viewed from an ivory tower, that country might be called a parasite, but I think we should just say it behaved like any shrewd businessman.

Can Austria be considered to have been sovereign up to the end of the Kreisky era from a military point of view? Definitely not, if we consider the innumerable written and unwritten regulations restricting the country's armament. The awareness that it could have withstood an attack for only a few days had the Warsaw Pact tanks stationed on its frontiers started moving, could not have bolstered self-confidence. I have already mentioned the shortcomings of its air defense. Essentially, its sovereignty depended on the three "nays" declared by others: foreign troops were not stationed on its territory, Soviet missiles (allegedly) were not targeting to its large cities, and it was no secret that NATO would not abandon a neutral good friend if it were attacked from the East.

For their part, the Austrians added a few tough "ayes" to these "nays." They announced that the declaration of neutrality, which prescribes the protection of this neutrality "with every available means," makes armament their duty. Later, "available" was replaced by the more forceful term of "expected," and Austria's military leaders did all they could to show how much the country's military budget lagged behind the military expenditure of countries of similar size, adding that it is to be "expected" of Austria to catch up. In 1975, a military doctrine was formulated to supplement the law on neutrality providing for circular defense worthy of a neutral country: strategic maps also studiously showed the possible NATO crossing routes as a potential threat. Even if Austria's neutrality did not emulate the Swiss model, its military organization certainly did. Compulsory military service was introduced, the reserve militia (*Landwehr*) was assigned an important role in defense in order to check incursion and hamper occupation by a possible aggressor. The budget allotted for the purchase of more modern military technology was gradually increased.

This notwithstanding, to feel really sovereign, Austria had to look East and compare itself with the Communist states. This was where it had to play the role of a small regional great power while enhancing the mythical nature of the common Central European fate, and where it had to gather strength for negotiations with the West. Communist leaders sought contacts with Vienna in the hope of gaining acceptance by points further west and, conversely, Austria became the gateway to the East. The two opposing sides needed Austria as much as they had needed Switzerland during World War II. Its only rival for this position was Finland, which started at a far worse position. All this probably would have been inconceivable without Kreisky, who proved to be the right man for overcoming the image of Austrian politicians as parochial by joining the Brandt-Palme duo, on the one hand, and by giving a Social Democratic (and, at the same time, European) ideological legitimation to the Austrian model, on the other, as well as for gaining an opening through the Iron Curtain which separated Austria from Hungary, the "happiest barrack"[36] in the East.

After a while Austria began to feel there were fewer restrictive rules and, therefore, it had a larger field for maneuvering. Since the occupation was the point of departure of its reasoning, it could measure the growth of sovereignty with relative precision—which is rare in history. It had influence, it could accomplish things; whatever Austria needed, it had the money, contacts, and cunning to acquire. Frequently, it was enough just to wait for offers to come, and then accept them. It had every right to think its sovereignty was real. If only the Common Market were less unwilling....

---

[36] See P. Haslinger, *Hundert Jahre Nachbarschaft: Die Beziehungen zwischen Österreich und Ungarn: 1895–1994* (Frankfurt, 1996). The K.u.K. (Kreisky und Kádár originally, "Kaiser und Königliche" referring to the institutions of Austria-Hungary) relationship is an exemplar: it tells everything there is to know about Austria's virtual sovereignty or, at least, how comparisons with its eastern neighbors helped this sovereignty: "the Russians had left our country, but they are still in yours and had in fact again overrun Hungary in 1956; we drive Volkswagens, you drive cheap East-German Trabants; you need our money but we don't need yours; we are in the vanguard of the Western world while you are, at most, in the Eastern, and—don't forget—we weren't so far apart in 1945..." We know that Austrians could spend hours repeating these commonplaces while constantly assuring the Hungarians how much they nevertheless (!) love the temperamental but hospitable *Ungar*. Condescendingly and pityingly, they say: "we in the Free World will help you when you restless people get into trouble again—remember 1956. But it seems you may have learned something from us under Kádár, and are getting the idea how to outwit the world."

A Country without Qualities[37]

> Freedom from democratic control,
> equality in leading bodies,
> brotherliness in pricing.
> *Robert Menasse*

It is now 1997, the Golden Age has long ended. National pride is more or less extant (though there is a noticeable change in the trend and fewer people consider themselves members of the Austrian nation), and no spectacular tragedy has occurred either, Austria is intact and prospering quietly. I cannot even say that there is a tremor beneath the surface and a new world is in the making which Austrians stubbornly refuse to take note of, that the ornaments of their national identity lie in the dust, their sovereignty is in ruins, and yet they continue believing that "they are different." On the contrary, the political and cultural elite—with no less practical acumen than before and making use of the inertia of national self-esteem—is almost imperceptibly leading the country toward an empire where the question, "how sovereign are we, Austrians?" no longer makes sense. More specifically, it is passing through an age when diminution of sovereignty, never firmly established (or literally bomb-proof) has become obvious. Even more specifically, Austria is acquiring surplus sovereignty before it has to face a deficit in its sovereignty, it forestalls possible defeat by victory or, at least for the time being, the Austrian state is successfully selling this strategy to the citizens. In the meantime, it is butchering, excuse me, putting to sleep, nice and slow, the sacred cows of national identity through its negotiations on European Union membership and in related disputes on the question of neutrality. It is sacrificing its identity for a new—more normal?—identity.

Before Europe appeared on Austria's horizon, a few things happened in the country leaving their imprint on the sovereignty-consciousness of the people. One does not have to be a psychologist trained in Vienna to suspect that in addition to pleasure in work well-

---

37   See Menasse's book bearing this title. R. Menasse, *Das Land ohne Eigenschaften.*

done, a great deal of luck and even more repression, self-deception, overcompensation was needed to create this previous harmony, which can readily boomerang when all is not so well, when Lady Luck turns away, and a new generation grows up. Perhaps I have dwellt too much on motifs that should be forgotten or relegated to the subconscious. So, let us take a look at Austria, this country favored by fortune. In retrospect it is hard to see clearly all the great risks Viennese politicians took when they put all their stakes on escaping from the occupation-zone system and the "common German fate."

After 1955, the Soviets remained within a sixty mile radius of Vienna in Hungary, and the lightnings of the storms of 1956 and 1968 struck very close to Austria. In 1955 it was hard to say whether the Soviets' westward expansion had ended. The threat of a third world war was real, and had it broken out, Austria would have stood in the midst of falling bombs waving the scorched pages of the Austrian State Treaty, trusting in the tacit promise of Western powers to come to the aid of their "Western-oriented ideological kin," as Austrian politicians liked to call their regime, from their nearest base in Bavaria. Eventually, Austria decided to bet on the continuation of the thaw in relations that began after 1953, on a future *détente*, hoping in the power of the self-fulfilling prophecy. In any event, it tried to set an example, in its own interest. At that time, mediation could have easily meant ending up between two chairs on the floor, and Austria could have been tormented by the old doubt whether, being a poor and small country, it was viable at all. When the politicians bet on long-range *détente*, they also assumed that the Germans would not overdo it and the conflict between the two German states would not really diminish that much. For this reason, and not only because of the sad consequences of the *Anschluss* nor because the world would have looked unfavorably on another all-German fraternizing, it was worth escaping the German past.

Austria's geostrategic views proved correct over the decades. Blocs were fixed, the Iron Curtain could be crossed only in one direction, from West to East. There was no threat of a military attack, business rivalry, economic refugees, or waves of criminals from the East. In this sense, Austria was indebted to the Communist system which cast Austria in roles that only improved its self-esteem even when the rare holes in the Iron Curtain appeared; the country was shown up as a generous source of aid, a teacher, it took in refugees, and gave sanctuary. Let's not waste words on the rich uncle and the Westernizer roles we know so well in Eastern Europe. We might say melancholically that it is easy to become a self-confident nation when everything is working for it. It is easy to become a sovereign state when no one really threatens it. It is easy to create the Austrian Miracle in the postwar period of spectacular reconstruction, to write the Austrian Model chapter in the success story of the Western welfare state. But what happens if the wind shifts from one day to the next in the immediate vicinity, at a time when the country begins to show signs of fatigue? What is to be done in the great East European earthquake that followed the awaited *détente* if Austria loses a part of its self-confidence in the meantime? If it finds that the virtual is no longer real?

What went wrong with the Austrian machinery during the past two decades? Something must have happened. Today one-fourth of the country backs Jörg Haider, who is flirting with the idea of pan-German nationalism, even Nazism, and who—counting on the fading influence of the establishment—has proclaimed the program of the Third Republic, an allegedly direct democratic and authoritarian "social community of people," a community without parties.[38]

1. The "other Austria," a small group of rather Leftist liberal and primarily Viennese intellectuals, had unsparingly repudiated the so-called "life lie," (Lebenslüge) the victim myth of the Second Republic, in the eighties, especially in the wake of the Waldheim scandal. Naturally, this did not mean an end to the myth but the beginning of a systematic reinterpretation of the past (*Vergangen-heitsbewältigung*), and also the polarization of public opinion. In the course of this self-examination they found the proverbial skeleton in the closet, sometimes even literally. The syrupy German-Austrian *Heimatfilms* (homeland movies) were replaced by *Anti-Heimat* literature, represented by authors like Peter Handke, Thomas Bernhard, and others.

2. Unification made Germany a real world power whereby even former East Germany—what a shame—outstripped Austria in many

---

[38] See C. Leggewie, "Millenniumsdämmerung: Notizen zur österreichischen Lage," *Transit,* no. 10 (1995); Scharsach, op. cit; János Mátyás Kovács, "Haider in Ungarn: Notizen zum postmodernen Populismus," *Transit,* no. 11 (1996).

respects which, compared to this new Germany, seemed again tiny, the size of a medium German state. Austrian self-esteem is now facing a new German self-confidence.

3. The two-party social partnership is showing cracks, the state sector is disappearing (being privatized), teeming with corruption scandals (*cf. Skandalrepublik*), tough modernization measures are postponed, the cumbersome parity system is slow to react to the challenge of globalism, the slimming of the top-heavy welfare state is dragged out. There are increasing quarrels between the "reds" and the "blacks," citizens turn away from politics and tend to succumb to the temptation of populism instead of to the lure of new—"green" and liberal—parties.

4. Austrian economic development has slowed, approaching stagnation. The new Asian competitors are rapidly overtaking Austria, which was caught unprepared for the information revolution. Overregulation, the bureaucratic welfare state, and the powerful union lobby behind it, are strangling the economy. The European Community is closing ranks, COMECON is dead and, although there is still some money to be made from the post-Communist transformation, East and Central European business rivals have also appeared on the scene.

5. As a result of the dissolution of the blocs, East-West mediation has largely lost its meaning. Eastern Europe wants to become a part of Europe and not Central Europe, and in the process (of joining NATO, for instance) tends to bypass Austria. Meanwhile Germany is becoming the Central European power. The Iron Curtain is no longer there to protect the Alpine country, for which it is difficult to see itself as the island of peace. It suddenly finds itself very much in the East (hitherto having been the easternmost western state; it may now become the westernmost eastern state) next to a powderkeg. Economic, instead of political, refugees pound (not knock) at the door. Due to the growing impoverishment of the United Nations and its accumulating failures, being the seat of a United Nations organization is no longer a source of pride. As for the Third World...sorry, what does the term mean?

6. Overshadowed by Germany, Austria, this cultural great power, again looks parochial, lowbrow and old-fashioned. Its museums, con-

cert halls are increasingly said to be boring. Austrian joviality is at times strained. The proud "we're doing well" conviction is fading while frustration and envy are on the increase, refugees are denied entry more often than not. Kaiserschmarren does not taste as good anymore at the Heuriger.

"What does it mean to be an Austrian today?" This question reflecting insecurity is again raised in the mid-nineties after a seemingly completed nation-building. Are the Germans who live in the Alps (and who feel increasingly uncomfortable) the Austrians? Or, are they people whom less and less self-respecting East European businessman will deal with anymore? Or, are they the people hanging onto their desks in some government office? I would not like to exaggerate for, actually, the problem is not so acute: Russia may yet find its own self, the new German epic may come to a standstill, and the need for happy Austria may yet arise. The millennial celebrations are here, historical consciousness is on the rise, and even if the political and cultural identities are shaken, no one can take away nature awareness from the tourist republic. There will always be a need for natural parks.

All the same, by 1989, the Austrian political elite drifted into an unusual situation: it had to make decisions. The questions involved were vital and similar in nature and magnitude to those they faced before signing the Austrian State Treaty. There were three options. One, follow the same traditional course of "let's keep going, something will happen" (*weiterwursteln*); two, follow Haider, who loudly criticizes certain elements of identity of the Austrian Golden Age (welfare state, parity system, etc.) while extolling others (Austria's innocence, Austrian virtues, etc.); or, three, escape forward to Europe. The rules of political competition excluded the second, though some of the ideas of the populist leader were quietly adopted (for instance, the tightening of regulations on aliens). The first gradually lost ground. As a local prophet of the Central European idea observed with self-directed irony: destitute refugees sleep under the symbolic East-West bridge swept by howling winds. If Austria insists on embarking on a separate course, it risks growing apart from the rest of the world, and join the dubious company of those fallen behind, those not going anywhere, those embroiled in wars. Despite the risks involved, Europe seemed very attractive.

Europe held out the promise of replacing the worn-out spare parts of the Austrian Model and the assurance that in case fundamental structural changes become necessary, it will alleviate the pains of transition and assume some of the political responsibility for reforms. The prospect it offered was in plain language and also hard to substantiate ("to remain Austrian in Europe"), a new national identity without having to discard the old.[39] Austria wished both to change (normalize) and not to change its identity. Instead of an either/or, it should be an either and or choice, was the way an uncommitted intellectual put it. However, there was still one problem. A basic element of the original model—neutrality, what else?—had stood in the way of Austria's admission to the European Union for about three decades. Viennese politicians began to ponder how to extricate themselves from this tricky situation. It would be unworthy and stupid to openly disown the ideology that created the state, indeed, the nation, since three-quarters of the people believed in it and, anyway, there is time enough to make concessions when negotiations begin. Stubborn insistence would be just as stupid because it would only intensify the already present aversion to Austria's captiousness. Besides, the former Soviet Union, the guardian of Austria's conscience, is indisposed for the moment; so it is now or never.

Creeping Commitment

> When Marshall Kulikov, with six times eighteen
> decorations on his chest and stomach, visited our
> Parliament, I considered perpetual neutrality
> important for the sake of Austria's security and
> independence.
> *Felix Ermacora*

Austria, which was highly sensitive to events in the East, reacted much sooner than the West to the onset of the agony of the Soviet regime. When in 1987–1988 it saw the unbelievably rapid expansion

---

[39] To those urging long-range and radical changes, Chancellor Vranitzky's advice was that those with visions should see a doctor.

proudly, to avoid having to say "adaptation by force of necessity" At the same time they could only stand by while even Portugal was admitted. It should be added that the Western powers also did not want to risk a confrontation with the Soviets over Austria.

By the second half of the eighties, first the Christian, then the Social Democrat politicians[42] began to realize that the advantages of flexible small economies were fast disappearing in the global market competition. A somewhat greater share of European integration would come in handy, the Austrians thought. In 1987, the government announced the slogan: "Global Approach." The "four freedoms" of the European Economic Area would do for a start, but once the

---

[42] The Austrian Industrial Alliance, close to the Christian Democrats, initiated the dispute (see W. Hummer and M. Schweitzer, *Österreich und die EWG: Neutralitätsrechtliche Beurteilung der Möglichkeiten der Dynamisierung des Verhältnisses zur EWG* (Vienna, 1987); Krejci, Reiter, and Schneider, eds., op. cit. In other words, the industrial lobby makes Europe presentable. Of the parties, the ÖVP had always taken greater initiative than the SPÖ and there is incessant competence and prestige rivalry between them as to which one will take Austria into the European Union. On the main stages of the dispute, see Ermacora, "Neutralität pointiert!" in Krejci, Reiter, and Schneider, eds., op. cit.; W. Hummer, ed., *Österreichs Integration in Europa 1948 bis 1989: Von der OEEC zur EG* (Vienna, 1990); H. F. Köck, *Ist ein EWG-Beitritt Österreichs zulässig? Die völkerrechtliche und verfassungsrechtliche Zulässigkeit eines Beitritts Österreichs zur Europäischen Wirtschaftsgemein-schaft* (Vienna, 1987); H. F. Köck, "Änderung und Aufhebung eines völkerrechtlichen Sonderstatus. Erörtert am Problem der dauernden Neutralität in Zusammenhang mit dem Antrag Österreichs auf Beitritt zu den EG," in A. Mock, ed., *Verantwortung in unserer Zeit: FS für Rudolf Kirchschläger* (Vienna, 1990); P. Luif, *Neutrale in die EG? Die wirtschaftliche Integration in Westeuropa und die neutralen Staaten* (Vienna, 1989); A. Noll, *Neutralität, Staatsvertrag, EG-Beitritt* (Vienna, 1989); M. Rotter, "Von der integralen zur differentiellen Neutralität," *Europäische Rundschau*, no. 3 (1991); E. Sucharipa, *Neutralität und EG, Bundeswirtschaftskammer* (Vienna, 1993:b); K. Zemanek, "The Chaotic Status of the Laws of Neutrality," in *Im Dienst an der Gemeinschaft: FS für Dietrich Schindler,* ed. W. Haller et al. (Basel, 1989); K. Zemanek, "1966–1989: Gedanken zur Dynamik der dauernden Neutralität," in *Verantwortung in unserer Zeit: FS für Rudolf Kirchschläger*, eds. A. Mock and H. Schambeck (Vienna, 1990) and also Ermacora, Hafner, Reiter, Rotter, and Schweitzer in Krejci, Reiter, and Schneider, eds., op. cit.

European Community really becomes a union, they would amount to mere charity. Therefore, Austria should gradually abandon a strict interpretation of neutrality unless it wants to lose its sovereignty some other way (as a result of economic stagnation and all its political consequences). For four years the Austrian political and scholarly elite debated the question whether they should make concessions at all, then concluded that actually concessions were not necessary. The change was brewing. The disputants found all the possible legal loopholes and formulated all the conceivable ideological twists explaining why the European Union and neutrality were in fact akin. Again they included the neutrality clause in the application—if less aggressively than previously—risking that negotiations would freeze a second time.

What were these loopholes and ideological twists? Austrian legal experts suddenly discovered that some—flexibly interpretable—points of the European Community agreement, specifically, the defense and state of emergency clauses, protect the member states should they decide not to obey the common will in case of war, threat of war, political crisis, etc. (if abuses are suspected, the Strassbourg Tribunal decides whether non-obedience is permissible). Similarly, majority decisions in the Community are few and far between, therefore, in most cases, proposals infringing upon neutrality may be vetoed. Consequently, if admitted, Austria would not be at the mercy of others. Moreover, the European Community basic treaty is very liberal where special wishes of new members are concerned, which means that there is nothing to prevent securing prior political acceptance of the principle of neutrality. If this could be achieved, the Tribunal could not intervene either. Ireland is neutral and nevertheless a member of the club. If poor countries are admitted for strategic reasons, why not Austria, which is a rich country and would be a net contributor. The Community would gain by Austria's admission. Is this not worth a little uncertainty in principle? Anyway, how could the Community imagine totalizing the internal market with a gap between Northern and Southern Europe where Switzerland and Austria are? Wouldn't these two countries be important export markets and crossroads?

Ideologies are the work of those who no longer dare to believe in loopholes and rather make concessions on the question of neutrality.

They chose the difficult task of somehow erasing the adjective perpetual. They curse their predecessors for not being satisfied with just "lasting neutrality." Their chief argument culminates in the wisdom of *tempora mutantur*, that is, neutrality used to be nice and useful, nowadays it tends to be just nice. "It has lost its addressees."[43] The answer is no longer granted when it comes to the question of "against whom are you neutral?" The Soviet Union not only demanded, but also respected neutrality. There is no reason why Slobodan Milosević, Saddam Hussein, or Muhammed al-Quaddafi would do the same. Instead of violating the constitution, Austria should return to the narrow interpretation therein (officially, to the military core of the concept). Namely, that a country which does not belong to any military alliance and does not allow foreign troops on its territory, is neutral. Although, of course, the constitution could be amended. Austria has not signed binding international agreements, it was Austria which declared itself neutral, therefore, it should be Austria who rescinds this. Of course, the world has acknowledged this declaration, it would be good therefore if the consent of the great powers were also gained, if for no other reason than out of courtesy. This should be accomplished in peacetime.[44] Actually, there is no need to rescind neutrality since Austria, too, can still have recourse to the old distinction, that is, playing with the policy of neutrality while maintaining the legal principles of neutrality. Anyway, solidarity has replaced neutrality as the correct form of behavior. In 1955, Austria did not choose neutrality for its own sake, but because it was the means of securing sovereignty. Today it must act in solidarity (i.e. it must adjust to others) to avoid damages to its sovereignty. Neutrality is not a thing for itself, not a prison. Solidarity is just as nice a feature (and it is certainly nicer than being a free-rider). In truth, Austria has been *de facto* in the European Community for a long time. Curiously, staying outside *de jure* would increase dependence. Finally, the gem of this pragmatic reasoning is that working for world peace could be more effective inside the European Community than outside.

---

[43] See statement by Vice Chancellor Erhard Busek, *Standard*, June 12, 1992.

[44] The disintegration of the Soviet Union voided the Austrian State Treaty, so neutrality may be quietly forgotten, a few outspoken Austrian politicians argued.

It is not hard to notice that the search for loopholes is addressed to Brussels, while ideological considerations are prepared for domestic consumption. The Austrian government has begun a game of duplicity: first, it tries to convince the Community that there is a way to eat one's cake and have it too, but to be sure it begins to distance itself from the myth of neutrality and to prepare public opinion. When, after two years of silence, the European Community tells Austria that it does not trust its promises, the political leadership is left with no choice but to explain to the Austrian people why the Community is preferable to neutrality. We might even think that it was due to the persuasive power of the government that the results of the 1994 plebiscite on the European Union membership showed a surprising two-thirds majority support. Similarly to other countries, the economic arguments, which opened the persuasion campaign, would have probably resulted in a fifty-odd percent in favor. The almost seventy percent needed a little help from the Soviets again.

To be precise, it was the post-Soviets and it was indirect help. Until its dying moments, the Soviet Union continued to criticize, though with diminishing force, Austria's aspiration to join the European Community. But this was not the essence of its assistance. After 1989, security-policy considerations increasingly replaced economic considerations on both sides of the negotiating table. Disintegration of the Warsaw Pact and of the Soviet Union, as well as the war in Yugoslavia made the European Community more accommodating, and Austria began hurried preparations for admission because it saw the weaknesses of the United Nations security system in Yugoslavia and hoped that a future European security system will be stronger. Just to be on the safe side, the European Community still showed reluctance and in a long-awaited reply dated August 1991 it notified Austria of its willingness to negotiate, adding that the latter had better forget its conditions concerning neutrality. Furthermore, it should start thinking about an eventual amendment to the Constitution because neutrality "raises problems," and, yes, Austria may request special treatment but, of course, it should also know that Brussels does not favor separate paths. They were not impressed even when in the meantime Austria demonstrated that it can forget the broad interpretation of neutrality. During the Gulf War, the taboos of neutrality toppled one after the other, when the Austrian government allowed the passage of American and Allied troops and war-material over territory under its jurisdiction in compliance with the Security Council resolution. Initially it said that it "voluntarily adopts" (i.e., it is not being servile to) United Nations resolutions, then, calling the war a "policing action" serving collective self-defense, took the side of the anti-Iraq forces and joined the sanctions.[45] Solidarity versus neutrality, that is, backing out of perpetual neutrality. Soon Austria was again party to sanctions implemented, in part or whole, against Yugoslavia, Somalia, Liberia, etc. (Already in the Falklands war Austria complied with sanctions against Argentina.) Thus, Austria in practice became part of the collective security system.

There were no demonstrations in the streets of Vienna chanting slogans like "What have you done with our neutrality?" or "Where is our perpetual identity?" Among others, because government politicians simultaneously spoke—with sorrow—about the superannuation of neutrality, yet—using the who-if-not-Austria argument—claimed that Austria is going to Brussels as a neutral state.[46] Furthermore, they incessantly scared an already apprehensive populace with Soviet secession wars, eastern maffias, Bosnian refugees. Sarajevo is closer to Vienna than Bregenz, Europe would protect us from fascism (!), they kept repeating, almost convincing themselves that the island of peace can only be protected from the enemy on the great European sea. With Europe, Austria would even join *Schengenland*," besides, collective security is considerably cheaper than armed neutrality. During the war in Slovenia, foreign aircraft again entered Austrian airspace; a missile may be launched in the Middle East and fall in Vienna any time—so why wait?

The magic mixture promoting accession was almost ready when the Maastricht Treaty was signed. Austrian politicians clutched at their heart: all their efforts have been in vain, they believed. It is impossible to smuggle neutrality into an integration which not only expands but

---

[45] The irony was that Iraq had recognized Austria's neutrality, while Kuwait had not.

[46] See Chancellor Franz Vranitzky's statement, *Standard*, January 27, 1993.

deepens relations, which plans a single European currency, common foreign and security policies, and advocates majority decision-making. Moreover, the SPÖ-ÖVP coalition was annoyed knowing it would not be able to sell this program domestically, no matter how much it talks about making the concept of neutrality "dynamic." Especially not with Haider convincing half the country of the ghastly deeds of the bureaucrats in Brussels. However, it also became obvious that to some extent Maastricht enhances the bargaining power of small outsiders because the European Union does not want to leave any (market or military) gaps on the map. Therefore, it sometimes relaxes the rules in order to ease access for neutral countries seeking admission. Sweden renounces its automatic neutrality, while Switzerland—which has always been more consistent in its interpretation of neutrality than Austria—wants no part of a centralized Europe. Both are ominous signs from the point of view of Austria, which adopted the strategy of "creeping commitment." Nevertheless, unswayed, it says it is better to be where the decisions are made and exert its influence on the members than to suffer the consequences of decisions made without it; that the obstructing minority and the principle of subsidiarity and also the plan for a "Europe of regions" will protect Austria from the many majority decisions; and, anyway, their bark is worse than their bite when it comes to a common security policy; it is enough to think of the public squabbles that have characterized the Western states since the outbreak of the Yugoslav conflict; since Austria is joining of its own free will, it may also withdraw anytime it chooses. In other words, Austria should join, wait things out, and perhaps depart. It has survived the United Nations as a neutral state, it will survive the European Union, too. And, off the record: no big deal if it will not.

However, Brussels proved generous. After the first shock of the results of the French and Danish referenda, it decided to expand the integration before deepening it. The question of neutrality was left out of the agenda when negotiations started early 1993; it was replaced by economic issues, such as transit traffic, agricultural subsidies, environmental protection regulations, etc. It was not mentioned in the accession agreement, yet (therefore) both sides seemed satisfied. It is peculiar that no one talked about neutrality, allowing the other side to interpret the concept as it likes, at the same time, they used it as a tacitly understood argument in the great admission bargaining. Brussels reasoned as follows: if we force them to rescind the maxim of neutrality, they will balk at issues where they have the most bargaining power, in transit agreements, and to boot, their constituents will vote them down on the accession referendum; therefore, it is better to demand "only" a declaration that they will take part in the common foreign and security policies without reservation and will eventually join the West European Union and Partnership for Peace; if they consent to this, they can call themselves whatever they like, even perpetually neutral. The Austrian position was a mirror image of this tactic: if we scare them by saying we shall only marry them as neutrals and we can wait for the wedding, then they will be more yielding in negotiations on other more delicate issues; it does not involve much of an obligation if we adopt the creed that we shall support the common foreign and security policies which do not even exist yet and, when they will, they are not likely to be anything more serious than a kind of "soft security"; and when we return home from Brussels, we can proudly say to the people that we have won without giving away anything.

In March 1994, when negotiations ended, Austrian politicians were exuberant: Austria stayed neutral, its identity unchanged, the West was forced to concur, persistence paid off. As to why Austria was silent about its most precious spiritual possession, they said that neutrality was such a natural characteristic and so compatible with Europe that, and I quote, "the government dispensed with making it the issue of negotiations."[47] Austria has shown goodwill and, imagine, it won four votes for itself in the Council of Ministers in return. Does anyone have any idea how many votes Germany has, being ten times as big? Only ten.[48]

---

[47] See the Austrian government report on the results of the negotiations *Bericht der Bundesregierung über das Ergebnis der Verhandlungen über den Beitritt Österreichs zur Europäischen Union* (Vienna, 1994).

[48] See Foreign Minister Alois Mock's speech delivered in the Austrian Parliament in March 1994 at the end of the negotiations. Ott, ed., op. cit., pp. 109–113.

Neutrality has died but no one dares to make out the death certificate, a Viennese journalist observed. An old business swindle, sneered another. An *Etikettenschwindel*: the label is old but instead of vintage wine the bottle contains vinegar. It may well be that the Austrian government missed a historical opportunity when it did not withdraw completely from the Russian sphere of interest by not rescinding the pledge of neutrality when it could easily have done so, say, between 1991 and 1993. Today, with the end of "Euro-phoria," it would not be easy to amend the constitution and discard the ballast of neutrality. It is possible that Austria could already have joined NATO also, but instead it doggedly crawls toward the non-existent security system of the European Union because it clings to a decreasingly realistic "real-fiction." In opting for creeping commitment, Austria bargained cautiously about its own sovereignty. It realized that the neutrality it had to assume by necessity as a restriction on its sovereignty in 1955, but which it later was able to use to enhance sovereignty, again began to impinge on its freedom of movement. Right now, with sudden concern for its internal sovereignty, all but forgotten in the Golden Age when it lived in comfortable coalitions and citizenry did not interfere from below, it is hoping that military security and economic growth within the European Union will bring "more" sovereignty than political subordination takes away. In the early nineties there was a risk that by not joining Europe on account of its adherence to neutrality-based sovereignty, the citizens will punish the government for an ensuing diminution of the country's economic or military sovereingty.

Therefore, it had better keep the traditional identity elements of internal sovereignty in reserve. Furthermore, Austria should not only not discard neutrality, but should proclaim that the country is a veritable gift for the members of the Union—Austrian politicians argued. They need Austria because it is rich, stable, cultured, and environment-friendly (as a matter of fact, the European Union adopted Austria's stricter environment protection standards, not vice versa), and also because it links the Union with the late Eastern bloc (a novel element in this argument is the claim that Austria introduces Eastern applicants to the integration). Let the whole world learn again that Austrians are not Germans. The evidence being that Austria accepted

German as one of the official languages of the Union only on the condition that it would be supplemented with Austrian words. An appendix was agreed upon, which includes the following words, among others: *Erdapfel* instead of *Kartoffel* (potato), *Faschiertes* instead of *Hackfleisch* (meatloaf), *Karfiol* instead of *Blumenkohl* (cauliflower), *Marille* instead of *Aprikose* (apricot), *Paradeis* instead of *Tomate* (tomato), *Ribisel* instead of *Johannisbeer* (currant).

A Change of Identity?

Austria's honeymoon in the European Union has ended. It is now figuring out how membership affects its sovereingty. It is comparing things which are partly non-existent yet: a future increase in security, a possible political subordination, expansion in the scope of economic opportunity in some respects, its diminution in others. Meanwhile, it compares the change in internal sovereignty with that of the external.[49] No one can be reasonably expected to ask intelligent questions in this conceptual chaos. Even Austria's previous virtual sovereignty was easier to grasp than its present "tensile" sovereignty.

Austria recently applied to the European Union for an observer status. Somewhat impatiently, it was asked if it would not rather be a member. Lately, leading Social Democrat politicians have also began to openly talk about NATO membership. No one mentions Waldheim anymore, though his book, *The Answer*,[50] just appeared without, however, any revelations about his past even after ten years. Well, he has done his duty. And not just during the war. The unheard-of international isolation at the time of the scandal helped his colleagues realize that the stubborn *mir san mir* (we are us, or, bluntly: who cares what you think?) attitude is an insufficient basis for sovereignty. The ex-president is still *persona non-grata* and still on the American watchlist. Everything is normal in Austria and getting more normal by the day.

---

[49] See Fritz Breuss, "Erste Spuren des EU-Beitritts in Österreichs Wirtschaft," *Wirtschaftspolitische Blätter*, nos. 3–4 (1996).
[50] Waldheim, op. cit.

Boldizsár Nagy

EPHEMERAL SOVEREIGNTY
AND THE LONGING FOR THE ABSOLUTE

If legal cognition perceives norms that are contradictory
in their contents, it strives to dissolve this contradiction,
through meaningful interpretation, as mere pseudo-contradiction.
If this attempt is unsuccessful, then it eliminates the interpreted
material as meaningless, and as such, non-existent in the
sphere of law, which is a sphere of meanings.*

Jurisprudential interpretation must carefully avoid
the fiction that a legal norm admits only of one as the "correct"
interpretation. Traditional jurisprudence uses
this fiction to maintain the ideal of legal security.
In view of the ambiguity of most legal norms this ideal
is only approximately attainable. It should not be denied
that the fiction of legal norms having but one meaning
may have great advantages from some political point of view.
But no political advantage can justify the use of this fiction
in a scientific description of positive law.**

Hans Kelsen

*Roadsign****

Two topics are the subject of the present study. The first concerns
the semantic confusion about sovereignty and is comprised of three
parts. The first is an enumeration of the usual—therefore, easily yet

---

* *Tiszta jogtan* [Pure law]. Publication of the Bibó István Szakkollégium
(1988), p. 76.

** Hans Kelsen, *Pure Theory of Law* (Berkeley, 1967).

*** I am indebted to the two commentators, Tamás Kende and Péter Szigeti,
for their discerning criticism, to the participants in the debate, and the editor,
Györgyi Várnai, for their inspiring comments. They deserve credit for
improvements in the text and my stubbornness is to blame where there are none.

seldom obviated—confusion about the uses of the concept. Then, delving a little deeper, the second part reveals why international law is incapable of coming to terms with the content of sovereignty. According to my proposition, the main reason is indecisiveness on the question whether the origins of the development of an international system should be sought in the individual will of the states or, on the contrary, states must find the scope of their freedom within the restrictions and regulations imposed by international law and relations. This contradiction, although real, cannot be resolved, therefore, the content of sovereignty remains extremely uncertain, always to be corrected with whatever element was neglected. The third component of the first topic is an illustration offered by surveying Hungarian reality in the form of two questions—"Is or was Hungary sovereign?" and "Who make up the sovereign Hungarian people?"—in order to demonstrate that it is almost impossible to speak intelligibly about "sovereignty."

In the second half of the study, after evoking the image of longing for sovereignty as the ultimate absolute, an "if" proposition is adopted, namely, "if it were possible to speak intelligibly about sovereignty" as the point of departure for the sake of dialogue. That is followed by an assessment of international legal factors, which are contrary to the dogma of bloc-like, indivisible, total, and unrestricted state sovereignty, with special attention to those phenomena of the past decade that reflect the enhanced role of the international community.

The conclusion, in view of the first half of the study, is that it is meaningless to assert the existence or loss of Hungary's sovereignty because proof is impossible. It would be worthwhile in another study to make a methodical and broadly comparative assessment of the factors in international life that strengthen or diminish the separate existence of individual states.

I. The Difficulties in the Discourse and the Possible Content, Criteria, Synonyms of the Concept of Sovereignty

Why is it so difficult to discuss sovereignty? I think it is difficult for two reasons. One of them is the definitional quagmire, the usual curse of the social sciences, habitually aggravated by lawyers. We must resign ourselves to the fact that the word sovereignty has no meaning of its own, cannot reveal its own content.[1] I shall list some categories and phrases which may mean the same thing as the word sovereignty:

Statehood, independence, autonomy, autarchy, self-government, jurisdiction, totality of domestic affairs, regional/political integration, (absolute) power, constitutional power, final decision-maker, legitimation/legitimacy, right to self-determination, supervision over territory and population.

Just like the concepts above used concurrently in different disciplines and professions, sovereignty itself does not have a single identifiable meaning, therefore, it cannot have a generic definition either. Political science, political philosophy, theory of international relations, and international law all use one or more of the terms above without defining their meaning in relation to one another and to sovereignty, to determine which terms may be used simultaneously (because they carry distinct intelligible meanings) and which, taken as synonyms, play no part in building the system. Moreover, even within a discipline, the meaning of the terms depends on the schools

---

[1] According to Csaba Gombár, internal and external sovereignties are traditionally distinguished. Internal sovereignty=centralized and recognized sovereignty, external sovereignty=internationally manifest and recognized authority (p. 7).

"A sovereign agent enacts laws and grants exceptions to the law; the one that is above everything and everyone—and is not under any power" (p. 8).

László Lengyel: Sovereignty=scope of mobility, end of dependent relation (pp. 97–98).

Ákos Szilágyi distinguishes totalitarian sovereignty and classical sovereignty. According to him, federative organizations may also be sovereign (pp. 161 and 159).

György Csepeli lists the following among the attributes of sovereignty: own currency, independent military, independent foreign ministry, national border guard, separate customs system, passport, state railways, standards, national postage stamp issue (p. 154).

In László Valki's definition, in international law "a state not legally subordinate, is sovereign" (p. 59).

(discourses) using them.[2]

By inference, there is no (poetic) metalanguage. When dealing with concepts, the author must link the term used with some more or less well-identified signification defining the medium in which it is used, or devise easily recognized contents and syntax.[3] In the present study I use sovereignty as understood in international legal phraseology, which means approximately the following:[4]

The state and only the state is sovereign. Other actors in international law either derive their legal personality from the state—for instance, intergovernmental, including integrational organizations—or, partly as a result of the doctrinal efforts of jurisprudence, become the subjects of international law without the question of attributes of international legal sovereignty even arising in connection with them.

---

[2] Krasner, for instance, distinguishes four basic meanings of sovereignty, as follows: a) the modern Westphalian system, that is, territoriality and autonomy; b) domestic supremacy; c) the capacity to control movement across borders; and d) international contractual capacity. He states that autonomy within the Westphalian system was never complete, because it was violated in four ways: via conventions, contracts, coercion, and imposition. Richard K. Ashley and R. B. J. Walker, "Reading Dissidence/Writing the Discipline: Crisis and the Question of Sovereignty in International Studies," *International Studies Quarterly* 34 (1996), pp. 116–119, 367–416.

[3] There is no single definition of sovereignty because the meaning of "the term depends on the theoretical context within which it is being used." D. Stephen Krasner, "Compromising Westphalia," *International Security* 20, (Winter 1995–96), pp. 115–151.

[4] See also László Valki's study in the present volume, especially pp. 59–63, or the brief summary by Cassese according to which: "Sovereignty, in addition to granting each State a set of powers relating to the territory under its jurisdiction, includes the following sweeping rights: first, that of claiming respect for the State's territorial integrity and political independence by other States, second, that of claiming sovereign immunity for State representatives acting in their official capacity...third, that of claiming immunity from the jurisdiction of foreign courts for acts or actions performed by States in their sovereign capacity." Antonio Cassese, *International Law in a Divided World* (Oxford, 1988), p. 130. For a detailed review of the changes in the meaning of sovereignty, see Martti Koskenniemi, *From Apology to Utopia: The Structure of International Legal Discourse* (Helsinki, 1989), pp. 206–212, particularly notes 49 and 50.

These are, for instance, the people exercising the right of self-determination, minorities, insurgents, belligerent, and perhaps also
humankind in connection with its common heritage and concerns.

State sovereignty does not depend on recognition, but if the international community as a whole denies recognition, then it is nonexis-
tent from the point of view of law, as was the case with the
Bantustans. According to international law, a sovereign state may perform legal acts on its own behalf and exercise the *iure imperii* acts of
the state, that is, conclude treaties, appoint and receive ambassadors,
control its borders, issue stamps, represent its territory and population
in international cooperation, from telecommunications[5] to health care.

The domestic legal acts of the sovereign state are accepted as
valid by other actors in the international sphere, that is, if they do not
challenge the legislation, judicial decisions, and administrative decisions of that state.[6]

Sovereignty is a rather formal category in international law, and
although there are traditional and current borderline cases (from the
Vatican through Taiwan to the Republic Srpska or the Turkish
Republic of Northern Cyprus), generally, the decision whether or not
a specific entity is sovereign from the point of view of international
law is not difficult to make.

The difficulty of discussing sovereignty has another, more serious
source than the trivial problem of definition which may be resolved by
artificial linguistic consensus: namely, the science and application of
international law is an area of perpetual confrontation between irrecon-

---

[5] By way of illustration: The first paragraph of the International Telecommunications Agreement "enacted as Act 18 of 1985, provides the keynote as
follows: ..."(Para. 1), then states that only those non-United Nations member
sovereign countries may become members of the Agreement whose admission
is supported by a two-thirds majority. (Para. 5.)

[6] There are exceptions. A state, by referring to law and order, may refuse to
take cognizance of certain rules of law of another state (for instance, those
allowing polygamy) or, without questioning the existence of the state, may
deny recognition of the government acting on behalf of the state, in which
event, it may also disregard the decisions of government agencies. I shall
return to the consequences of such a measure in the later discussion of
Hungary's sovereignty in the early Kádár period.

cilable approaches wherein the dilemmas cannot be resolved.[7] In order to decide whether the application of a measure restricts state sovereignty, we should first ascertain the "natural" and "inviolable" scope of sovereignty. This, in turn, demands that we identify the basis of sovereignty, that from which it springs and which may define its limits.

Concerning the source of sovereignty, two contradictory arguments are known to international legal discourse. According to one of them, the source of sovereignty is the factual existence of the state, the aggregate of facts outside the sphere of law. It is the will of states that creates international law which sanctions and makes sovereignty its fundamental principle. According to the other, however, the legal order surrounding the states vests in them the attributes of sovereignty as determined—and, therefore, restricted—by international law. Defining the scope of sovereignty again evinces the divergence of views concerning its origin and foundation. The positive, apologetic reasoning starts from facts, and will refer everything not forming part of another state's sovereignty to the sovereign authority of the state, and, in case of dispute, will accept only facts (actual possession) to decide the issue. In the negative, utopistic reasoning, which approaches the question from the international system, the scope of sovereignty, that is, the extent of the freedom of action of states, depends on the competence-distributive function of international law and order. In other words, freedom of the state is the sum total of what the international system grants, or does not restrict.

The dilemma cannot be resolved, due to the fact that at one point reasoning on both sides is compelled to use the other side's opposite argument. When the question is: why a sovereign state cannot deviate from its previous declaration of will, that is, why treaties and customary law are binding, even the positive, apologetic reasoning can only answer that it is imposed by the system of international law. On the other hand, when the question concerns the origin of the force of authority of international law and order, utopistic reasoning can only say—if it wants to avoid taking a position based on pure natural law

---

[7] The following argument is, for the most part, a simplified abstract of Martti Koskenniemi's lucid and well-documented analysis. For more detail, see Koskenniemi, op. cit., pp. 193–263.

(derived from either the divine principle or the principle of reason)—
that it arises from empirical facts, from the behavior of states.

Consequently, the "natural" scope of sovereignty cannot be described in abstract terms in reference to a state, and much less can the dispute between two states on the use of natural resources or the competence for action by the supreme authority, be solved merely on the basis of the legal category of sovereignty.[8]

It is worth recalling some of the characteristic international legal disputes of the post-World War II period that show both sides using sovereignty as their argument, yet find that it could not be used as a basis for a solution; thus, either the dispute remained unresolved, or the tribunal of arbitration applied some other principle to settle the dispute.

In the *Right of Passage* case (1960) brought before the International Court of Justice, Portugal and India both relied on sovereignty to claim mutually exclusive jurisdiction: Portugal claimed the right of passage for its troops and arms through the territory of India to reach Portuguese colonial enclaves in order to exercise its right to use force, a prerequisite of sovereignty, for suppressing the rebellion against Portuguese authority; India, on the other hand, claimed the right to prohibit the passage of foreign troops and armament through territory under its jurisdiction. Their dispute could have been resolved in two ways: either inductively by reference to the will of the two countries—as expressed in treaties—or deductively on the basis of the needs of the international system and general customary law— provided that either of them would furnish an answer. In the end, however, facts decided the dispute: by the time decision was reached

---

[8] To decide boundary disputes without violating sovereign equality, we are limited to criteria that are hierarchically more important than statehood to provide a justification for drawing its limit in some particular way. This is perhaps most vividly illustrated in conflicts over territory or natural resources.

In such cases, the disputing states unilaterally devise an interpretation of their statehood that covers the desired assets. Because statehood implies no particular limit to the state's sphere of freedom, such cases cannot be understood as simply recognizing a limit that is somehow 'already' there. As the practice of the International Court of Justice has shown, such disputes require the construction of an 'equitable' solution rather than a determination of any rights and duties existing *ex ante*." Koskenniemi, op. cit., p. 408.

six years later, India had annexed the Portuguese colonies. At the same time, characteristically, the decision avoided taking a general stand on the question of sovereignty, with the conclusion that there exists a bilateral authoritative practice (*lex specialis*) which did not entitle Portugal to unconditional right of passage. The unanswerability of the question is reflected by the eight to seven vote on this part of the decision.[9]

In the Nuclear Tests cases,[10] Australia and New Zealand questioned whether atmospheric nuclear tests may be held in the Pacific region by asserting that the nuclear fallout over their territory violates their sovereignty. France, on the other hand, maintained that it had a sovereign right to maintain its military capability and carry out nuclear tests on islands under French rule in the Pacific Ocean. The question finally did not come up for decision because France unilaterally halted atmospheric nuclear tests and the International Court of Justice discontinued the case.[11]

This same dilemma characterizes the Gabčikovo-Nagymaros Project awaiting decision by the International Court of Justice. Slovakia questions Hungary's right to change in 1992 its 1977 decision concerning the construction of the hydroelectric dam project on the Danube (in other words, it uses the bilateral treaty as an argument against Hungary's decision to terminate). At the same time, it denies that the general rules of environment protection or the treaties for the protection of biological diversity and the general customary law prohibiting harmful practices can restrict Slovakia's sovereign right to utilize the hydropotential of the Danube. (In these arguments of Slovakia the freedom of the sovereign state is set against the prescriptions established by the international system.) The Court will pronounce judgment, but it will not be setting a precedent, because it is impossible to decide what sovereignty is based on, therefore, the questions of what does and does not constitute sovereignty, what is reconcilable with

---

9 See Koskenniemi, op. cit., p. 208; Vanda Lamm, *A Nemzetközi Bíróság ítéletei és tanácsadó véleményei: 1945–1993* (Budapest, 1995), p. 99; and *Summaries of Judgments, Advisory Opinions and Orders of the International Court of Justice: 1948–1991* (New York, 1992), pp. 52–54.

10 For a brief description, see Lamm, op. cit., pp. 205–211.

11 *Summaries of Judgments*, pp. 97–99.

what, acts to restrict "absolute sovereignty," and should remain vague.

II. Is Hungary Sovereign and, if so, When Is It Sovereign? To Whom Does Sovereignty Belong to?

If we are incapable of grasping reality in conceptual terms or of describing it step by step then, by nature of the language, we may substitute reality by linking the subject to a point in the past, assuming[12] that, given sufficient time and the availability of source material, the speaker and the listener would reconstruct the subject in the same way in a lengthy verbal description. Thus, although the phrase "Hungary in 1989" has no formally or linguistically identified content, statements that "After 1989 Hungary also became a sovereign state," and "Since 1989, it also possesses the formal attributes of sovereignty"—as Csaba Gombár writes—becomes subject to interpretation. According to László Lengyel, events after 1989 led to the establishment of independence, while previously, in the Kádár period, "the state lacked both external and internal sovereignty" Looking beyond Hungary, Gombár believes that the "state formations established within the sphere of influence of the Soviet empire" were not sovereign after 1945 because for them sovereignty was "only a distant purpose, a vague ideal."[13]

---

[12] Mostly without any justification, which I cannot go into here.

[13] So many pitfalls in a simple statement! —What would the list of state formations contain? Do Albania, China, Korea, Yugoslavia, Romania always belong there? What is the subject of the sentence? The countries concerned? Their legislatures? The formal or actual power centers of the communist parties? Does the sentence suggest that the Hungarian Socialist Workers Party led by János Kádár longed for sovereignty but was unable to attain it? Or, does it suggest that the party leaders (the parliament and the government) were puppets who were not part of the country, therefore, the country longed to be sovereign in opposition to the politicians, behind their backs? Can it be said that there was no law and order in Hungary and the executives of state functions arrogated the right to authority to themselves between 1945(?) and 1989? What should the first date be? 1945, 1947, 1948, or as late as 1949?—If the non-democratically selected leaders of a country—including dictators—do not embody state sovereignty, then must we conclude that no dictatorship is sovereign?

Are they right or wrong? We do not know and, in my view, shall never know. By way of an experiment, I questioned a group of twelve social scientists, including some authors of the present volume, and sixteen fourth-year law students of Budapest University about the fundamental facts of Hungary's sovereignty.[14] First I asked if in their opinion Hungary was "essentially not sovereign," "sovereign in a limited sense," or "completely sovereign" in 1996, 1968, 1957, and 1946?

There was complete agreement that before 1996 the Hungarian state was not completely sovereign.[15] However, the respondents were

---

Yugoslavia, Romania always belong there?

What is the subject of the sentence? The countries concerned? Their legislatures? The formal or actual power centers of the communist parties? Does the sentence suggest that the Hungàrian Socialist Workers Party led by János Kádár longed for sovereignty but was unable to attain it? Or, does it suggest that the party leaders (the parliament and the government) were puppets who were not part of the country, therefore, the country longed to be sovereign in opposition to the politicians, behind their backs?

Can it be said that there was no law and order in Hungary and the executives of state functions arrogated the right to authority to themselves between 1945(?) and 1989? What should the first date be? 1945, 1947, 1948, or as late as 1949? —If the non-democratically selected leaders of a country—including dictators—do not embody state sovereignty, then must we conclude that no dictatorship is sovereign?

[14] The polling, of course, was not a sociologically meaningful survey, since the notion of a representative sample does not even arise. Nevertheless, I think, it proves irrefutably that neither the experts, nor the knowledgeable public has formed an instinctive common idea concerning the existence and extent of Hungary's sovereignty.

[15] Concerning 1968 the ratio of "not sovereign" to "had restricted sovereignty" was 16:12, concerning 1957 the ratio was 26:2, concerning the post-war coalition period preceding the Warsaw Pact and COMECON the ratio was 14:13 (plus one "I don't know" response). In other words, no one believed that there was even one moment of unrestricted sovereignty in the history of Hungary after 1945 up to at least 1968. This is not as self-evident as it may seem. If sovereignty is independence from the great powers and opposition to the international community—as many believe—then Hungary was considerably sovereign in 1957 when it opposed—behind the protective shield of the Soviet Union, of course—the official position of the United Nations and its dominant member, the United States. Think of Cuba's position today.

not unanimous on whether Hungary has achieved complete sovereignty by now.[16]

Two-thirds of the respondents said that the proposals and decisions of the IMF and the World Bank have restricted Hungary's sovereignty, and similar skepticism was expressed about large organizations of which Hungary is a member or aspires to join.[17] In comparison, on the question of satellite television broadcasts (which cannot be controlled) only one-fifth of the respondents believe that they restrict state sovereignty (including the right to protect youth from undesirable influences), while four-fifths do not think that these broadcasts, which impact on the cultural life of the country, affect sovereignty.[18]

---

[16] The distribution of responses was as follows: "essentially not": 2, "restrictively": 11, "completely": 15.

[17] The question was this: "Did, does, or would our (voluntary) membership in he organizations listed below and the concomitant obligations restrict Hungary's sovereignty?" There were three possible responses: restricts, does not restrict, don't know. This table shows the distribution:

	Restricts	Does not restrict	Don't know	
United Nations	4	23	1	
European Union	21	7		
NATO	19	9		
Warsaw Pact	27	1		
Paris Union for the Protection of Industrial Property	5	11	11	(did not answer: 1)
UEFA*	3	17	7	(did not answer: 1)

* The topicality of this question springs from the decision of the European Community Court in Luxembourg, which shook the very foundations of the UEFA rule demanding strict obedience and was also applied in national competitions, according to which the number of foreigners playing on a team may be restricted and the original club may ask to be paid for the player. The Court pronounced that in the European Community a soccer player is an employee like anyone else, therefore, may seek employment under local conditions anywhere within the European Community in compliance with the principle of freedom of movement.

[18] This was the only question which revealed a significant difference between the scholars and the university students. All five of those who responded that satellite broadcasts restrict sovereignty were university students.

What this rudimentary test shows is that there is no tacit consensus in Hungarian public opinion on the question whether the country is sovereign, except in connection with the Warsaw Pact and 1957. It is remarkable how many people think that the objects of Hungarian aspirations, that is, membership in the European Union and NATO, would actually restrict sovereignty.[19] At the same time, only four respondents said that the United Nations, which makes implementation of sanctions binding on Hungary without the latter's consent, restricts sovereignty; and none of the social scientists expressed concern about state supremacy in relation to international television broadcasts most likely to undermine cultural integrity.[20]

One would expect that, even if the views about Hungarian state sovereignty are profoundly divided, there would be agreement on the questions as follows: whom does state sovereignty serve, whom does it protect and from what, and who are invested with the historical, political, and constitutional right to determine the fundamental tenets of domestic arrangements and foreign relations of the sovereign state. Language deceptively suggests that the sovereign Hungarian state obviously belongs to the Hungarian people. Yet, the question "Who is Hungarian?" was found just as unanswerable as the question "Who is sovereign?"[21] The answer depends on the context in which the question is raised. A certain person may be considered Hungarian in one context and foreign in another. This holds true even if many are forced to decide by tragically extreme circumstances—or let others decide for them, without regard for the consequences—to what group they "really" belong. This covers everything from anti-Jewish laws to the practice of issuing permits to return home for Bosnian refugees,

---

[19] United Nations measures will be discussed in detail further on.

[20] Being an international lawyer, I found this surprising, because it is one of the most important issues in the debate the basic principles of satellite broadcasting on the agenda of the United Nations; specifically, the question is whether transmission to another country is reconcilable with national sovereignty. Some of the states were so firmly opposed to it that the International Telecommunications Union deciding on satellite locations and frequencies adopted the general rule prohibiting transmission via satellite to another country, except in the technically unavoidable case of overspill.

[21] See György Csepeli's study in the present volume.

and still there is no "unequivocal criterion" in sight.

It is interesting to examine international and Hungarian legal proposals from this point of view.

In international law, citizenship is the dominant criterion of nationality status. The decisive principle in selecting the officials of an international organization based on national quota is formal citizenship, and not self-identification or ethnic origin. Similarly, diplomatic protection is granted only to those who are citizens of the state granting protection at the time of the injury as well as at the time when protection is exercised.[22] Private international law (for instance, from the point of view of the conditions of marriage) defines also as alien a person who is not a Hungarian citizen, irrespective of common culture, customs, etc.[23]

However, this basic principle contains certain nuances. In the *Nottebohm* case[24] the International Court of Justice pronounced that citizenship must express actual relationship. Hence, Liechtenstein could not extend diplomatic protection to Nottebohm, who became a naturalized citizen during World War II in order to avoid the confiscation of his assets in Guatemala—which was nevertheless done, because he was an ethnic German and previously a German citizen.

Hungarian law also recognizes the situation whereby the authorities treat a person who is a Hungarian citizen as if that person were an alien. This holds for those millions of people of Hungarian background who were born abroad and who may be unaware that they are

---

[22] Thus, whether the head of the Hungarian government (in spirit) considers himself the prime minister of ten million Hungarians or of fifteen million, the fact remains that the foreign minister can grant diplomatic protection to only ten million. (The late Prime Minister József Antall stated that in his spirit he was prime minister of fifteen million Hungarians, in reference to some five million ethnic Magyars living abroad, mostly in the neighboring countries.)

[23] The situation is even more complicated in the case of legal persons and the shareholders who own them. The designations, "Hungarian company" and "Hungarian product," are not merely part of the patriotic or chauvinistic rhetoric, but also a criterion fundamentally influencing access to European Community markets. Those preparing for integration know that the examination by customs law of "what is Hungarian" and the question of "who is Hungarian" are equally important.

[24] *ICJ Reports* (1995), p. 4.

members of the Hungarian political nation, that is, that they are Hungarian citizens under the law, even if they are fourth-generation descendants, and for those who took up permanent residence abroad and under the laws on foreign exchange and suffrage cannot exercise the same rights as other Hungarian citizens who live in Hungary.

There are also examples of the opposite situation when the law guarantees preferential treatment for aliens, of Hungarian origins. The laws governing immigration and citizenship both ensure preferential treatment for the one "claiming to be a Hungarian national and whose ancestor was a Hungarian citizen."[25]

Neither the terminology, nor the practice it is based on, that is, the interaction between the state and the international community, nor the concrete case of Hungary point to a clear concept of sovereignty. Hence, reason turns to emotions for help, arguing that it is impossible that something does not exist when it should, and thus postulates sovereignty.

III. Sovereignty as the Concept of an Ultimate Absolute

Let us review the attributes with which everyday imagination, as well as important series of studies in constitutional and international law, invested the concept of sovereignty.

The sovereign state is free, unrestricted, complete, invulnerable, free to decide at will, free of intervention, "master of its own house." The sovereign state is undisputed, its dictates (the word of its parliament and courts) are final, is not subject to control or review, declares the truth and needs no additional proof. The constitution—if there is one—is a sacred text, its tenets are the ultimate standard.

The sovereign state is beautiful because it is majestic, it is supreme, creates symbols for its own exclusive use; it has a poetic, indeed spiritual substance; it is often the embodiment, the alter ego of

---

[25] Para. 27 of Govt. regulation 64/1994 (IV.30) and Para 4 of Act LV of 1993. The former exempts such immigrants from the three-year residence requirement, the latter reduces the naturalization requirement from an eight-year waiting period to one year.

collective consciousness, of the nation; it is the exalted representation of ourselves with which we identify; it draws the dividing line between "us" and "them" by way of legislation.

The sovereign state is powerful, more powerful than anyone else, because, second to God or by the grace of God, it possesses ultimate secular power, it is the military and the police whose power shields, punishes the guilty and protects the innocent.

The sovereign state is the embodiment of predictability, order, and harmony, primarily in the form of law and order which predicts the consequences of personal behavior and, at the same time, maps out the spatial scope of activity, that is, the state borders which filter out unpredictable external forces bent on disorder and allow them entry only if they adapt to internal order.

The sovereign state is good because through state welfare agencies it aids and supports the ill, comforts the elderly, provides for the needy, protects against epidemic, recognizes and certifies qualification, operates public utilities and services, educates and entertains as well.

In other words, the sovereign state is a god second to God or in lieu of God, endowed with the attributes and presumed limitations of the Almighty.[26] The attitude to sovereignty does call to mind the different images of God, granting even atheism, or denial of sovereignty in this case. We long for something ultimate, something unquestionable, an origo, the measure for everything, something that is identical with itself and has no source, yet is capable of creation, has energy without being nourished, appears under always new forms but unaltered in its essence, something that is a certainty without proof, an answer complete in itself, the Archimedean point.

Yet, we must understand that while the aspiration this display of poetic imagination conveys is real, the idea of sovereignty itself is not.

> Discourses on sovereignty cannot relate to their object, sovereignty, as anything but a problem or question....When pronounced in a religious tone of desire, the word "sovereignty" is often used ideologically, as if it represented some source of

---

[26] The question is familiar: Can God create a stone He cannot lift?

meaning, some effective organizational principle, some mode of being already in place, some simply and obviously given resolution of paradoxes of space, time and identity. Yet this word is only spoken amid and in reply to a crisis of representation where paradoxes of space, time and identity displace all certain referents and put all origins of truth and meaning in doubt. As this is so, sovereignty cannot really represent any of these things.[27]

IV. Sovereignty, Independence, Intervention, the Limits to Freedom

Returning to international legal discourse—which knows little of doubts and acknowledges even less—we must answer the question whether signing an international agreement, hence joining an international organization, restricts sovereignty.

The answer, whether affirmative or negative, seems trivial and true. Naturally, the scope of activity of a state diminishes when it signs an agreement under the terms of which it must tolerate or do something it otherwise would not (for instance, allow the passage of ships through a canal built on its own territory, or use specified radio frequencies in military communication).[28]

On the other hand, we may say it is evident that a treaty or membership in an organization cannot have a negative effect on sovereignty, since signing and implementing a treaty, or carrying out obligations pertaining to membership in an international organization are in effect an exercise of sovereignty. Every decision is an exclusion of incompatible alternatives, relinquishing other theoretically possible outcomes, but it may not be considered as an avoidable restriction for

---

[27] Ashley and Walker, op. cit., pp. 367–416.

[28] The first example refers to the case of the Kiel Canal where the question was this: is Germany obligated to obey the contractual command of neutrality in the case of ships passing through the canal if it is contrary to its national interest, that is, "could it give up sovereignty in this respect?" The second anticipates Hungary's membership in NATO; when it happens, only the use of NATO-compatible communications systems will be allowed in the military.

the simple reason that it is given ontologically.

László Valki, in his seminal book on the integration then known as the Common Market, had in essence distinguished political sovereignty from legal sovereignty, recognizing the gradual nature of the former, that is to say, he interpreted political sovereignty as a measure of dependence along an axis indicating gradations from "completely dependent," "relatively dependent," "mutually dependent," to "holding the other in dependence." In turn, he applied the binary code to interpret legal sovereignty showing that it either exists or it does not, and rejected the notion that a state may be "partially sovereign" in legal terms.[29]

Indeed, it becomes confusing if every factor acting counter to independence is seen as violating sovereignty. For instance, the economy of a state may depend on importing strategic goods, its geographical position such as the lack of seaports may make it dependent on transit permits from its neighbors, its financial system may recognize the right of veto by other states or organizations, a significant proportion of its population may live on foreign aid, which can be withheld. Nevertheless, according to international legal criteria, material restrictions due to mutual dependence, or arising from collusion between "nature" and "history"—such as the wealth or poverty of a state in natural and human resources, including climate and geographic conditions—must not be listed among the factors restricting sovereignty because conceptually they do not belong there.

Human-made factors of interdependence do not affect sovereignty either, not even if some of them infringe upon the independence of the state. Indeed, most of them leave both sovereignty and independence intact. Independence may be called restricted in terms of law if an international agreement stipulates the extradition of a person to another state, or if a state has to tolerate the presence of foreign warships in its territorial waters, or if it has to refrain from introducing protective tariffs. It is unnecessary to double the nature of this restriction by interpreting it as a restriction on sovereignty as well. There is a difference: in these situations "complete independence" may be

---

[29] László Valki, *A nemzetközi jog társadalmi természete* (Budapest, 1989), pp. 415–418.

regained by unilateral measures, since all that is required is withdrawal from the given legal commitment.

Jus cogens and general customary law are interesting exceptions from the point of view of legal doctrine. The former refers to unconditional, peremptory rules (for instance, the prohibition of the use of force), the latter to rules that may be disregarded only by those who have been persistently opposed to them from the time of their conception (for instance, the regulations governing the right of passage in coastal waters). A state may not ignore *jus cogens* or general customary law; in this sense it cannot attain "complete independence," which may seem a restriction on sovereignty. At this point the problem becomes a game of words. I think it is more appropriate to postulate that the command of obedience to *jus cogens* and general customary law is inherent in the sovereignty of every state, and does not violate that sovereignty, since it does not take away anything that belongs to it. Thus, the sovereignty of a state created recently cannot extend to the introduction of slavery, nor to the prerogative of intentional *mala fide* violation of commitments.

In my view, actions implemented by some states or even by the international community as a whole at the expense of any state against its express political will, reduce independence without affecting sovereignty, in the form of legally regulated sanctions.

V. Events in the Period between the Two World Wars Already Contradicted the Concept of Bloc-like Sovereignty

We do not know when Hungary was ever a sovereign state, or even if it is sovereign today, indeed, there is uncertainty as to who the agents of this doubtful sovereignty may be. Moreover, it is questionable whether sovereignty is in fact the hinge around which international relations revolve. The idea that the Westphalian system will come to an end and sovereignty will need to be reassessed is not new. World War I upset contemporary ideas just as much as the cataclysm of World War II, or the realization of interdependence in the sixties and seventies or, more recently, the end of the bipolar world order.

It is worth recalling some of the institutions, events, and ideas of the interwar period in order to put contemporary views on the depreciation and fading of sovereignty in proper perspective.

Some of these concerned the status of the individual and set limits on the exercise of territorial authority over the individual. The system for the protection of minorities instituted by the League of Nations is a case in point. Although it did not allow the individual to appeal directly to the organs of the League of Nations, the submission of a petition, if supported by a member of the Council, did set the international machinery into motion. Hence, the authority of the territorial sovereign over its subjects became limited. The practice of certain joint commissions also protected the rights of individuals. Both in the Americas and Europe there were bilateral, or trilateral, joint commissions before which the citizens or legal persons of a state could appear to file a complaint against another state as, for instance, the Hungarian Péter Pázmány University did against Czechoslovakia on the basis of the Trianon peace treaty.

Among the cases restricting territorial supremacy the following deserve mention: the solution of the question of Upper Silesia in which the ruling of a special court, or Claims Commission, with the participation of a third party, restricted the authority of both Poland and Germany; the case of the Saar district, under international (League of Nations) administration for fifteen years; and the case of mandated territories. The nation commissioned to administer a mandated territory was not given unrestricted authority; it was, above all, assigned the task of preparing the territory for independence and was under the obligation to report on its activities to the League of Nations; furthermore, the inhabitants of the mandated territory could file complaints against the nation holding the mandate.[30]

These developments shook the very foundations of nineteenth-century positivist doctrines and gave way to a sweeping modernist trend according to which sovereignty was outdated and, henceforth, it became the international community's responsibility to create the

---

[30] The examples are many, including the arrangement concerning the Äland Islands, which is instructive from the Hungarian point of view because it contains important minority-protection regulations.

new, internationalist, activist basis for international relations by way of legal measures facilitating change.[31]

VI. International Legal Standards Restricting the Freedom of Action of States, in Particular Qualitatively New Developments in International Law

Naturally, public opinion in Hungary is more concerned with how Hungary's membership in the European Union and NATO will restrict its freedom of action than with the events between the two world wars. I believe the formal argument according to which membership as well as possible termination of membership in these organizations are free decisions made by the Hungarian Republic is irrefutable (member states of the organizations, of course, must approve admission, but not secession); consequently, rather than restricting, they represent a way of exercising legal sovereignty.[32] However, if we look beyond and analyze relations of power, decision-making, and influence in practice, we discover the trivial fact that these two organizations merely add to the long list of organizations and treaties restricting state legislative and executive power, from GATT, which governs tariffs and deprives states of the right to employ arbitrary protectionist means,[33] through

---

[31] Two outstanding essays about this process, representing the critical legal school, were written by David Kennedy, *Some Reflections on The Role of Sovereignty in the New International Order,* manuscript, 1992, pp. 6–8; and Nathaniel Berman, "Modernism, Nationalism and the Rhetoric of Reconstruction," *Yale Journal of Law and Humanities* 4 (1992), pp. 362–363.

[32] Csaba Gombár also mentions this dilemma, but does not say whether or not the proposition, "right to secede=assertion of sovereignty" is to be accepted. We lose track of the answer in a puzzling footnote. (See note 54, which says that we cannot know what this situation would actually involve, since no state has yet seceded from the European Union.) Debates around the study reveal a lack of agreement on the right of secession. Some authors recognize it, others not.

[33] Given extraordinary circumstances, the state may introduce, for instance, protective tariffs or take measures against a company/state that undercuts competitors, but may not introduce them as a purely economic policy measure to build a protective wall around a country.

monetary organizations to the International Labor Organization (ILO), which fundamentally influences labor relations, or to Interpol, which deals with the most sensitive issues of state life.

In the following I shall discuss issues which are remarkable, because they go beyond commitments pertaining to membership in an international organization or the fulfillment of a multilateral treaty. This means either that the partial surrender of the freedom of action by the state is not reciprocated by a similar self-imposed restriction by the other state (as opposed to tariff agreements for instance) or, a situation whereby the state loses its right to independent decision and cannot evade compliance with a rule regardless of mutual advantages.

According to the fundamental principle of international law, formulation of international legal rules requires the express or tacit consent of equal states. These provisions are binding if and insofar as the state concerned recognizes them as such. The Roman maxim, *par in parem non habet imperium*, is the fundamental principle defining relations between sovereign and equal states: no state among them shall exercise power over its equals; obligations become binding only with the consent of the state concerned, which consent may be formulated in a treaty or customary law.[34]

Nevertheless, there is a trend in international law, which has become more pronounced over the past twenty years, to regard certain standards as general customary law and in some cases as peremptory norms, i.e., *jus cogens*, that expressly prohibit any deviation, which restrict the freedom of decision and action of states and the states must accept the binding force of these standards.

Let us review some of the areas where international law interferes with the unlimited freedom of action of individual states (regarded by many as traditional sovereignty) or goes as far as to

---

[34] This same notion is expressed by Tomuschat as follows: "Our rough and sketchy description of a development that took more than 300 years to come to its final point may not permit many conclusions. It shows, however, that sovereign equality has always been the *leitmotif*. States *superiorem auctoritatem non recognisunt*." Christian Tomuschat, "Obligations Arising for States Without or Against Their Will," *Recueil des Cours* 241, no. 4 (1993).

impose indisputable restrictions on it.

A) Internationalized Territories, the Common Heritage and Common Concern of Mankind

The territoriality of sovereignty is obvious,[35] even if extraterritorial jurisdiction and national legislation and the conflicts arising from them are of long-standing and seem to be spreading.[36] The unlimited expansionist wish of states is held in check not only by the frontiers the other states, but also by territories recognized as coveted subjects for appropriation and freely accessible to all. The high seas have been such a territory for centuries and, undoubtedly, outer space is now also a *res communis omnium usus*, that is, for the free use of all. Theoretically, sovereignty claims over the Antarctic are not ruled out but, in effect, the treaty system in force has frozen these claims.[37]

It is worthwhile to review briefly the contention concerning "national possession vs. international status" as a new development in the concept of sovereignty. Respective states extended their jurisdiction over the continental shelf after World War II as well as over the

---

[35] See, for example, Krasner, op. cit., pp. 115–151.

[36] In the much analyzed Lotus case, Turkey extended its jurisdiction over a French naval officer held responsible for a collision of ships on the high seas, which the Permanent International Court approved in 1927 despite protest by the French government. PCIJ: *Lotus Case*, Ser. A. 10. Most modern litigations are due to the expansion of the scope of trade and tax regulations, as a result of which the authorities of a given state vindicate the right to regulate the business policy of companies operating on the territory of and according to the laws of another state, as did the United States when, on June 22, 1982, it prohibited the exportation of oil and gas production equipment to the Soviet Union by extending the jurisdiction of the regulation over American-controlled companies, but which were European in terms of law. The European Community unequivocally stated that "The US measures as they apply in the present case are unacceptable under international law because of their extraterritorial aspects." (21 ILM (1982), cited by Barry E. Carter and Phillip R. Trimble, *International Law* (Boston, 1991), p. 752.

[37] Seven states have partly overlapping territorial claims in Antarctica. The Hungarian Foreign Minister published the Antarctic Treaty, ratified in 1959, under serial number 7, in *Magyar Közlöny*, no. 22, 1984.

so-called exclusive economic zone in the two hundred-mile range from the coast, mostly during the 1970s.[38] These two developments meant a strengthening of territoriality, national expansion at the expense of the international one.

The elaboration of the category of common heritage of humankind opened a reverse course. In 1967, Malta proposed at the United Nations that whatever is found on the sea-bed falling outside national jurisdiction be declared the common heritage of mankind and benefits derived therefrom be turned toward decreasing the gap between developed and developing countries. The United Nations Law of the Sea Convention of 1982 states that the sea-bed beyond national jurisdiction (called "the Area") and its resources form the common heritage of humankind. This means, among others things.

> 1) Article 137 (1) No state shall claim or exercise sovereignty or sovereign rights over any part of the Area or its resources, nor shall any State or natural or juridical person appropriate any part thereof. No such claim or exercise of sovereignty or sovereign rights nor such appropriation shall be recognized....
> 2) "All rights to the resources of the Area are vested in human-kind as a whole, on whose behalf the Authority shall act."[39]

Similarly, the 1979 Moon Agreement[40] declared that the planets and other celestial bodies (except the Earth) of the solar system, the Moon, and the satellite orbits around them constitute the common heritage of humankind—implying not only that they cannot be sub-ject to sovereign rule, but that they must be utilized commonly.

Two important conventions, one on climate change and one on

---

[38] They do not have complete and exclusive jurisdiction either over the con-tinental shelf, or in the exclusive economic zone. Foreigners may enter, sail in, fly over, and lay cables in this region. For this reason, we must be wary of using of the term, "exercise sovereignty," which explains the choice of the more moderate "jurisdiction" in the text.

[39] A/CONF.62/122. The sea-bed authority, called "Authority" was created by the agreement and given the prerogative to regulate exploitation within the framework defined by the agreement.

[40] A/RES/68; 18 ILM (1979) p. 1434.

biological diversity, presented for signature in Rio de Janeiro in 1992, define the safeguarding of the climate and of biological diversity as the common concern of humankind.[41]

These conventions radically affect the use of resources, one of the main objects of the drive for sovereignty. Hitherto, territorial states had an exclusive right to regulate the use of resources on their territory with the exception of shared or common resources (e.g., boundary rivers or lakes) which were and are frequently subject to customary rules or formal agreements between the affected parties. The wealth and resources of international territories were subject to the first come first served principle, including the potential for overuse or degradation, except in the case where international agreements restricted or prohibited the trapping, hunting, or fishing of certain species and special agreements outlawed air- and sea-polluting practices.

The doctrine of the common heritage and of the common concern of humankind not only forbids sovereign appropriation, but expressly prescribes uses to benefit of humankind as a whole, as well as rational management and development. Thus, it imposes a hitherto unknown restriction on the appetites of sovereign states: it is no longer possible—in collusion with other states—to preempt territories defined as international nor to usurp their resources on the principle of "might makes right."[42]

B. Human Rights and Protection of the Individual

Until the mid-twentieth century the doctrine of international law deemed the relationship between the individual, or subject, and the sovereign (state)—with the exception of regulations protecting minorities and a few special rules such as labor regulations—to be the domestic affair of states falling under their internal jurisdiction and not subject to

---

[41] Change, 31 ILM (1992) 849, and the Convention on Biological Diversity, 31 ILM (1992) 822, Hungary enacted Acts LXXXI and LXXXII of 1995.

[42] "First come, first served" may sound more sophisticated, but in the area of fishing, for instance, it means the same, namely, well-equipped fishing fleet can plunder the sea so efficiently as to leave nothing, including the fish population necessary for reproduction, for less well-equipped coming from geographically closer shores.

international authority.[43] Individuals residing abroad were in a more advantageous position because if their rights were violated by the respective state they were entitled to diplomatic protection by the state of which they were citizens, provided intervention on their behalf was not in conflict with the political interests of the home state.

As an after-effect of World War II three areas of international law evolved, which explicitly restrict the supremacy of the territorial state over the population whether they are citizens or foreigners.

The battles and conquests of the war were directly conducive to rewriting the law concerning the victims of war in the form of the four Geneva Conventions in 1949 and the two Protocols in 1977.[44] Their significance, among others,[45] lies in that even in case of a distinctly internal civil war, certain regulations are applicable to protect individuals and the civilian population against the arbitrary actions and atrocities of the combatants exercising authority over the territory.[46]

Broadly interpreted, the Nuremberg principles also challenged the doctrine of unrestricted sovereignty, since they ordered the punishment of acts that would have been permissible under the laws of the Third Reich.[47]

---

[43] Gábor Kardos, *Emberi jogok egy új korszak határán* (Budapest, 1995), p. 12–13.

[44] Act 32 of 1954 and Act 20 of 1989.

[45] Géza, Herczegh, *A humanitárius nemzetközi jog fejlődése és mai problémái* Budapest, 1981), offers a general commentary.

[46] The unprecedented(?) massacres in Bosnia are painful reminders of the limits of law, but do not prove that law is meaningless: in the event some of the perpetrators are brought to trial and sentenced, it will be done on the basis of the Geneva Convention supplemented by the Protocols which play an important part in the litigation of Bosnia-Hercegovina against Yugoslavia (Serbia-Montenegro) at The Hague International Court of Justice. The same may serve as the basis for punishment of the perpetrators of the atrocities in 1956 in Hungary.

[47] Deng cites the fierce dispute on this question between Oxford Professor H. L. A. Hart and Harvard Professor L. L. Fuller in the 1958 volume of the *Harvard Law Review*. They agreed that the acts of the Nazis should be punished. Their dispute concerned the problem whether Nazi law should be revised by retroactive legislation (Hart) or simply should not be regarded as law (that would legalize acts committed in conformity with that law) on grounds of immorality (Fuller). Francis M. Deng, "Frontiers of Sovereignty: A Framework of Protection, Assistance, and Development for the Internally Displaced," *Leiden Journal of International Law* 8, no. 2 (1995), pp. 261–262.

The horrors of the war also spurred codification of the refugee law, and the Cold War accelerated the process. The Geneva Convention relating to the status of refugees adopted by the United Nations in 1951[48] restricts the freedom of action of the territorial state in a number of ways. On the one hand, it obliges the state to examine the case of each person who appears at the border of the state and claims to be a refugee, and decide whether the person is in fact entitled to protection by the Convention. This normally entails permission to enter the state territory, at least for the duration of the procedure.[49] On the other hand, the Convention obliges the state to refrain from expelling anyone if it means that the person would have to go to a country or to the frontier of a territory where "his/her life or freedom would be threatened on account of race, religion, nationality, membership in particular social groups, or political opinion."[50]

The most comprehensive and most frequently analyzed development restricting previous freedom of action of the state[51] is the codification of human rights and the establishment of control mechanisms. In Europe, the European Convention on Human Rights[52] is the most important but not the only instrument which allows the individual (and not only the other contracting party) to bring complaints before an international forum. In addition, there are universal conventions that, given the right conditions, guarantee the right of the cit-

---

[48] Proclaimed in Hungary by Act 15 of 1989.

[49] Let me add that I agree with this broader interpretation. According to another opinion, the legal obligation of the state begins after the refugee manages to enter the state.

[50] 1951 Convention on Status of Refugees, Para. 1, Article 33.

[51] See, for instance, Tom J. Farer's and Felice Gaer's study which begins with the following sentence: "Until World War II, most legal scholars and governments affirmed the general proposition, albeit not in so many words, that international law did not impede the natural right of each sovereign to be monstrous to his or her subjects." "The UN and Human Rights: At the End of the Beginning," in *United Nations, Divided World,* eds. A. Roberts and B. Kingsbury (Oxford, 1993), p. 247.

[52] Act XXXI of 1993. On the interpretation of the convention in practice and decisions made in wake of the complaints, see, for example, Viktor Mavi, *Az Európa Tanács és az emberi jogok* (Budapest, 1993).

izen of a state as well as aliens to initiate proceedings against the state if the state (through its organs) violates the civil and political rights of the person or practices inadmissible discrimination.[53] An even wider circle of conventions, though not allowing direct appeal to an international forum by the injured person, stipulates the obligation of the parties of the convention to submit periodical reports on the implementation of the guarantees and on violations of rights, if there were any.[54]

The growing system of protection for the victims of war, refugees, and people whose human rights have been violated, substantively restricts the supreme power of the territorial state over persons who reside in, or wish to enter, that state. In developing these legal fields, international law abandons the concept of sovereignty protecting autocratic or totalitarian regimes and democracies alike, and embodies a value-based normative preference for democracy.

C. Democratic Foundations of Government

The reaction of the international community to the collapse of East and Central European states, which imply admission to the international community conditional on democratic requirements, testifies to the normative preference for democracy. The December 1991 decision of the European Union named five conditions for recognizing

---

[53] Complaints against the cosignatory states of the first Facultative Report of the International Convention on Civil and Political Rights may be brought to the United Nations Commission on Human Rights and, according to article 14 of the International Agreement on the Abolition of All Forms of Racial Discrimination—if signed by the state—to the eighteen-member committee established by the Agreement. For details, see Leo F. Zwaak, *International Human Rights Procedures Petitioning the ECHR, CCPR and CERD* (Nijmegen, 1991); and Manfred Nowak, "Egyéni panaszeljárások az ENSZ emberi jogi egyezményei alapján," *Acta Humana*, nos. 15–16 (1994), pp. 112–125. The American Convention also established a committee and a court where individuals may bring complaints. In its first substantive decision in July 1988 the court ruled against Honduras. Carter and Trimble, op. cit., p. 910.

[54] The UN Convention on the Rights of Children ratified on November 20, 1989, is one example (enacted in Hungary as Act LXIV of 1991), see article 44.

the successor states of the Soviet Union and Yugoslavia.[55] These were: respect for human rights to freedom and minority rights; observation of the inviolability of borders; the obligation of peaceful settlement of disputes; observation of the obligation of arms control and the ban on nuclear weapons; and respect for the fundamental principles of democracy.[56]

The Council of Europe also demands that its future members accept and observe traditional European democratic values. At the time of writing this study, the Council is deliberating the question whether Russia will be able to realize the goals set down in the Statute of the Council, namely, to demonstrate her adherence to "the spiritual and moral values which are the common heritage of her people, and the true sources of individual freedom, political liberty, and the rule of law—the principles which form the basis of all genuine democracy." Between 1976 and 1996 the number of European countries qualifying for membership increased from eighteen to thirty-nine.

In the euphoria characterizing 1989 and 1990, the Eastern and Western signatories of the Paris Charter for a New Europe[57] declared in the first sentence after the preamble: "We undertake to build, consolidate, and strengthen democracy as the only system of government of our nations."

If we add that both the European Convention on Human Rights and the International Covenant on Civil and Political Rights demanded decades ago general, free, democratic, and secret elections on the territories of the parties[58] (by no means a common practice between the two world wars even in traditional democracies), then it is easy to discern the reason for the opinion formulated in the study of interna-

---

[55] See *International Legal Materials* 31, no. 6, (1992), p. 1487.

[56] In the present volume, Ákos Szilágyi gives an analysis of this decision but draws different conclusions.

[57] See Boldizsár Nagy, ed., *Nemzetközi jogi szerződések és dokumentumok* (Budapest, 1991), pp. 70–87.

[58] Article 3 of the first auxiliary report in 1952 of the European Convention states the obligation to hold periodical, secret and free elections. Article 25 of the PPEO declares the right of citizens to "vote and elect on the basis of general and equal franchise in genuine and secret elections which guarantee the free expression of the will of voters."

tional law in the early 1990s according to which the democratic legitimation of the governing power within the states is now becoming the condition for joining the community of states.

Thus, in 1992, Professor T. Franck of New York University and, in 1994, J. Crawford, a faculty chairman at Cambridge University, published important studies[59] on the development of a new customary law in international law which would stipulate that beyond their de facto existence, states must also meet the minimum requirements of democracy for admission into the international community.[60] In my view, this is a welcome development even though it makes the political traditions of the Euro-Atlantic region the universal norm and thus may be viewed as yet another expansionist policy of the industrialized powers. The generations who grew up in the stronghold of socialist sovereignty may find the presence of international observers at elections in East and Central Europe unusual but not humiliating, especially if viewed in a global context recalling their earlier presence in Namibia, Vietnam, and Eritrea.[61]

---

[59] See Thomas Franck, "The Emerging Right to Democratic Governance," *American Journal of International Law* 86, no. 1 (1992), pp. 46–91; James Crawford, "Democracy in International Law," Inaugural Lecture Delivered 5 March 1993 (Cambridge, 1994).

[60] In the 1995 winter issue of the *Harvard International Law Journal*, G. H. Fox and G. Nolte, close associates of T. Franck, were already discussing the question whether it is permissible, and to what extent, to impose restrictions on the democratic rights of the enemies of democracy (as was done in the case of Algeria, for instance, when the fundamentalists were on the verge of winning democratic elections). See Gregory H. Fox and Georg Nolte, "Intolerant Democracies," *Harvard International Law Journal* 36, no. 1 (Winter, 1995), pp. 1–70.

[61] People in distant regions of the world may want to hear impartial reports on Central European developments just as much as we like to hear the confirmation by international observers that elections in Eritrea were clean, and not merely an emphatic declaration by Eritrean diplomats. The sending of international observers long predates the political changes at the end of Cold War. The League of Nations sent observers to the plebiscites after World War I, and the United Nations, too, adopted the practice early on by sending United Nations observers, for instance, to British Togoland, British Cameroon, and the then Belgian East Africa (Ruanda-Urundi) in the fifties. See Franck, op. cit., p. 114.

Perhaps all this means only that we have reached the third stage in a process.

In the first stage, the international community gave the right to self-determination to oppressed peoples, then to colonies, breaking down the *de facto* sovereignty and empires of external powers.

In the second stage, the international community guaranteed the human rights of every individual against the state exercising territorial control and, in certain regions in Europe and America, created international mechanisms for the effective protection of the individual.

Lastly, in the present third stage, the international community expects the legitimacy of the power fundamentally controlling natural and human resources to be of a certain type, namely, democratic.

D. European Union Citizenship

The Maastricht Agreement, which created the European Union, added a new article to the Treaty of Rome governing the European Community. Article 8 (8–8e, to be specific) in force as of November 1, 1993, declares that the citizens of member states are also citizens of the Union. Although Article 8a repeats the restrictions stipulated by the subsidiary legislation in providing for the right of free change of residence, these restrictions are actually very few. It may be said that with the exception of persons not entitled to welfare benefits and medical care, jobholders as well as pensioners and students are free to take up residence anywhere within the European Union, from Taormina to Uppsala and beyond. Wherever the person chooses to settle, he or she has the right to vote in municipal elections and the elections of members of the European Parliament, as well as the right to diplomatic and consular protection by any one of the European Union member states in a third state where the person's home country has no representation.

Although, the traditional methods of acquiring citizenship are not applicable to Union citizenship, because it is not inherited and not a birthright but a concomitant of citizenship of a member state, it contains a number of elements belonging to a political nation, from the freedom of taking possession to the pursuit of political representation, on two levels (local and European), regardless of member-state boundaries. Thus, Union citizenship shows a marked difference from the familiar models of international relations wherein citizenship determines the person's affiliation to a given state.[62] The express aim of Union citizenship is to double—rather than divide—loyalty, but it also contains the potential that, when it comes to indivisible rights, European Union citizenship, as opposed to the national, will prove decisive. The above-mentioned municipal elections illustrate the point, that a local community cannot exclude resident foreign citizens from participation in public affairs, that is, from exercising local and European rights jointly; an alien who is a permanent local resident as well as a citizen of another European Union member state.[63]

E. The Right to Secede and the Right to Self-Determination

The scope of the present study does not allow for a review of the easily misinterpreted and often reinterpreted relationship between the right of self-determination and the disintegration of states and, in some cases, ensuing secession. I do not intend to dwell on conceptual controversies, nor on the doctrinal disputes concerning the rules of state succession. Let it suffice to draw the conclusions of my reasoning—open to debate, of course.

The principle of the equality of peoples and the right of self-determination demolished bloc-like sovereignties, because between 1945 and 1990 it authorized and assisted the inhabitants of colonies

---

[62] Dual or multiple citizenship is a statistically insignificant exception that a series of agreements tries to avoid. It is a cumbersome anomaly in international law—and also from the point of view of the national legal system. Many states—like Germany, for example—explicitly prohibit granting citizenship prior to renouncing former citizenship.

[63] Schreuer welcomes this process. His article, "The Waning of the Sovereign State," emphatically states: "The fading of nationalism should add rationality to international relations. The distribution of identification offers several levels of political organization rather than an exclusive commitment to a fatherland, la patrie, or the flag will curtail the potential for irrational or dangerous mass psychology." Christoph Schreuer, *European Journal of International Law* 4, no. 4 (1993), pp. 447–471.

and other similarly dependent peoples to secede from the mother country and establish independent states in over one hundred cases. In the struggle between sovereignty or territorial integrity versus self-determination, the latter proved superior, which the international community could justifiably support even against sovereignty.[64]

The right of self-determination means something else, if it has an identifiable meaning at all, in the Euro-Atlantic context and in the post-colonial era in general. In this region and age it recalls some of the ideals of the Wilsonian era, when the right of self-determination was the means and ideology for creating the independent state of an ethnically-based nation. However, I think that after the role it played in the liberation of colonies, it is no longer possible to return[65] to the meaning it had after World War I—which in the meanwhile has become obsolete —and it is impossible to interpret it as a principle of pure ethnicity guaranteeing every ethnic group a state of its own. The rhetoric causing and following the disintegration of states in Central and Eastern Europe made frequent use of the word, but what actually happened is more readily interpreted within the framework of state disunion based on non-self-determination. The right to peaceful secession based on consensus cannot be disputed; at most, the national constitutional restrictions must be recognized. International law does not stand in the way of separation from the mother state unless it takes place with the help of external force and intervention.[66] Furthermore, the post-1990 Euro-Asian practice seems to rewrite to a degree the rules of state succession; in other words, what

---

[64] For more detail, see Nagy, ed., op. cit., pp. 72–74.

[65] Saying "no longer possible" denotes only an impossibility in the international dogmatic legal sense. In the wake of the permissible method of interpretation of facts influencing the formulation of international customary law, it is impossible to arrive at the conclusion that, at the close of the twentieth century, self-determination is the universal principle (equally applicable in and outside of Europe) authorizing each ethnic group to establish its own state. The phrase means no more than this.

[66] The secession of Québec or of Scotland is not prohibited by international law, just as the break-up of Czechoslovakia was not prohibited that is, not to be prevented by other states.

took place in the region was a reformulation of the right of secession.[67] There are limits to exercising this right, otherwise the emergence of a new form of tribalism, a type of post-modern fragmentation would be in the offing.[68]

Analyzing territorial integrity versus the right of self-determination, Franck raises the most important question on sovereignty:

> Both are specific products of another time and place, yet
> both are being used frequently and freely in the debate
> about the most important political-legal issue of our time:
> what should be the posture of the international community
> towards a post-modern tribal population inhabiting a part of
> a recognized State which seeks to break away to constitute
> a separate, new State or to join another State?[69]

If Croatia could become independent, why not Krajina, if
Moldavia could become Moldova, why not the Republic of Trans-
Dniestr, if Russia could, why not Chechnia, if Canada could (in

---

[67] Although an agreement on contractual state succession was signed in 1978,
the unification of Germany, as well as the disintegration of Yugoslavia,
Czechoslovakia, and the Soviet Union resulted in a different practice from the
one defined in the provisions of the agreement. Instead of general succession,
the bilateral re-negotiation of contracts (with temporary implementation or
suspension of implementation until negotiations were closed), and the admission as new members into international organizations became the guiding rule.

[68] "Post-modern tribalism which will be used generically...to include politically assertive clans, 'nations,' denominations and ethnic groups that do not
necessarily see themselves as 'tribal' seeks to promote both a political and
legal environment conducive to the break-up of existing sovereign States. It
promotes the transfer of specified parts of the populations and territories of
existing multinational or multicultural States in order to constitute new unina-
tional and unicultural that is postmodern tribal States." Franck, op. cit., p. 126.
Although Gombár does not use the term "tribalism" and concentrates on relations within individual states, the debate he initiated in *Politikatudományi
Szemle* in 1994–1995 on the development of new ethnicity offers many interesting facts. See Csaba Gombár, "Társadalomszemléletünk etnicizálódása,"
Politikatudományi Szemle 3, no. 4 (1994), pp. 78–115.

[69] Franck, op. cit., p. 126.

1867?, 1931?, 1982?),[70] why not Québec?

The answer is that neither the right of self-determination as currently defined, nor minority rights contain any reference to the right of aggressive secession (possibly even externally abetted). Presumption is in favor of state integrity which loses ground only when the internal conflict on the question of secession becomes so grave that it is said to threaten international peace and security. In this situation the international community may enter the conflict—a step justified on the basis of the United Nations Charter and the yet incompletely formulated requirement of democratic legitimacy—either on the side of the secessionists or to help keep the country together.[71] If the international community supports the establishment of a new state, it may prescribe the conditions of membership.

On the whole, international law is indifferent, even if the majority of the states are not, about the peaceful, constitutional ways of secession. As we know, there are a number of federative states from India to Nigeria that emphasize state and territorial integrity on all occasions. At the same time, there is no standard which would oblige the international community to prevent the peaceful partitioning of a state or the secession of a region.

Whether separation is achieved through peaceful settlement or through conflict, the trend seems to be that the international community will accept the new state on the condition that it meet a certain set of minimum requirements of democracy, and providing that the seceding part, or the successor states of the disintegrated state, keep within the former administrative boundaries, even if they are the

---

[70] 1867: British dominion; 1931: complete independence; 1982: after bringing it home, the Constitution could be modified without approval by the British Parliament.

[71] Nathaniel Berman's study offers a fascinating analysis of this attitude in connection with the Spanish Civil War and the Bosnian conflict. He points out that active intervention, as well as localization of the conflict and the "injunction" that the states refrain from assisting either side, are radical innovations compared to the pre-World War I doctrine, and both are based on the right of the international community to determine the posture of individual nation-states in relation to the conflict within the state. See Nathaniel Berman, "Modernism, Nationalism and the Rhetoric of Reconstruction," *Yale Journal of Law and Humanities* 4 (1992), pp. 351–380, and especially pp. 484–487.

result of a "historically unjust" decision.[72] *Uti possidetis*, that is, the principle of accepting previous administrative boundaries as interstate boundaries, was the concept governing the liberation of Spanish colonies in the first quarter of the nineteenth century. In the broader sense it means that the previous condition determines the physical boundaries of the change in legal status, that is, it means the possession of what is actually occupied. The principle was applied in this sense to the case of the newly independent African colonies where the boundaries of the new countries were an expression of power relations between the colonialist powers instead of following ethnic composition. According to competent authorities and the currently evolving practice, this principle is also being applied in the Euro-Asian region, that is, a new common law is being formulated.[73] This may explain why law does not support the further division of former socialist federated member states or the redrawing of their boundaries.[74]

Summarizing the impact of self-determination and state succession on the meaning of sovereignty, we may say that the general recognition of the right of colonial and dependent peoples to self-determination and thus even to the establishment of an autonomous state was the first large-scale attack on integral sovereignty. Furthermore, German unification and the disintegration of the former federated socialist states demonstrated that state sovereignty is not supreme even in a non-colonial context. Although the international community sets conditions on the establishment of a sovereign state, under certain circumstances it also supports it.[75]

---

[72] Schreuer calls attention to the fact that during the disintegration of Yugoslavia the Security Council expressly prohibited the forced change of administrative boundaries. Schreurer, op. cit., pp. 447–471, n. 97, p. 468.

[73] Thomas Franck, *Fairness in the International Legal and Institutional System, Recueil des Cours 240* (Dordrecht, 1993), pp. 147–148.

[74] There is no end to such proposals, from Krajina which wanted to leave Croatia to join Serbia, through the Crimea, to Ossetia. For more details, see Ákos Szilágyi's study in the present volume.

[75] It is worth recalling that many may have cherished the dream of German unification or the independence of the Yugoslav constituent republics even before 1989, yet in 1989 the French president still believed that German unification was impossible, and in 1991 the United States still endeavored to hold Yugoslavia together.

F. Coercion by the United Nations

In both NATO and the European Union, decision-making on substantive foreign- and security-policy questions requires consensus whereby every member state may prevent the implementation of some highly important measure,[76] thus also prevent the organization from turning against one of its own members, or from taking steps against a non-member state whose interests are of special concern to a member state. In contrast, the United Nations may radically restrict the freedom of action of a state.

On the one hand, it may implement measures against member states if it decides that the actions of the particular state threaten or violate peace and security or deems them acts of aggression. The only practical restraint on the execution of sanctions is exercised by the five permanent members of the Security Council who may veto the adoption of a resolution on sanctions if directed against the permanent member or its ally.

On the other hand, it may bind member states to cooperate in enforcing adopted sanctions against states that threaten or violate peace, even at the cost of incurring economic losses.[77]

Another option affecting the sovereignty of states where the government becomes incapable of carrying out state functions, as it had in Somalia, Rwanda, and Bosnia, is to take over administration or to take steps toward checking anarchy and providing for the basic needs

---

[76] The Maastricht Treaty which brought the European Union into being and which codified the rules of framing the common foreign and security policies of the European Union, provides in Para. 2 of Article J.3 only that majority decisions may be made on measures connected with the execution of joint operations if the Council decides so by unanimous vote. An interesting analysis of the past twenty-five years of the cooperation of European Union member states on foreign policy issues, also revealing their disagreements, was published by Tamás Kende, ed., *Európai közjog és politika* (Budapest, 1995), pp. 146–156.

[77] As a member of the United Nations, Hungary did not have the right to weigh whether or not it should observe the sanctions against Serbia and thus sustain damages costing billions, according to some. Of course, the attitude of member states toward the implementation of such sanctions would be more positive if they were compensated by the international community.

of the population—with or without the formal consent of the "legitimate government." The end of the Cold War revived rights,[78] provided by the Charter but previously used only against two outlaw states, Rhodesia, and the Republic of South Africa, showing that the collective security system presupposes submission to the authority of the system on the part of its creators; in this context, when it is a choice between sovereignty and international authority, the latter wins out.[79] It is worth emphasizing what is already known: the United Nations Security Council of fifteen members may, by nine votes (including the votes of the five permanent members), impose obligations—for instance, the obligation to severe economic relations—on all of the 185 member states! It was precisely this special prerogative that made United Nations measures with regard to Haiti questionable, because they gave the United States a green light for intervention.

Three Security Council resolutions—which may easily become landmarks— may affect traditional sovereign prerogatives more seriously than any regional integrational decision, since they are irreconcilable with the concept of the inviolability of bloc-like sovereignty.

One of the resolutions[80] calls on Lybia to extradite its citizens indicted in the United States and Scotland for blowing up the PanAm airliner near Lockerbie. The other two contain the Security Council proposal to establish international criminal courts for the punishment of war crimes and crimes against humanity in former Yugoslavia and Rwanda.[81]

---

[78] In the Hungarian literature László Valki gives the most authoritative analysis of United Nations practice up to the turn in world politics in 1989. He also discusses special features of United Nations operations in Korea and Congo. See Valki, op. cit., pp. 319–328.

[79] Naturally, if the Security Council vetoes a proposal, or if the political will for joint action is absent, there will be no joint reaction. I do not mean that the collective system enjoys priority in every case, only that, given the political conditions not analyzed here, it restricts the freedom of action of a state more radically than regional integrations with voluntary membership whose decisions are based on consensus.

[80] SC Res 731 (January 21, 1992) 31 ILM (1992) p. 732.

[81] SC Res 827 (May 25, 1993) set up the court for indicting Yugoslav suspects and SC Res 995 (November 8, 1994) set up the court for indicting Rwandan suspects.

All three resolutions affect the hard core of sovereignty: they restrict the criminal jurisdiction of the state and break with the tradition—put aside only in the Nuremberg trials—according to which states will not extradite their own citizens to another state.[82]

VII. Guidelines for Analyzing the Condition and Nature of Sovereignty

The process of formation of a new sovereign state, the determination of the degree of sovereignty of the state joining the international community and the question of the legitimacy, the right to representation invested in the entity (monarch, dictator, government) embodying the sovereign are frequently used in analyses without distinctions.

International law makes a sharp distinction between entities considered already states and those that have yet to qualify, in other words, the conditions for joining an international community and the conditions for maintaining membership in the community are not the same. The conditions, presently in the process of being elaborated,[83] concerning recognition as a member of the community of states, do not apply to old member states whose status as autonomous legal entities shall not be questioned even if they are represented by totalitarian regimes. Regarding democratic minimum requirements, the

---

[82] Lybia appealed to the International Court of Justice at The Hague against the United Nations Security Council resolution demanding that Lybia extradite its citizens, as a result of which the Court will bring a decision whether the resolution is permissible or interdictory. This, in essence, raises the question of judicial control over the executive power of the Security Council, which would require the reconsideration of the whole philosophy of the United Nations. On facts and "constitutional" questions see, for instance, Alvarez, op. cit. The first alleged Serbian war criminal to be indicted raised similar constitutional questions when he questioned the lawfulness of the establishment of The Hague Court by the Security Council, but without success. The International Criminal Court of Appeals passed judgment dismissing the plea contending default in jurisdiction. 35 ILM (1996), pp. 35–74.

[83] See above regarding on the evolving customary law on democratic legitimation.

condition that links the old and emerging states is the accession to power of a despotic government by illegitimate means in a democratic state, in which case the international community may deny recognition of the government—leaving recognition of the state itself intact—that is, regard the government as without authority to represent the state. An example of this was what occurred after 1917 when no one questioned the existence of the Russian/Soviet state, only the right of the Bolshevik government to speak on its behalf was disputed. In 1957, no one denied Hungary's existence and legal entity status. The question was whether János Kádár and his government should be recognized or not?

In a few cases over the past two decades humanitarian intervention contributed to this situation insofar as it showed an increasing, but by no means universal, tendency to concede the legitimacy of the use of external force to overthrow extremely anti-democratic regimes which were deemed a threat to international peace and security.

As opposed to the illegitimate government of an existing state, the question in the case of the Bantustans, the Baltic states, the Turkish Republic of Northern Cyprus, or Taiwan concerns autonomous statehood and not the legitimacy of government.

The following is one of the observations governing the theoretical approach to sovereignty: it is worth remembering that African, Latin-American, and Asian processes differ from the European insofar as the equivalent to the magnetic power embodied in the European Union and other "European"[84] organizations (NATO, OSCE, Council of Europe) and the OECD, is absent in those regions. Little is said in European or Hungarian literature about the workings of organizations there: it is hard to determine how Paraguay's membership in MERCOSUR and SELA[85] affects its sovereignty, or Australia's in APEC,[86] not to mention the obscurity surrounding the better known organizations (Organization of African Unity, Organization of American States, Arab League, United Nations). All this leads to the

---

[84] As we know, NATO and OSCE are not geographically limited to Europe.

[85] Mercado Común del Cono Sur and Sistema Económico Latino-Americano. See *Officina World Yearbook 1994–1995*, p. 24.

[86] Asian-Pacific Economic Cooperation.

conclusion that it would help us to understand reality if we were to study world processes as a complex matrix with multi-dimensional interaction, rather than along the single trend of globalization and the single concept of sovereignty. In this case, the question would no longer be whether joining integration organizations diminishes Hungary's sovereignty or leaves it intact, but what is the origin of the forces of interdependence and disintegration that affect the country, what factors enhance or diminish its freedom of action. Put in general terms, I conceive analysis of international processes and the fate of individual states along the following broad categories:

Summary of the Influences Impacting on the Freedom of Action of the State

		Disintegration		
		Fragmentation	Entropy	Strengthening of the sub-national level
Interdependence	Integration		Sensitivity Vulnerability	
	Trans-nationalization			
	Regime			

Suggested definition of the concepts:

Integration: Deep interrelatedness based on intentional, regulated, mostly intergovernmental contact, usually assuming an organizational form.

Transnationalization: Across the border cooperation between subnational participants, the networks, including transnational actors they create.

Regime: A complex system regulating the use of a given resource (including geographical regions), including rules, customs, expectations, applied to all users, state and private enterprise alike.

Fragmentation: Reviving nationalism, separatism, new tribalism, all aspirations to secede.

Entropy: Complete collapse, implosion, functional incapacitation of state organizations, systems of international relations, as in Somalia or earlier in Lebanon.

Strengthening of the subnational level: The need for decentralization of the decision-making process, regional aspirations (aimed at creating a different decision-making structure, that is, redistribution within the nation, rather than separation).

Sensitivity: Shows the extent to which a state is exposed in the short-range to changes in the international system, and its (negative) influences.

Vulnerability: Long-term sensitivity of the state, that is, the measure of adaptability, regeneration in sensitive areas, or the persistence of an open wound at the point of thrust.[87] Perhaps, application of this more intricate system would cast light on mysteries globalization failed to explain, or interpreted fallaciously, and help to understand what the United Nations Secretary General phrased as follows in connection with the role of the state in his 1992 report:

> The time of absolute and exclusive sovereignty, however, has passed; its theory was never matched by reality. It is the task of leaders of States today to understand this and to find a balance between the needs of good internal governance and the requirements of an ever more intendependent world.[88]

---

[87] The meaning of sensitivity and vulnerability closely approximates Rusett and Starr's definitions. See Rusett and Starr, op. cit., p. 488.

[88] Boutros-Boutros Ghali, *An Agenda for Peace* (New York, 1992).

BIOGRAPHIC INDEX

AFANASEVSKY, Nikolai Nikolaevich (b. 1931)
Diplomat, chief of the First European Departmentof USSR's Ministry of Foreign Affairs, 1986– 1991; deputy minister of foreign affairs, 1994.

ALTHUSIUS, Johannes (1557–1638)
Dutch Calvinist; political thinker and the intellectual father of modern federalism; advocate of popular sovereignty.

ARAFAT, Yasser (b. 1929)
Palestinian leader; formed the "al-Fatah" movement, and organization; chairman and leader of Palestinian Liberation Organization (PLO) since 1968. Head of the Palestine Authority.

ARISTIDE, Jean Bertrand (b. 1953)
Former clergyman and politician, present president of Haiti.

BEETHOVEN, Ludwig van (1770–1827)
German composer of Flemish descent; ranks as one of the greatest figures in the history of Western music.

BIBÓ, István (1911–1979)
Hungarian political thinker, politician; co-founder of the National Peasant Party; minister of state in 1956.

BISMARCK, Otto von (1815–1898)
Founder and chancellor of the German Empire. At his best in foreign affairs, he was the principal architect of an age that gave Europe twenty-six years of peace after the Congress of Berlin (1878).

BODIN, Jean (1530–1596)
French political philosopher and economist best known for his avant-garde theory of ideal government.

BREZHNEV, Leonid Ilich (1906–1982)
Leader and Communist Party official who, with Aleksey Kosygin, replaced Nikita Khrushchev as general secretary of the Central Committee of the Communist Party of the Soviet Union. Governed the Soviet Union, 1977–1982.

BULGAKOV, Mikhail Afanasevich (1891–1940)
Russian playwright, novelist, and short-story writer. Author of the novel *Master and Margarita*.

CHURCHILL, Sir Winston (1874–1965)
British author, and statesman who, as prime minister from 1940 to 1945, led Britain from near defeat to victory in World War II.

CLINTON, Bill (William) Jefferson (b. 1946)
American Democratic politician; twice elected president of the United States.

CONCHA, Győző (1846–1933)
Hungarian lawyer, author in the fields of international law and political science.

DELORS, Jacques (b. 1925)
French politician and economist. President of the Committee of European Communities (now European Commission) 1985–1994.

DOLLFUSS, Engelbert (1892–1934)
Austrian statesman; chancellor of Austria, 1932–1934; destroyed the Austrian Republic and established an authoritarian regime based on conservative Roman Catholic and Italian Fascist principles.

DUDAEV, Bekmuraz (b. 1949)
Mayor of Grozny; brother of President Dudaev.

DUDAEV, Dzhokar Mussaevich (1944–1996)
Chechen army officer and politician; president of the Chechen

Republic, 1991–1996; Chairman of Government, 1992–1996.

EICHMANN, Adolf (1906–1962)
Nazi official, active in the extermination of millions of European Jews during World War II. Convicted of war crimes by an Israeli court, he was hanged.

FIGL, Leopold (1902–1965)
Austrian politician; chancellor of Austria, 1945–1953.

FRANCIS JOSEPH I (1830–1916)
Habsburg emperor of Austria from 1848 and king of Hungary from 1867; one of the longest reigning monarchs in European history.

FREUD, Sigmund (1856–1939)
Austrian neurologist and psychiatrist; founder of psychoanalysis.

GORBACHEV, Mikhail Sergeevich (b. 1931)
Russian politician. Last president of the Union of Soviet Socialist Republics, 1990–1991.

GÖRING, Hermann (1893–1946)
Official of the Nazi Party in Germany and one of the prime architects of the Nazi police state, its air force, rearmament, and wartime economy.

GROTIUS, Hugo (1583–1645)
Dutch jurist and scholar whose works are of fundamental importance in international law.

HAIDER, Jörg (b. 1950)
Austrian politician; leader of the right-radical Freedom Party.

HAYDN, Franz Joseph (1732–1809)
Austrian composer, one of the most important figures in the development of classical music during the eighteenth century.

HEGEL, Georg Wilhelm Friedrich (1770–1831)
German philosopher who developed the concept of dialectics.

HERZL, Theodor (1860–1904)
Hungarian-born politician; founder of Zionism, a movement to establish a Jewish homeland.

HITLER, Adolf (1889–1945)
Leader of the National Socialist German Workers' Party and dictator of Germany, 1933–1945.

HOBBES, Thomas (1588–1679)
Philosopher and political thinker, an advocate for absolute monarchy.

HUSSEIN, Saddam (b. 1937)
Iraqi politician; member, then deputy secretary of the regional leadership of the Baath Party, 1963–79. President of Iraq since 1979; prime minister since 1994.

KAFKA, Franz (1883–1924)
German-speaking Czech writer, author of *The Trial, The Castle,* and other shorter works.

KELLOGG, Frank Billings (1856–1937)
U.S. secretary of state, 1925–1929; in 1928 signed the Kellogg-Briand Pact, a multilateral agreement designed to outlaw war as an instrument of national policy; in 1929 received the Nobel Peace Prize for his peacekeeping efforts.

KELSEN, Hans (1881–1951)
Austrian-American legal philosopher, professor of law, jurist and writer on international law, formulated a kind of positivism known as the "pure theory" of law.

KENNEDY, John F. (1917–1963)
Served as United States congressman, 1953–1961; the first

Roman Catholic to be elected president, 1960–1963; assassinated in Dallas.

KHRUSCHEV, Nikita Sergeevich (1894–1971)
Russian politician; general secretary of the Communist Party of Soviet Union, 1953–1964.

KLAUS, Josef (b. 1910)
Austrian lawyer, politician. Chancellor of Austria, 1964–1970. Former chairman of the Austrian People's Party.

KREISKY, Bruno (b. 1911)
Austrian statesman; joined the Austrian foreign service after World War II. Chairman of the Socialist Party; chancellor of Austria, 1970–1983.

LOCKE, John (1632–1704)
Influental political philosopher who laid the epistemological foundations of modern science.

LUEGER, Karl (1844–1910)
Politician, co-founder and leader of the anti-Semitic Austrian Christian Social Party, and mayor of Vienna, 1897–1910. He transformed the Austrian capital into a modern city.

MACHIAVELLI, Niccolò (1469–1527)
Writer, statesman, Florentine patriot, and original political thinker whose acute psychological observations brought him a reputation of an amoral cynic.

MADISON, James (1751–1836)
Fourth president of the United States, 1809–1817, and one of the founding fathers of his country.

MAO TSE-TUNG (1893–1976)
Principal Chinese Marxist theorist, soldier, and statesman, led his nation's revolution that established it as on of the twentieth

century's foremost Communist nations; chairman of the republic and chairman of the Party; and reasserted his control during the upheaval known as the Cultural Revolution.

MARIA THERESA (1717–1780)

Archduchess of Austria, queen of Hungary, queen of Bohemia, and wife of the Holy Roman Emperor Francis I; one of the most capable rulers of the Habsburg dynasty.

MARSHALL, George C. (1880–1959)

Was United States secretary of state, and of defense. In 1947 he proposed the European Recovery Program, the Marshall Plan. He received the Nobel Peace Prize.

MARX, Karl (1818–1883)

A German socialist and revolutionist, sociologist, and economist. Author of *The Communist Manifesto*.

MATTHIAS CORVINUS (1440–1490)

King of Hungary, 1458–1490; known as a Renaissance ruler.

MONNET, Jean (1888–1979)

French political economist and diplomat who, after World War II, initiated comprehensive economic planning in Western Europe. In France he was responsible for the successful plan designed to rebuild and modernize that nation's crumbled economy.

MONTESQUIEU, Charles-Louis de (1689–1755)

Outstanding French political philosopher of the eighteenth century whose major work, *De l'espirit des lois*, was a seminal contribution to political theory.

MOZART, Wolfgang Amadeus (1756–1791)

Austrian composer; together with Haydn he represents the apogee of the late eighteenth-century Viennese classical style; by virtue of the extraordinary quality of his broad achievements in opera, chamber music, symphonies, and piano concerti is regarded as one of the great musical geniuses of all times.

RAAB, Julius (1881–1964)
Chancellor of Austria, 1953–1961.

ROUSSEAU, Jean-Jacques (1712–1778)
French political philosopher; his *Du contrat social* (1762) had a major influence on the French Revolution.

SCHARF, Adolf (1890–1965)
Austrian politician; vice-chancellor, 1950–1957; president of Austria, 1957–1965.

SCHUMAN, Robert (1886–1963)
French statesman who founded the European Coal and Steel Community and worked for economic and political unity.

SCHWARZENEGGER, Arnold Alois (b. 1947)
Austrian-born American actor, businessman and former body-builder.

SEBŐK, Zsigmond (1861–1916)
Journalist and author of many children's books.

SHAMIL (1799–1871)
The third imam of Dagestan and Chechnia, a leader of the war for independence from Russia.

STALIN, Iosif Visarionovich (1879–1953)
General secretary of the Communist Party of the Soviet Union; ruled the Soviet Union dictatorially for a quarter of a century transforming it into a major world power.

TITO, Josip Broz (1892–1980)
Effective head of the Yugoslav state from 1943 and its president from 1953. Determined to maintain the independence of his country, he led the Yugoslav partisans against the German invaders in

World War II; and in 1948 became the first Communist national leader to successfully defy the Soviet Union.

TOCQUEVILLE, Alexis Comte de (1805–1859)
French political thinker, historian, and politician, best known for his perceptive analysis of the American political system in the early nineteenth century, in *Democracy in America.*

TRUMAN, Harry S. (1884–1972)
Vice president under Franklin D. Roosevelt, 1945; 33rd president of the United States, 1945-1953; led his nation into international confrontation with Communism while defending the New Deal reform tradition.

WALDHEIM, Kurt (b. 1918)
Austrian politician; foreign minister, 1968–1970; ambassador to the United Nations, 1964–1968, 1970–1971; fourth secretary general of the United Nations, 1972–1981.

WIESENTHAL, Simon (b. 1908)
Austrian investigator of Nazi crimes and former architect; director of the Jewish Documentation Center since 1961.

WILLIAM II (1859–1941)
German emperor, 1888–1918, commonly regarded in Allied countries as the prime instigator of World War I.

YELTSIN, Boris Nikolaevich (b. 1931)
Russian politician; official of the Communist Party of the Soviet Union; Deputy of the Supreme Soviet of the Union of Soviet Socialist Republics; Head of Committee on Construction and Architecture, 1989-1990; elected to the Congress of People's Deputies of the Soviet Union, 1989; president of the Russian Federal Republic since 1991.

ZAVGAEV, Doku Gapurovich (b. 1940)
Russian politician; official of the Communist Party of the Soviet

Union; first secretary of Checheno-Inglush Obkom; chairman of
the Checheno-Inglush Republic's Supreme Soviet from 1991;
People's Deputy of the Russian Federal Republic from 1991.

ZRINYI, Miklós (1620–1664)
Hungarian statesman, military leader, and author of the first outstanding epic poem in Hungarian literature.

INDEX

LIST OF CONTRIBUTORS

GOMBÁR, Csaba
> Director of Korridor Center for Political Research. Professor, Political Science Department, Eötvös Loránd University, Budapest.

CSEPELI, György
> Professor, chair of the Department of Social Psychology, Institute for Sociology, Eötvös Loránd University, Budapest.

HANKISS, Elemér
> Director of the Institute of Sociology, Hungarian Academy of Sciences, Budapest. Professor, Political Science Department, Eötvös Loránd University, Budapest.

KOVÁCS, János Mátyás
> Tenured fellow, Institute for Human Sciences in Vienna. Member of the Institute of Economics, Hungarian Academy of Sciences, Budapest. He teaches history of Eastern European economic thought at Eötvös Loránd University, Budapest.

LENGYEL, László
> Economist, president and chief executive of Pénzügykutató Rt. [Financial Research, Inc.].

NAGY, Boldizsár
> Associate professor of international common law, Department of International Law, Eötvös Loránd University, Budapest.

SZILÁGYI, Ákos
> Poet, aesthetician. Assistant professor, Institute of Aesthetics, Eötvös Loránd University, Budapest.

VALKI, László
Professor, chairman of the Department of International Law,
Eötvös Loránd University, Budapest.

VÁRNAI, Györgyi
Sociologist, executive secretary, Korridor Center for Political
Research, Budapest.

VOLUMES PUBLISHED IN "ATLANTIC STUDIES ON SOCIETY IN CHANGE"

No. 1   *Tolerance and Movements of Religious Dissent in Eastern Europe.* Edited by B. K. Király. 1977.

No. 2   *The Habsburg Empire in World War I.* Edited by R. A. Kann. 1978.

No. 3   *The Mutual Effects of the Islamic and Judeo-Christian Worlds: The East European Pattern.* Edited by A. Ascher, T. Halasi-Kun, B. K. Király. 1979.

No. 4   *Before Watergate: Problems of Corruption in American Society.* Edited by A. S. Eisenstadt, A. Hoogenboom, H. L. Trefousse. 1979.

No. 5   *East Central European Perceptions of Early America.* Edited by B. K. Király and. G. Bárány. 1977.

No. 6   *The Hungarian Revolution of 1956 in Retrospect.* Edited by B. K. Király and Paul Jonas. 1978.

No. 7   *Brooklyn U.S.A.: Fourth Largest City in America.* Edited by Rita S. Miller. 1979.

No. 8   *Prime Minister Gyula Andrássy's Influence on Habsburg Foreign Policy.* János Decsy. 1979.

No. 9   *The Great Impeacher: A Political Biography of James M. Ashley.* Robert F. Horowitz. 1979.

No. 10   *Special Topics and Generalizations on the Eighteenth and*
Vol. I*   *Nineteenth Century.* Edited by B. K. Király and Gunther E. Rothenberg. 1979

* Volumes no. I through XXXVII refer to the series War and Society in East Central Europe.

No. 11
Vol. II
East Central European Society and War in the Pre-Revolutionary 18th Century. Edited by Gunther E. Rothenberg, B. K. Király, and Peter F. Sugar. 1982.

No. 12
Vol. III
From Hunyadi to Rákóczi: War and Society in Late Medieval and Early Modern Hungary. Edited by János M. Bak and B. K. Király. 1982.

No. 13
Vol. IV
East Central European Society and War in the Era of Revolutions: 1775–1856. Edited by B. K. Király. 1984.

No. 14
Vol. V
Essays on World War I: Origins and Prisoners of War. Edited by Samuel R. Williamson, Jr. and Peter Pastor. 1983.

No. 15
Vol. VI
Essays on World War I: Total War and Peacemaking. A Case Study on Trianon. Edited by B. K. Király, Peter Pastor and Ivan Sanders. 1982.

No. 16
Vol. VII
Army, Aristocracy, Monarchy: War, Society and Government in Austria, 1618–1780. Edited by Thomas M. Baker. 1982.

No. 17
Vol. VIII
The First Serbian Uprising 1804–1813. Edited by Wayne S. Vucinich. 1982.

No. 18
Vol. IX
Czechoslovak Policy and the Hungarian Minority 1945–1948. Kálmán Janics. Edited by Stephen Borsody. 1982.

No. 19
Vol. X
At the Brink of War and Peace: The Tito-Stalin Split in a Historic Perspective. Edited by Wayne S. Vucinich. 1982.

No. 20
Inflation Through the Ages: Economic, Social, Psychological and Historical Aspects. Edited by Edward Marcus and Nathan Schmuckler. 1981.

No. 21
Germany and America: Essays on Problem of International Relations and Immigration. Edited by Hans L. Trefousse. 1980.

No. 22
Brooklyn College: The First Half Century. Murray M. Horovitz. 1981.

No. 23   *A New Deal for the World: Eleanor Roosevelt and American Foreign Policy.* Jason Berger. 1981.

No. 24   *The Legacy of Jewish Migration: 1881 and Its Impact.* Edited by David Berger. 1982.

No. 25   *The Road to Bellapais: Cypriot Exodus to Northern Cyprus.* Pierre Oberling. 1982.

No. 26   *New Hungarian Peasants: An East Central European Experience with Collectivization.* Edited by Marida Hollos and Béla C. Maday. 1983.

No. 27   *Germans in America: Aspects of German-American Relations in the Nineteenth Century.* Edited by Allen McCormick. 1983.

No. 28   *A Question of Empire. Leopold I and the War of Spanish Succession, 1701–1705.* Linda and Marsha Frey. 1983.

No. 29   *The Beginning of Cyrillic Printing—Cracow, 1491. From the Orthodox Past in Poland.* Szczepan K. Zimmer. Edited by L. Krzyanowski and I. Nagurski. 1983.

No. 29a   *A Grand Ecole for the Grand Corps: The Recruitment and Training of the French Administration.* Thomas R. Osborne. 1983.

No. 30
Vol. XI   *The First War between Socialist States: The Hungarian Revolution of 1956 and Its Impact.* Edited by B. K. Király, Barbara Lotze, Nandor Dreisziger. 1984.

No. 31
Vol. XII   *The Effects of World War I, The Uprooted: Hungarian Refugees and Their Impact on Hungary's Domestic Politics.* István Mócsy. 1983.

No. 32
Vol. XIII   *The Effects of World War I: The Class War after the Great War: The Rise of Communist Parties in East Central Europe, 1918–1921.* Edited by Ivo Banac. 1983.

No. 33
Vol. XIV   *The Crucial Decade: East Central European Society and National Defense, 1859–1870.* Edited by B. K. Király. 1984.

No. 35   *Effects of World War I: War Communism in Hungary, 1919.*
Vol. XVI   György Péteri. 1984.

No. 36   *Insurrections, Wars, and the Eastern Crisis in the 1870s.*
Vol. XVII   Edited by B. K. Király and Gale Stokes. 1985.

No. 37   *East Central European Society and the Balkan Wars, 1912–*
Vol. XVIII *1913.* Edited by Béla K. Király and Dimitrije Djordjevic.
            1986.

No. 38   *East Central European Society in World War I.* Edited
Vol. XIX   by B. K. Király and N. F. Dreisziger, Assistant Editor
            Albert A. Nofi. 1985.

No. 39   *Revolutions and Interventions in Hungary and Its Neigh-*
Vol. XX   *bor States, 1918–1919.* Edited by Peter Pastor. 1988.

No. 41   *Essays on East Central European Society and War, 1740–*
Vol. XXII   *1920.* Edited by Stephen Fischer-Galati and B. K. Király.
            1988.

No. 42   *East Central European Maritime Commerce and Naval*
Vol. XXIII *Policies, 1789–1913.* Edited by Apostolos E. Vacalopoulos,
            Constantinos D. Svolopoulos, and B. K. Király. 1988.

No. 43   *Selections, Social Origins, Education and Training of*
Vol. XXIV   *East Central European Officers Corps.* Edited by B. K.
            Király and Walter Scott Dillard. 1988.

No. 44   *East Central European War Leaders: Civilian and*
Vol. XXV   *Military.* Edited by B. K. Király and Albert Nofi. 1988.

No. 46   *Germany's International Monetary Policy and the Euro-*
            pean Monetary System. Hugo Kaufmann. 1985.

No. 47   *Iran Since the Revolution—Internal Dynamics, Regional*
            Conflicts and the Superpowers. Edited by Barry M. Rosen.
            1985.

No. 48   *The Press during the Hungarian Revolution of 1848–*
Vol. XXVII *1849.* Domokos Kosáry. 1986.

No. 49   *The Spanish Inquisition and the Inquisitional Mind.* Edited by Angel Alcala. 1987.

No. 50   *Catholics, the State and the European Radical Right, 1919–1945.* Edited by Richard Wolff and Jorg K. Hoensch. 1987.

No. 51   *The Boer War and Military Reforms.* Jay Stone and Erwin
Vol. XXVIII A. Schmidl. 1987.

No. 52   *Baron Joseph Eötvös, A Literary Biography.* Steven B. Várdy. 1987.

No. 53   *Towards the Renaissance of Puerto Rican Studies: Ethnic and Area Studies in University Education.* Maria Sanchez and Antonio M. Stevens. 1987.

No. 54   *The Brazilian Diamonds in Contracts, Contraband and Capital.* Harry Bernstein. 1987.

No. 55   *Christians, Jews and Other Worlds: Patterns of Conflict and Accommodation.* Edited by Philip F. Galagher. 1988.

No. 56   *The Fall of the Medieval Kingdom of Hungary: Mohács,*
Vol. XXVI *1526, Buda, 1541.* Géza Perjés. 1989.

No. 57   *The Lord Mayor of Lisbon: The Portuguese Tribune of the People and His 24 Guilds.* Harry Bernstein. 1989.

No. 58   *Hungarian Statesmen of Destiny: 1860–1960.* Edited by Paul Bődy. 1989.

No. 59   *For China: The Memoirs of T. G. Li, Former Major General in the Chinese Nationalist Army.* T. G. Li. Written in collaboration with Roman Rome. 1989.

No. 60   *Politics in Hungary: For a Democratic Alternative.* János Kis, with an Introduction by Timothy Garton Ash. 1989.

No. 61   *Hungarian Worker's Councils in 1956.* Edited by Bill Lomax. 1990.

No. 62   *Essays on the Structure and Reform of Centrally Planned Economic Systems.* Paul Jonas. A joint publication with Corvina Kiadó, Budapest. 1990.

No. 63   *Kossuth as a Journalist in England.* Éva H. Haraszti. A joint publication with Akadémiai Kiadó, Budapest. 1990.

No. 64   *From Padua to the Trianon, 1918–1920.* Mária Ormos. A joint publication with Akadémiai Kiadó, Budapest. 1990.

No. 65   *Towns in Medieval Hungary.* Edited by László Gerevich. A joint publication with Akadémiai Kiadó, Budapest. 1990.

No. 66   *The Nationalities Problem in Transylvania, 1867–1940.* Sándor Bíró. 1992.

No. 67   *Hungarian Exiles and the Romanian National Movement, 1849–1867.* Béla Borsi-Kálmán. 1991.

No. 68   *The Hungarian Minority's Situation in Ceauescu's Romania.* Edited by Rudolf Joó and Andrew Ludanyi. 1994.

No. 69   *Democracy, Revolution, Self-Determination. Selected Writings.* István Bibó. Edited by Károly Nagy. 1991.

No. 70   *Trianon and the Protection of Minorities.* József Galántai. A joint publication with Corvina Kiadó, Budapest. 1991.

No. 71   *King Saint Stephen of Hungary.* György Györffy. 1994.

No. 72   *Dynasty, Politics and Culture. Selected Essays.* Robert A. Kann. Edited by Stanley B. Winters. 1991.

No. 73   *Jadwiga of Anjou and the Rise of East Central Europe.* Oscar Halecki. Edited by Thaddeus V. Gromada. A joint publication with the Polish Institute of Arts and Sciences of America. New York. 1991.

No. 74
Vol. XXIX   *Hungarian Economy and Society during World War Two.* Edited by György Lengyel. 1993.

No. 75   *The Life of a Communist Revolutionary, Béla Kun.* György Borsányi. 1993.

No. 76
Yugoslavia: The Process of Disintegration. Laslo Sekelj. 1993.

No. 77
Vol. XXX
Wartime American Plans for a New Hungary. Documents from the U.S. Department of State, 1942–1944. Edited by Ignác Romsics. 1992.

No. 78
Vol. XXXI
Planning for War against Russia and Serbia, Austro-Hungarian and German Military Strategies, 1871–1914. Graydon A. Tunstall, Jr. 1993.

No. 79
American Effects on Hungarian Imagination and Political Thought, 1559–1848. Géza Závodszky. 1995.

No. 80
Vol. XXXII
Trianon and East Central Europe: Antecedents and Repercussions. Edited by B. K. Király and L. Veszprémy. 1995.

No. 81
Hungarians and Their Neighbors in Modern Times, 1867–1950. Edited by Ferenc Glatz. 1995.

No. 82
István Bethlen: A Great Conservative Statesman of Hungary, 1874–1946. Ignác Romsics. 1995.

No. 83
Vol. XXXIII
20th Century Hungary and the Great Powers. Edited by Ignác Romsics. 1995.

No. 84
Lawful Revolution in Hungary, 1989–1994. Edited by B. K. Király and András Bozóki. 1995.

No. 85
The Demography of Contemporary Hungarian Society. Edited by Pál Péter Tóth and Emil Valkovics. 1996.

No. 86
Budapest, A History from Its Beginnings to 1996. Edited by András Gerő and János Poór. 1996.

No. 87
The Dominant Ideas of the Nineteenth Century and Their Impact on the State. Volume I. Diagnosis. József Eötvös. Translated, edited, annotated and indexed with an introductory essay by D. Mervyn Jones. 1996.

No. 88
The Dominant Ideas of the Nineteenth Century and Their Impact on the State. Volume 2. *Remedy.* József Eötvös.

Translated, edited, annotated and indexed with an introductory essay by D. Mervyn Jones. 1997.

No. 89   *The Social History of the Hungarian Intelligentsia in the "Long Nineteenth Century," 1825–1914.* János Mazsu. 1997.

No. 90   *Pax Britannica: Wartime Foreign Office Documents Re-*
Vol. XXXIV   *garding Plans for a Postbellum East Central Europe.* Edited by András D. Bán. 1997.

No. 91   *National Identity in Contemporary Hungary.* György Csepeli. 1997.

No. 92   *The Hungarian Parliament, 1867–1918: A Mirage of Power.* András Gerő. 1997.

No. 93   *The Hungarian Revolution and War for Independence*
Vol. XXXV   *1848–1849. A Military History.* Edited by Gábor Bona. 1998.

No. 94   *Academia and State Socialism: Essays on the Political History of Academic Life in Post-1945 Hungary and East Central Europe.* György Péteri. 1998.

No. 95   *Through the Prism of the Habsburg Monarchy: Hungary*
Vol. XXXVI   *Hungary in American Diplomacy and Public Opinion during World War I.* Tibor Glant. 1998.

No. 96   *The Appeal of Sovereignty. Hungary, Austria and Russia.* Edited by Csaba Gombár, Elemér Hankiss, László Lengyel and Györgyi Várnai. 1998.

No. 97   *Hungarian Initiatives for Cooperation in the Danube Region, 1848–1996.* Edited by Ignác Romsics and Béla K. Király. 1998.

No. 98   *Hungarian Agrarian Society from the Emancipation of Serfs (1848) to Re-privatization of Land (1998).* Edited by Peter Gunst. 1998.